THE
SAN FRANCISCO
GOLF GUIDE

**Covering 10 Counties, plus
the Monterey Peninsula**

D1157366

Daniel Wexler

Published by MT III Golf Media
El Segundo, CA   USA
Midd23@aol.com

Also by Daniel Wexler:

The Missing Links: America's Greatest Lost Golf Courses and Holes

Lost Links: Forgotten Treasures From Golf's Golden Age

The Golfer's Library: A Reader's Guide to Three Centuries of Golf Literature

The Book of Golfers: A Biographical History of the Royal & Ancient Game

The World Atlas of Golf (with Michael Clayton, Ran Morrissett, et al)

A Timeless Game: Some Thoughts On Golf Topics Old And New

The Black Book

The Black Book is a series of national and regional golf course guidebooks which offer the most candid and detailed course descriptions available in American golf. With a particular focus on each layout's history and design evolution, they also include our exclusive Collectability Ratings, a unique tool for the traveling golfer. Information on the Black Book's *Private Club Guide*, as well as numerous regional titles, can be found at Amazon.com or DanielWexler.com.

MT III Golf Media

In addition to producing our comprehensive golf course guidebooks ("The Black Book"), MT III Golf Media also offers customized public relations and promotional materials for public courses, resorts and private clubs. Please visit us at www.danielwexler.com.

TABLE OF CONTENTS

INTRODUCTION

By no means is this the first guidebook ever penned covering the golf courses of a particular region of the United States; such volumes are, in fact, fairly common, both in major metropolitan areas and destination locales readily identifiable as golfing hotbeds.

The Black Book, however, is different.

To begin with, this volume includes every facility within reasonable driving distance of San Francisco for which verifiable information was available at the time of its writing. From the ritziest private club to the tiniest nine-hole par 3, all courses within the 10 immediate counties around San francisco are included, with a bonus section added to cover every facility on the famed Monterey Peninsula as well.

Second, these volumes are focused upon the golf courses – their layouts, histories, architectural evolutions, great (and not-so-great) holes, and whatever other salient points come to mind on a course-by-course basis. What they are *not* about is all manner of ancillary items that often clog mainstream guidebooks. There will, for example, be no discussions of food, tennis facilities, nearby hotels or the quality of beverage cart service. These books are for avid, serious golfers; the course is what matters here.

Significantly, course conditioning is not a factor is our assessment simply because it is a transient thing which can vary by season, greenkeeper and maintenance budget.

Perhaps most importantly, these guidebooks are intended to live up to a pithy little phrase of my own creation:

"Candid, but not opinionated."

And this to me is the heart of the undertaking because what the golf world does not need is another book calling every layout a "gem," or passing off regurgitated public relations copy as insightful descriptive material. The goal of The Black Book, then, is to provide an accurate picture of each course's overall attributes based upon a mix of objective factors (e.g., style of design, USGA ratings and slope, invasiveness of hazards, etc.), and a consensus of less formalized ones (a wide range of published rankings and commentaries). What is *not* factored in are my personal preferences regarding a course's "quality" relative to rankings, designer, style, region or period. This goal is furthered by the book's use of our exclusive Collectability Rating (see page 3), a unique evaluation method that essentially measures how desirable a "get" each facility is for the discerning golfer's personal list of courses played. The only place where my opinion becomes relevant, then, is in calculating how the above criteria add up relative to that scale.

As for The Black Book's accuracy, while periodic renovations of courses are inevitable, numerous sources have been utilized in order to present the most accurate information possible at the time of writing. One notable point, however, concerns individual hole yardages and course ratings. Where possible, the information herein comes directly from the courses themselves, generally via website. Failing this, it has been culled from either regional golf associations or the USGA's national database – sources which often show minor differences based on a variety of factors. Hole yardages can vary similarly, often due only to a recent re-measuring, or the addition of new tees. Therefore while the numbers presented are deemed substantially accurate, the occasional minor variance is unavoidable. And also unavoidable, particularly in golf's present economic climate, is the occasional variance in course classification, often in the form of traditionally private clubs allowing limited outside play. Thus, how a course is classified, while usually accurate, is always subject to potential change.

Regarding "ratings" in the larger sense, at the end of each applicable entry are a course's current rankings in the three American publications that perform this service, *Golf* magazine (biennial domestic and worldwide top 100s), *Golf Digest* (biennial domestic top 200, state-by-state rankings and top 100 public) and *Golfweek* (annual top 200s for both modern and classic layouts, plus resort courses). They are abbreviated as G, GD and GW respectively.

Now, a final note regarding bias and perspective.

As mentioned above, the great majority of the material presented herein is *objective* – the scale and style of a course's bunkering, or the statement that a layout measures 7,700 yards, or has been hugely altered since the Golden Age, are all impartial facts and not matters of opinion. But to the extent that one's personal tastes must inevitably poke around at the edges, it seems only fair to lay out my own, as follows:

1) I place an enormous emphasis on strategic design. Being able to hit a golf ball solidly is one important skill that the game requires; being able to think one's way around a well-conceived layout is an entirely different one. For me, the game is infinitely more engaging when both are fully in play.

2) I place a similar level of emphasis on variety, because even the greatest hole would get dull if played repeatedly. Courses with varied lengths and strategic challenges are, to me, much more appealing.

3) I prefer my golf relatively gimmick-free. Granted, this is a somewhat more subjective area, but generally speaking, 700-yard par 5s and artificial waterfalls in the middle of deserts tend not to inspire.

4) Ambience and setting count – not, perhaps, in assessing the strategic merits of a layout, but certainly in weighing the overall experience.

Obviously, readers may disagree with any or all of these perspectives – indeed, that's part of what makes a book like this fun – but either way, at least you'll know which comments might best be taken with a grain of salt when our tastes differ.

Safe travels!

DW

COLLECTABILITY RATING

Among the many qualities that make golf unique, none stands out further than the endless variety of its playing fields. Indeed, for most avid golfers, the chance to experience the game's vast array of courses – layouts built by all sorts of designers, in all manner of styles and settings – represents the lynchpin of golf's visceral, lifelong appeal.

In this light, we are all, in effect, collectors of golf courses, hoping to add as many significant facilities to our personal portfolios as time and circumstance will allow. It is with such an acquisitive sense in mind that The Black Book employs its original Collectability Rating, a one-to-five diamond scale which assesses each profiled facility's relative importance to the golfer's personal collection, based upon the following criteria:

1) The general perception of a course's overall quality as determined by various published rankings and commentaries, both national and regional.

2) A course's historical significance, measured primarily in terms of major competitions held, as well as period or social prominence/prestige, famous professionals or members, etc.

3) A course's architectural significance, judged by its design pedigree, its place within a particular designer's portfolio and, for older facilities, how much of their original layout remains in play.

4) An especially high (or low) degree of scenery or golfing ambience.

Each club's rating appears in the initial line of its entry, and can be defined as follows:

One of the game's absolute elite. A must-see.

An internationally prominent facility. Well worth a special visit.

♦♦♦♦

A nationally prominent facility. First-class design and/or major history.

A regionally prominent facility, often worth traveling for.

♦♦♦

A significant facility worth finding, should one be in the neighborhood.

A stronger facility offering flashes of notable design or history.

♦♦

A mid-range facility, perhaps standing out in a narrow market.

A basic facility, but one rated somewhat above the mundane.

♦

It beats a driving range.

LEGEND

Each course's entry offers a range of information on its various golfing attributes. Per the arrows shown below, these include (1) the course's designer(s), (2) its internet address and (3) its Collectability Rating (outlined on page three). If applicable, at the bottom of each entry, current positions in each of the major magazine rankings are shown (4), as detailed in the Introduction.

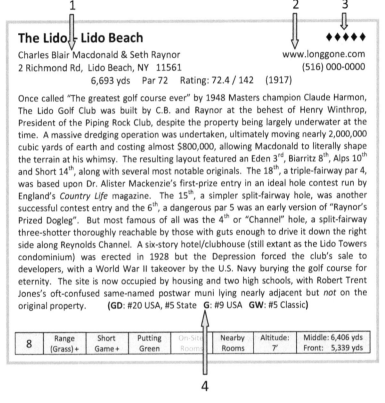

1

2 **3**

The Lido – Lido Beach ◆◆◆◆◆

Charles Blair Macdonald & Seth Raynor www.longgone.com
2 Richmond Rd, Lido Beach, NY 11561 (516) 000-0000
6,693 yds   Par 72   Rating: 72.4 / 142   (1917)

Once called "The greatest golf course ever" by 1948 Masters champion Claude Harmon, The Lido Golf Club was built by C.B. and Raynor at the behest of Henry Winthrop, President of the Piping Rock Club, despite the property being largely underwater at the time. A massive dredging operation was undertaken, ultimately moving nearly 2,000,000 cubic yards of earth and costing almost $800,000, allowing Macdonald to literally shape the terrain at his whimsy. The resulting layout featured an Eden 3rd, Biarritz 8th, Alps 10th and Short 14th, along with several most notable originals. The 18th, a triple-fairway par 4, was based upon Dr. Alister Mackenzie's first-prize entry in an ideal hole contest run by England's *Country Life* magazine. The 15th, a simpler split-fairway hole, was another successful contest entry and the 6th, a dangerous par 5 was an early version of "Raynor's Prized Dogleg". But most famous of all was the 4th or "Channel" hole, a split-fairway three-shotter thoroughly reachable by those with guts enough to drive it down the right side along Reynolds Channel. A six-story hotel/clubhouse (still extant as the Lido Towers condominium) was erected in 1928 but the Depression forced the club's sale to developers, with a World War II takeover by the U.S. Navy burying the golf course for eternity. The site is now occupied by housing and two high schools, with Robert Trent Jones's oft-confused same-named postwar muni lying nearly adjacent but *not* on the original property.   **(GD**: #20 USA, #5 State **G**: #9 USA **GW**: #5 Classic)

8	Range (Grass)+	Short Game+	Putting Green	On-Site Rooms	Nearby Rooms	Altitude: 7'	Middle: 6,406 yds Front: 5,339 yds

4

The facilities grid at the bottom of each entry provides information on (from left to right):

● A course's difficulty, on a 1-10 scale (based upon USGA rating, commentaries, etc.).

● A course's practice range. Tee surface is indicated as "grass," "mats" or "both." A plus sign indicates an especially strong facility. A minus sign indicates an undersized or "irons-only" range.

● A course's short game practice area (must include at least one bunker). A plus sign indicates an especially strong facility.

● A course's putting green(s).

● Whether the course offers on-site accommodations. Resort courses are deemed to have such accommodations if owned by a hostelry, even if the hotel is more than two miles distant. For private clubs, such accommodations are only recognized if listed on the club's website.

● Whether non-RV accommodations are available within a two-mile radius of the club.

● A course's altitude above sea level (estimated based on a representative mean point).

● A course's total yardages from representative middle ("white") and front ("red") tees.

Unshaded boxes within the grid mean that a course does not possess this particular component.

A BRIEF HISTORY OF SAN FRANCISCO GOLF

The San Francisco Bay Area is geographically different from most major American cities in that with San Pablo, San Rafael and San Francisco bays extending northward and southward from the Golden Gate, and mountains consuming considerable acreage in several directions, the amount of land suitable for golf development has always been limited. As a result, even during the go-go days of the 1920s, when real estate remained inexpensive and course construction spiked in many major cities, far fewer courses were built in and around San Francisco and Oakland than in nearly any of the nation's large metropolitan areas. Yet despite this relative paucity of courses, the Bay Area – with an undeniable boost from the outlying Monterey Peninsula – has enjoyed a golfing history that very few comparably sized cities can equal.

The game's roots actually run quite deep here; indeed, the three holes reportedly constructed by the Burlingame Country Club in 1893 stand as the first golf development ever recorded west of the Mississippi River. The formation of the San Francisco Golf Club was soon to follow, and it is a testament to the early nature of its 1895 founding that the club's initial nine-hole course was actually situated *within* the borders of the Presidio army base – a fascinating statement as to the somewhat less-regimented nature of military and civilian interaction during the 19th century.

Several more nine-hole layouts would spring up around the Bay Area during the century's final years, with the relatively short-lived Oakland Golf Club being constructed in 1897, the San Rafael Golf Club following in 1898, and the less-documented San Mateo Hunt Club also opening its doors during this period. And then there was the nine-hole course affiliated with Monterey's Hotel Del Monte, which also joined the fray during 1897. Still in play today (in somewhat revised form), the Del Monte layout would be expanded in 1903, giving it the historical distinction of being California's first 18-hole facility.

By 1905, the desire of the Presidio's Commandant to at least occasionally use his base's western expanse for military purposes became a problem for the San Francisco Golf Club membership, many of whom opted to pick up stakes and head south. Leasing a considerably larger site within the city's Ingleside district, they constructed a member-designed 18-hole facility which was well-received within an admittedly novice-filled golfing market. In their wake, however, some of the sturdier Presidio members elected to carry on, redesigning their facility into a short 18-holer and operating as the private Presidio Golf Club. Add to this the municipal layout at nearby Lincoln Park (which began with six holes in 1909 before eventually being expanded) and San Francisco had three courses operating within city limits by the onset of World War I.

The Northern California Golf association was founded in 1901, ushering in an era of organized competition which began with the staging of the first Northern California Amateur in 1903. But Bay Area competitive golf only entered the national limelight in 1915, when the San Francisco Golf Club hosted major professional and amateur tournaments in conjunction with the Pan-Pacific Exhibition, a World's Fair-like event held to commemorate the opening of the Panama Canal. These tournaments drew strong enough fields that the winner of the 72-hole professional contest was reigning U.S. Open champion Walter Hagen, who enjoyed a $1,000 payday. The amateur side was taken by one Harry Davis Jr. of The Presidio, who bettered a match play field which included Hall-of-Famer Chick Evans.

A year later, in 1916, the Western Amateur made its first trip west of the Rocky Mountains, being hosted by the Del Monte Golf Course in Monterey. Then, in 1917, San Francisco debuted its City Championship, an amateur event which, undeterred by two World Wars, a Depression, a Summer of Love, and whatever other challenges have come its way, has been contested annually, without interruption, ever since.

Though obviously only a one-time thing, the 1916 Western Amateur also had a major impact on the game's development throughout the region, for it represented a proverbial dip into the golfing waters by the powers-that-be on the Monterey Peninsula. In its aftermath, Del Monte Properties boss Samuel Morse elected to prioritize golf within his fledgling development, hiring Western Amateur runner-up Douglas Grant and fellow local amateur star Jack Neville to design America's foremost seaside golf course, Pebble Beach. Their creation would open in 1919, and while some subsequent alteration and maintenance enhancements were necessary to bring it fully into its modern form, Pebble Beach drew the sort of widespread attention necessary to help the Peninsula become one of the world's great golfing destinations.

The 1920s would witness golf's greatest-ever rush of course construction throughout the United States, and while the aforementioned geographic issues limited the Bay Area in this regard, some very significant developments did take place. The first of these involved the San Francisco Golf Club which, faced with the prospect of losing their leased land in Ingleside during 1918, opted to purchase acreage nearby, with a committee of members once again laying out a new course. But by now, the notion of hiring a known architect was commonplace in American golf so, not entirely satisfied with their in-house creation, the club decided to retain the up-and-coming A.W. Tillinghast to perform a renovation. Tillinghast's redesign opened in 1920 and while some subsequent changes would be made (notably within the layout's copious bunkering), his work gave the Bay Area its first high-end, "modern" golf course.

The second major development took place just west of the new San Francisco Golf Club property, where another recent addition, the Lakeside Golf Club, had opened in 1916. Lakeside would struggle economically, however, and only two years into its existence, it was purchased by the Olympic Club, a venerable downtown San Francisco organization which desired a country facility that would include golf. Having secured plenty of adjacent acreage as well, Olympic hired William Watson to redesign the Lakeside layout into a 36-hole facility, with its new Lake course lying entirely east of Skyline Boulevard and its Ocean course straddling Skyline and including several holes routed along the bluffs above the Pacific. Both layouts opened in May of 1924 with the Ocean, in particular, drawing national acclaim. Sadly, heavy storms during the winter of 1925-1926 would cause major landslide damage, leading to a facility-wide redesign in 1927 by Watson's construction foreman Sam Whiting. What resulted, inevitably, was a somewhat diminished Ocean course, its once-spectacular nature largely neutered by an entirely inland routing – but also a revamped Lake course that would soon take its place among the strongest tournament venues on the West Coast.

Meanwhile, there were also big doings going on under the watchful eye of Samuel Morse on the Monterey Peninsula, as the latter half of the 1920s saw the addition of two more golf clubs to join Pebble Beach. The first, the Monterey Peninsula Country Club, was completed in 1926 and featured a layout routed across both forest and seaside terrain; its scenic aspects were superb, while its challenge was tailored mostly towards recreational play.

The second club was Cypress Point.

Laid out by Dr. Alister MacKenzie in 1928 over a site which included an unmatched mix of dense forest, imposing sand dunes and oceanfront acreage set spectacularly upon rocky clifftops, Cypress Point immediately staked its claim as an elite venue, with its famed par-3 16th hole becoming one of golf's most photographed landscapes. Cypress Point drew massive coverage from several period-prominent national golf publications and, along with neighboring Pebble Beach, gave the Peninsula two world-class layouts practically within walking distance of one another. If the Eastern bluebloods hadn't taken California golf seriously up to this point, Samuel Morse certainly made sure that they did now.

But beyond a developer like Morse, the man most responsible for the growth of Northern California's golfing reputation was Alister MacKenzie. A Cambridge-educated doctor and a veteran of the Boer War, Mackenzie had made his name working with legendary British course architects H.S. Colt and C.H. Alison before venturing out on his own, eventually leaving his most prominent design footprints in the United States and Australia. MacKenzie would move to America in 1927 and eventually settle in Santa Cruz during the latter years of his life, a period in which, in addition to Cypress Point, he added such regional gems as Pasatiempo, the Meadow Club and the municipal Sharp Park, as well as major redesigns of the California Golf Club, Claremont and Lake Merced. Seldom has so talented a golf course designer accomplished so much in so limited a geographic area, and in so short a span of time.

But also worthy of mention among architects was William Watson, a Scottish native born near St Andrews who came to the United States in 1898. After working for a number of years as a professional and greenkeeper in the Midwest (while wintering in Pasadena), Watson settled permanently in California circa World War I and began a full-time design practice that flourished in both the northern and southern parts of the state. His most prominent Bay Area creations would include the 36 holes at the Olympic Club, Harding Park, the Orinda Country Club and the Diablo Country Club, as well as redesigns of both the Claremont and Burlingame Country Clubs, and it can be safely said that were it not for the massive, attention-drawing presence of Dr. MacKenzie as a period competitor, Watson's name would be far better remembered in Northern California golfing circles today.

One more architect who profoundly affected the region (though on a much smaller scale) was two-time U.S. Amateur champion H. Chandler Egan. A Harvard graduate, Egan moved to Oregon in 1911 and there began a design practice which apparently caught Samuel Morse's attention, for it was Egan who was hired to perform a major renovation of Pebble Beach ahead of its hosting of the 1929 U.S. Amateur. Though retaining the layout's original figure-eight routing, Egan added bunkers and rebuilt virtually every green complex, in several cases adding visually striking faux dunes around putting surfaces. These dunes would return to grass during the austerity of the Depression, but it can be argued that nearly a century later, Pebble Beach's current playing characteristics owe more to Chandler Egan than anyone else.

Egan's work was well-received and helped make the 1929 U.S. Amateur the Monterey Peninsula's introduction to much of the golfing world east of Salinas, but the event's run of play didn't hurt either. Indeed, while Harrison "Jimmy" Johnston's 4 & 3 finals triumph over Dr. O.F. Willing was all fine and good, history would far more loudly record the stunning first round departure of two-time defending champion Bobby Jones, who arrived as a heavy favorite before being dispatched by 19-year-old Johnny Goodman at the 18th green. Jones' loss surely drew more attention to the Amateur than Johnston's ultimate victory but regardless, Pebble Beach was now very much on the national map.

Though amateur golf generally enjoyed an equal degree of popularity during this period, the professional game was just beginning its meteoric rise during the 1920s, a development not lost on the Bay Area. San Francisco did not immediately launch a long-running PGA Tour event in the manner undertaken in Los Angeles, San Diego, Phoenix and Tucson, but it did witness several short-term tournaments boasting national-level fields. These included Jock Hutchison's runaway victory in the 1922 Northern California Open (played at the San Francisco Golf Club), a 1926 victory by "Lighthorse" Harry Cooper in the first major professional event hosted by Pebble Beach (the Monterey Peninsula Championship), and a 1926 triumph by Bill Mehlhorn in San Jose's one-time Santa Clara Valley Open.

Of a somewhat more lasting nature was the San Francisco Match Play (aka the National Match Play Open), which made its debut at the Olympic Club in 1930 and was played annually (save for 1933) over various Bay Area venues through 1941. Hall-of-Famer Leo Diegel beat Monterey native Al Espinosa 6 & 4 in the final of the inaugural edition, and he would be followed by more big-name champions such as Craig Wood (1932), Jug McSpaden (1935), Jimmy Demaret (1938 and 1940) and Johnny Revolta (1941) before the event lapsed with the onset of World War II.

Also emerging victorious in the Match Play was a man with local ties, Lawson Little, who took the 1937 edition at the old Ingleside Golf Club. Though born in Rhode Island, Little spent most of his formative years in the Bay Area and in Monterey, and it was from there that he emerged in the mid-1930s as the region's first great golfing prospect. Indeed, while Little's overall amateur record couldn't match that of Bobby Jones, he utterly trumped Jones in one regard, becoming the only player ever to win both the U.S. and British Amateurs in back-to-back years, accomplishing this remarkable feat in 1934 and '35. Little would turn professional in 1936 and while his PGA Tour career was a shade less grand, a ledger which included eight official victories (including the 1940 U.S. Open at Canterbury) could hardly be considered disappointing.

While much of the nation suffered, American professional golf actually fared quite well during the Depression, a circumstance demonstrated by a new slate of events which called the Bay Area home. The first new arrival was the Oakland Open, which debuted at the Claremont Country Club in 1937, and saw its inaugural edition carry the historical footnote of being the great Sam Snead's first-ever victory outside of West Virginia. Thereafter, the tournament would be contested at the Sequoyah Country Club for six more editions, with names like Harry Cooper, Jimmy Demaret, Byron Nelson and Jim Ferrier all being etched upon the trophy.

The San Francisco Match Play event was indeed retired in 1941 but it was immediately replaced by a new tournament, the San Francisco Open, a year later. Ben Hogan won this debut edition (beating Sam Snead by three at the California Golf Club) before the event observed wartime darkness in 1943. Perhaps surprisingly, only three more playings would follow, all of them won by Byron Nelson, with the first two coming at Harding Park and the last, in 1946, being a nine-shot runaway at the Olympic Club. Also joining the fray during the 1940s was the Richmond Open, which was contested across the bay at the Richmond Country Club in 1944, and then again from 1946-1948. While Sam Snead, Toney Penna and Dutch Harrison would all emerge as winners here, the tournament carries the historical burden of its 1948 edition, where pioneering African-American golfers Bill Spiller, Ted Rhodes and Madison Gunter were denied spots in the field, with their resulting lawsuit representing the first step in the eventual demise of the PGA of America's notorious "caucasians only" clause in 1961.

However, the most significant tournament addition during this period – easily – was the arrival of the Bing Crosby Pro-Am, an event begun by Crosby near San Diego in 1937, but which the legendary crooner moved to the Monterey Peninsula in 1946. Initially contested over a three-course rotation which Included Pebble Beach, Cypress Point and the Monterey Peninsula Country Club, its pro-am format was an instant hit with celebrities, athletes and prominent business people, making the tournament one of the West Coast's most prestigious and, eventually, a winter television ratings bonanza. In the mid-1960s, the brand-new Spyglass Hill Golf Course would replace Monterey Peninsula, and the Northern California Golf Association's Poppy Hills Golf Course would take over for Cypress Point in 1991, with Poppy Hills then being removed in favor a renovated Monterey Peninsula Country Club Shore course in 2011. Boasting a ledger of champions that includes more than 20 Hall-of-Famers, the event would change its name to the AT&T Pebble Beach National Pro-Am in the years after Crosby's death, and it remains today a centerpiece of the PGA Tour's winter schedule.

The USGA had made its regional debut with the 1929 U.S. Amateur, and it returned several times over the ensuing quarter-century, with events including the 1937 U.S. Amateur Public Links (at Harding Park), the 1940 and '48 U.S. Women's Amateurs (won by Betty Jameson and Grace Lenczyk respectively at Pebble Beach), the 1947 U.S. Amateur (claimed by Robert "Skee" Riegel, also at Pebble Beach) and the 1952 U.S. Girls' Junior, which represented the national breakthrough of a 17-year-old Mickey Wright, at the Monterey Peninsula Country Club.

But in 1955 the region took a big step up in class when the U.S. Open made its Northern California debut at the Olympic Club, and this would prove one of the more memorable events in Open history. For this would be represent the peak of a 42-year-old Ben Hogan's pursuit of his Holy Grail, a fifth U.S. Open victory, and after rounds of 72-73-72, he held a one-shot 54-hole lead. In most any other period Open, Hogan's closing 70 would have comfortably done the trick but on this occasion, little-known Jack Fleck birdied the 72nd hole to card a stunning a 67, tying Hogan on 287 and necessitating an 18-hole playoff. In something of a surprise, Fleck jumped out to an early playoff lead and never looked back, and while a Fleck bogey at the 17th narrowed the margin to one, Hogan promptly unraveled with a double-bogey at the short par-4 18th and, in one of the great upsets of all time, Jack Fleck was the U.S. Open champion.

The USGA would bring several more events to the region in the years immediately to follow, most prominently returning to Olympic for the 1958 U.S. Amateur (won by Charles Coe), then taking the Amateur to Pebble Beach in 1961, where Jack Nicklaus routed Dudley Weysong 8 & 6 to claim the title for the second time. But as the 1950s turned to the 1960s, an equally big story was the debut of two new PGA Tour events in the region, the Lucky International and the Almaden Open. The Almaden would be the shorter lived and less-prestigious of the pair, being played from 1960-1965 at the Almaden Country Club, with only four of those six editions today recognized as official by the PGA Tour. The Lucky International, on the other hand, found significant status on the PGA Tour while it was played at Harding Park from 1959-1969, producing a list of champions that included Hall-of-Famers Gary Player, Gene Littler, Jack Burke Jr., Billy Casper and Chi Chi Rodriguez, as well as local favorites George Archer and Ken Venturi.

Venturi is of particular importance as he, and soon thereafter Tony Lema, would emerge as the Bay Area's first great golfers of the postwar era. In Venturi's case, after learning the game at Harding Park, he was ticketed for greatness at a young age, losing in the finals of the inaugural U.S. Junior Amateur in 1948, winning the first of two California Amateur titles in 1951, and finishing second at the 1956 Masters prior to turning professional. He would go on to win 14 times on the PGA Tour but had his career famously derailed by severe cases of carpal tunnel syndrome in both of his wrists – only to mount one of the game's great comebacks in winning the 1964 U.S. Open at Congressional. Wrist issues would ultimately end his playing career, however, setting up a long and very popular run as lead golf analyst for CBS sports.

Lema, on the other hand, was more of a late developer, learning the game at the Lake Chabot Golf Course before enlisting in the Marine Corps at age 17 and serving in Korea. Only after his military discharge did he get serious about golf and by the late 1950s, he was winning events against quality fields. By the early 1960s, he had found a place on the PGA Tour, where he would go on to claim 12 victories and pick up the nickname "Champagne Tony" after serving champagne to the press following a victory at the 1962 Orange County Open. Tragically, Lema was killed in a plane crash near Chicago in 1966, but not before becoming one of the Tour's best and most popular players – and, in an odd bit of symmetry with his fellow San Franciscan Venturi, also winning a Major championship in 1964, the British Open at St Andrews.

Another 1960s Major development took place in 1966, when the U.S. Open returned to the Olympic Club for the second time, and once again the club's Lake course generated a highly memorable result. This was because for 63 holes, the Open appeared to well in the grasp of Arnold Palmer, who'd begun the final round three ahead of Billy Casper and then extended the lead to seven after turning in 32. But as history well records, Palmer collapsed on the final nine, Casper carded two late birdies to tie him on 278, then fell behind early in their Monday playoff before mounting one more comeback to ultimately claim the title by four shots.

The later years of the 1960s saw the arrival of what would be the last new Bay Area PGA Tour event for nearly four decades when what was originally known as the Kaiser International Open made its debut in 1968 at Napa's Silverado Resort. Initially a January event before moving to the fall in 1970, the Kaiser regularly drew strong fields and produced big-name winners – plus it also managed the rare feat of having 14 official playings in a 13-year span, this owing to a 36-hole rainout in January 1969 that somehow managed to be counted as official, with the 72-hole version that was added that autumn to make up for it also holding a spot in the record book. Also making its debut at decade's end (1969) was a tournament known as the Lincoln-Mercury Open, an event played at Alamo's Round Hill Country Club and sponsored by the LPGA.

From the time of its 1950 founding, the LPGA had made several brief appearances in the region, beginning with the two-year run (1950 and '51) of the Pebble Beach Weathervane, which was won by Babe Zaharias and Patty Berg respectively. There followed three playings of the Richmond Open between 1951-1955, the one-off San Francisco Weathervane (won by Louise Suggs) in 1953, and the equally brief United Voluntary Services Open (won by Wiffi Smith at The Presidio) in 1957. The Lincoln-Mercury, however, would have a tad more staying power, being played seven times over a 10-year span (the last two as the Sarah Coventry) and finally giving women's professional golf a lasting foothold in the region.

Indeed, following the Sarah Coventry's 1978 expiration, the LPGA wasted little time in creating a new event, the Inamori Golf Classic, two years later. Played at the Almaden Country Club, the Inamori would be contested three times (and boast a trio of Hall-of-Fame winners in Amy Alcott, Hollis Stacy and Patty Sheehan) before moving to San Diego in 1983. Undaunted, the LPGA immediately replaced it with still another new event, the Konica San Jose Classic, which was also played at Almaden, and which would run from 1983-1989.

The 1970s, meanwhile, began with Jack Nicklaus winning a thrilling 1972 U.S. Open at Pebble Beach (clinching the title with a 1 iron which famously hit the flagstick at the 218-yard 17th) and later witnessed Lanny Wadkins defeating 47-year-old Gene Littler in a playoff for the 1977 PGA Championship (also at Pebble Beach). But in between, the decade featured the rise of the greatest golfer ever produced within the region, Johnny Miller.

A San Francisco native, Miller first entered the national spotlight upon winning the 1964 U.S. Junior Amateur, then, after his freshman year at Brigham Young, claiming low amateur honors at the 1966 U.S. Open at the Olympic Club, where he finished in an impressive tie for eighth. After turning pro in 1969, Miller claimed individual PGA Tour victories in 1971 and '72 before becoming a household name at the 1973 U.S. Open at Oakmont, where he stood six off the lead through 54 holes before closing with perhaps the finest round of competitive golf ever played, a scorching 63 which proved just enough to edge John Schlee by one for the title. What followed was an eight-win Player of the Year campaign in 1974, four more wins in 1975 and three in 1976, the latter season including a six-stroke British Open victory at Royal Birkdale. Though he cooled considerably thereafter, Miller's career totals of 25 PGA Tour wins (including two Majors) made him an easy choice for Hall of Fame induction in 1998.

The 1980s, of course, are best remembered for the U.S. Open's 1982 visit to Pebble Beach, an event in which, like Ben Hogan at the Olympic Club in 1955, Jack Nicklaus appeared primed to win a record fifth Open title. Nicklaus stood three off the lead after 54 holes, then launched himself into contention via five straight front nine birdies, and eventually shot 69 to post a four-under-par 284 total. His chances of at least getting into a playoff looked good when Tom Watson reached the 17th tied at four under, then pulled he tee shot into some deep rough left of the green. But in one of the Open's all-time iconic moments, Watson proceeded to chip in for birdie before adding another birdie at the par-5 18th to win by two.

The '80s also included two important events contested at the Olympic Club, the 1987 U.S. Open (wherein Scott Simpson closed with a 68 to edge Tom Watson by one) and a victory by Bing Crosby's son Nathaniel in the 1981 U.S. Amateur, a compelling story but also something of a shocker given that local product Crosby did not appear on anybody's list of favorites entering play. The decade also witnessed a 1988 visit to Pebble Beach by the PGA Tour's Tour Championship (won by Curtis Strange) as well as the arrival of the senior-oriented Champions Tour, who made a one-time visit to Harding Park in 1981 before kicking off 14 straight playings of the TransAmerica Senior Championship at the Silverado Resort in 1989. The Champions would remain a regular presence in the region thereafter, initially adding a second event for two years in Morgan Creek (the 2001 and '02 Siebel Classic), then debuting a tournament at Pebble Beach in 2004 which, through multiple names and sponsors, remains active today.

While the 1990s would include a victory by David Gossett in the 1999 U.S. Amateur at Pebble Beach, the decade is best recalled for professional events, most prominently Tom Kite's wind-driven victory in the 1992 U.S. Open at Pebble Beach and Lee Janzen's one-shot triumph over Payne Stewart in the 1998 Open at Olympic. The Tour Championship also visited Olympic in 1993 and '94 (with Jim Gallagher Jr. and Mark McCumber raising trophies), though of far greater local interest was the 1994 ATT&T Pebble Beach National Pro-Am, which saw a 46-year-old Johnny Miller come out of nowhere to record his 25th and final PGA Tour victory, outdueling 44-year-old Tom Watson and three additional contenders by one.

Absent from this recounting since before World War II is mention of golf course development for the simple reason that relative to most major American cities, rather little took place within the region during the postwar years. Indeed, only two regulation-sized facilities of genuine note were constructed during the 1950s, the Bayonet course on what was then the sprawling Ford Ord military facility near Monterey (1954) and the Almaden Country Club (a future PGA Tour venue) in 1956. New arrivals picked up a bit during the 1960s, though the most noteworthy entries tended to be constructed in outlying regions. Most prominent on this list was surely Robert Trent Jones' Spyglass Hill Golf Course, whose difficulty found near-instant fame upon its 1966 opening when it was immediately added to the rota of the Bing Crosby Pro-Am. Also arriving on/adjacent to the Monterey Peninsula was Robert Muir Graves' layout for the Quail Lodge Resort (1963) and a second course at Fort Ord, the Blackhorse (1964), which, like its older sibling, was designed by the base's golfing commander, General Robert McClure.

The 1960s and '70s saw considerable growth in resort course development nationwide and this trend was also felt within the region, notably in Napa (a Robert Trent Jones remodeling of an earlier 18 into the 36-hole Silverado Resort), Half Moon Bay (a 1973 Arnold Palmer layout with an oceanfront 18th hole) and, to the north, at Bodega Bay, which constructed a Robert Trent Jones II nine in 1978, with a second loop added nine years later.

The 1980s saw continued development around the Monterey Peninsula, first at the Pete Dye-designed Carmel Valley Ranch (1981), then at the Northern California Golf Association's Poppy Hills Golf Course (1986) and, most notably, at the Links at Spanish Bay, an oceanfront layout designed by Robert Trent Jones II, former USGA President Sandy Tatum and Tom Watson in 1987. Half Moon Bay would add a second 18 in 1997, and a future U.S. Women's Open site, CordeValle, would further deepen the resort ledger in 1999. But as the new millennium approached, the region fell more in line with nation trends towards upscale public course development, frequently on sites well removed from the heart of San Francisco or Oakland. Of course, in so affluent a region, private club development remained an inevitability, and if Jack Nicklaus's well-received Mayacama Golf Club (2001) enjoyed an enviable site, more frequent was the usage of acreage whose availability was tied to either its remoteness or a lack of suitability for other purposes. The result was some spectacular golf in elevated, often rugged locations, such as a pair of courses situated above Carmel (Jay Morrish's 1999 design at Tehama and Tom Fazio's 2000 layout at The Preserve) as well as the David McClay Kidd-designed TPC Stonebrae, which sits in the mountains above Hayward and Union City.

From a competitive perspective, the new millennium began in epic form with Tiger Woods' mind-boggling performance in the 2000 U.S. Open at Pebble Beach, wherein he broke Old Tom Morris' 138-year-old margin-of-victory record upon running away from Ernie Els and Miguel Angel Jimenez by an astonishing 15 shots. The Open would return to Pebble Beach in both 2010 (with Northern Ireland's Graeme McDowell breaking through) and 2019 (when Gary Woodland turned back Brooks Koepka's heroic bid for an Open threepeat), while also making a visit to the Olympic Club in 2012, where Webb Simpson emerged victorious. Also added to the region's big event ledger were a quartet of tournaments played at Harding Park, the 2005 WGC American Express Championship (won by Tiger Woods), the 2009 Presidents Cup, the 2015 WGC-Match Play (claimed by Rory McIlroy) and the 2020 PGA Championship, where Collin Morikawa raised the trophy on tournament which, due to the COVID pandemic, was played without spectators. And on the women's side, the 2016 U.S. Women's Open was played at CordeValle, where Brittany Lang defeated Anna Nordqvist in a three-hole aggregate playoff.

At the time of this writing, both the PGA and LPGA Tours have annual stops scheduled in the region, the men's Safeway Open being contested (since 2014) at Silverado and the women's Mediheal Championship visiting the Lake Merced Golf Club. Pebble Beach, of course, will always be a desired Major championship venue (the 2023 U.S. Women's Open and the 2027 U.S. Open are currently on the schedule) and it is presently joined on the USGA docket by the Olympic Club (which will host the 2025 U.S. Amateur) and Cypress Point, which will make a rare return to the tournament spotlight by entertaining the 2025 Walker Cup.

PROMINENT ARCHITECTS OF
THE SAN FRANCISCO AREA

Arranged alphabetically, the following are the course designers who have left the largest footprints upon the golfing landscape of the San Francisco Bay Area. Courses are referred to by their current names and are listed chronologically, with the designation "BO" indicating that it has been built over (i.e., a different course exists upon the site today). "DU" indicates that the course's date of construction is unknown.

Bob Baldock – A prolific architect often credited with the completion of well over 300 design projects, Robert Earl Baldock (1908-2000) was a native of Omaha, Nebraska who plied his trade primarily the American West from the 1950s through the 1990s. A former club professional who cut his design teeth working for Billy Bell, Baldock's output was mostly functional in style, and thus seldom garnered major regional or national praise. Indeed, his marquee project, the Shore course at Northern California's Monterey Peninsula Country Club, has been comprehensively renovated by Mike Strantz in the new millennium, leaving Baldock's footprints there as a thing of the past. He remains notable, however, for having built numerous courses (often free of charge) for the military and the Veterans Administration – no small design legacy indeed.

Bob Baldock In the San Francisco Area:

Lone Tree G & Events Center – Antioch	1957
Corral de Tierra CC – Corral de Tierra	1959
GC at Moffett Field – Sunnyvale	1959
Monterey Peninsula CC (Shore) – Pebble Beach (BO)	1961
Diablo Creek GC – Concord	1963
Foxtail GC (South) – Rohnert Park	1963
Redwood Canyon GC – Castro Valley	1966

Jack Fleming – A native of County Galway, Ireland, John Francis Fleming (1896-1986) had moved to England and worked his way into a construction foreman's position with Dr. Alister MacKenzie by the age of 24. Thus in 1926 he was dispatched to California to oversee the building of MacKenzie's Marin County project at The Meadow Club and, finding the area to his liking, soon emigrated permanently after MacKenzie did the same. Fleming would thus supervise construction on a number of the Good Doctor's regional layouts including, most prominently, Cypress Point. With the onset of the Depression arrived, he took a job as the head greenkeeper with the San Francisco Parks Department where he would toil for roughly 30 years, with his course design career serving as a fairly prolific sidelight. As a part of this second job, he built a number of courses in Northern California, many of them par-three or "executive" designs. Among the strongest of these regional layouts were Menlo Park's Sharon Heights Golf & Country Club and San Jose's Almaden Golf & Country Club (a future PGA Tour site), and Fleming also performed modest renovations at the Olympic Club. His nine-hole executive layout at San Francisco's TPC Harding Park was eventually named in his honor.

Jack Fleming In the San Francisco Area:

Blue Rock Springs (West) – Vallejo	1949
Golden Gate Park GC – San Francisco (9, Par 3)	1951
Almaden G & CC – San Jose	1956
Santa Rosa G&CC – Santa Rosa	1958
Boulder Creek G&CC – Boulder Creek (Executive)	1961
TPC Harding Park (Fleming) – San Francisco (9, Executive)	1961

14

Jack Fleming Cont'd.	
Gleneagles GC at McLaren Park – San Francisco	1962
Sharon Heights G&CC – Menlo Park	1962
Meadowood Napa Valley – St. Helena (9, Executive)	1965
Pruneridge GC – Santa Clara (9, Executive)	1967
Napa GC at Kennedy Park – Napa	1968

Herbert Fowler – Tottenham native William Herbert Fowler (1856-1941) was the product of an upper-class English family and possessed the height (6'4") and athleticism to initially make his name as a force at cricket. Golf didn't enter his life until age 35, though in characteristic fashion, he was playing to scratch and joining both the R&A and the Honorable Company of Edinburgh Golfers with relative dispatch. A banker by trade, Fowler only entered the field of golf course design when a group led by his brother-in-law financed the construction of the Walton Heath Golf Club in 1904 and, as has so often been the case in the design world, he built what many consider to be his best course right out of the box.

More work naturally followed, and Fowler soon formed an architectural partnership with a young Tom Simpson, Fowler handling the British designs, Simpson those located in continental Europe. Easily too old for military serviced, Fowler spent time in the United States during World War I, becoming involved in a handful of projects. He then returned in 1920 when he completed the North course at the Los Angeles Country Club and Cape Cod's ultra-natural Eastward Ho!, and it was on this visit that much of his San Francisco area work took place – including the conversion of Pebble Beach's 18th from a relatively nondescript par 4 into the world's most famous par 5. Fowler's British résumé is considerably more extensive as he continued practicing there well into the 1930s, supplementing original layouts with redesigns of such standards as Saunton, Royal North Devon, Ganton and Royal Lytham & St Annes. J.F. Abercromby and A.C.M. Croome would also join Fowler and Simpson, though most of Fowler's designs were completed without their input. Once referred to by Bernard Darwin as "perhaps the most daring and original of all golfing architects," Fowler bore the interesting dichotomy of always being known as Herbert in golfing circles, but being listed as Bill in many cricket records.

Herbert Fowler In the San Francisco Area:	
Lincoln Park GC – San Francisco (Redesign)	1920
Del Monte GC – Monterey (Redesign)	1921
Presidio GC – San Francisco (Redesign)	1921
Crystal Springs GC – Burlingame	1924
Menlo CC – Redwood City (Redesign)	DU
Sequoyah CC – Oakland (Redesign)	DU

Robert Muir Graves – A native of Trenton, Michigan, Robert Muir Graves (1930-2003) stood among a group of postwar American architects (see Arthur Jack Snyder, Gary Roger Baird, etc.) who evidently saw the prominent use of a middle name as an integral aspect of Robert Trent Jones's dominance of the period market. Educated at the University of California-Berkeley, Graves began his career working primarily as a landscape designer before later transitioning full-time into golf. Indeed, to quote Cornish & Whitten: "Although he was not the first landscape architect to become a golf course planner, Graves was generally felt to have ushered in the era of landscape architecture as the preferred academic background for course designers." A lecturer on landscape and golf architecture at several universities, Graves also co-authored (with Geoffrey Cornish) two prominent contemporary works, *Golf Course Design* (John Wiley & Sons, 1998) and *Classic Golf Hole Design* (John Wiley & Sons, 2002).

While Cornish & Whitten cite his involvement in somer 650 projects, Graves established himself primarily as a West Coast designer, building more than 45 new courses in California, Oregon and Washington, and finding considerably more work in the remodeling of perhaps four times that many within the region.   A mostly functional designer, he was comfortably the most prolific architect in San Francisco Bay Area history, where his résumé included the Sea Ranch Golf Links and, perhaps most famously, the Golf Club at Quail Lodge, near Pebble Beach.

Robert Muir Graves In the San Francisco Area:

Blackberry Farm GC – Cupertino (9, Executive)	1962
Monterey Pines GC – Monterey	1963
GC at Quail Lodge – Carmel	1963
Lake Merced GC – Daly City (Redesign)	1964
Saratoga CC – Saratoga (9) (Redesign)	1966
Las Positas GC – Livermore	1967
Diablo Hills GC – Walnut Creek	1968
Franklin Canyon GC – Hercules	1968
San Jose Municipal GC – San Jose	1968
Villages G&CC – San Jose	1968
Villages G&CC (Short) – San Jose (9, Par 3)	1968
Boundary Oak GC – Walnut Creek	1969
Moraga CC – Moraga (9)	1973
Sea Ranch GL – Sea Ranch (9 + Add 9, 1995)	1974
Rossmoor – Walnut Creek (9)	1977
Paradise Valley GC – Fairfield (w/D. Pascuzzo)	1983
Las Positas GC (Executive) – Livermore (9)	1990
Blue Rock Springs (East) – Vallejo	1994
Rancho del Pueblo CC – San Jose (w/D. Pascuzzo) (9, Executive)	2000
Buchanan Fields GC – Concord (9, Executive)	(DU)

Robert Trent Jones II –   The older of Robert Trent Jones's two sons, "Bobby" (b.1939, in Montclair, New Jersey) graduated from Yale and initially gave Stanford Law School a try before electing instead to pursue the field of golf design. He joined his father's firm in 1960, eventually taking over its active West Coast office in Palo Alto, California. In 1972 he went out on his own, and has since completed more than 200 designs in 38 countries, on all six golfing continents.

Beyond an accent on tactically engaging design that regularly exceeded that of his father, an additional reason for this worldwide success lies in Jones's involvement with the furthering of international relations and environmental causes. He served in the American delegation to the 1975 Helsinki Accords, and has enjoyed close relationships with many foreign leaders, helping his company to gain a foothold in far-off locales like Russia, where he built that nation's first course in 1992. Jones's Northern California works have included CordeValle (site of the 2016 U.S. Women's Open) as well as two projects completed on the Monterey Peninsula, the Poppy Hills Golf Course (which he also renovated in 2014) and the Links at Spanish Bay.

Robert Trent Jones II In the San Francisco Area:

Laguna Seca G Ranch – Monterey (w/R.T. Jones)	1970
L at Bodega Harbor – Bodega Bay (9 + Add 9 in 1987)	1978
Shoreline GL – Mountain View	1983
Poppy Hills GC – Pebble Beach (+ Redesign, 2014)	1986
L at Spanish Bay – Pebble Beach (w/T. Watson & S. Tatum)	1987
CordeValle – San Martin	1999
Dublin Ranch GC – Dublin (Executive)	2004

Dr. Alister MacKenzie –   Perhaps the most famous name in the history of golf course design, Dr. Alexander "Alister" MacKenzie (1870-1934) was of Scottish blood, though born and raised near Leeds, England. A graduate of Cambridge who earned degrees in medicine, natural science and chemistry, MacKenzie served in the Boer War, where he keenly observed the camouflage techniques employed by Afrikaner soldiers to outflank their more regimented British opponents.   Surviving the hostilities intact, he then returned to Leeds and took up medical practice before branching into golf course design, where he drew early attention by winning *Country Life* magazine's 1914 contest for the best design of a hypothetical par 4, a high-profile competition judged by no less than Bernard Darwin, Horace Hutchinson and Herbert Fowler.

Though he would become a partner with the legendary design firm of Colt & Alison, MacKenzie found his true glory working on his own and primarily abroad, with his first great venture being a 1926 trip to Australia, where he provided plans for the design or alteration of nearly a dozen courses, including a new 18 at Royal Melbourne and the addition of bunkering, on a massive scale, at Kingston Heath.   A brief visit to South America yielded four projects in Argentina (including Buenos Aires' famous Jockey Club) before MacKenzie moved full-time to the United States where, between 1927 and his 1934 death, he would complete more than 20 projects, with household names like Cypress Point, Crystal Downs and Augusta National (with Bobby Jones) heading the list.   During these years MacKenzie resided primarily in Santa Cruz, CA, in a modest home adjacent to Pastiempo's sixth fairway, a base of operations which allowed him to produce Bay Area standouts like the Meadow Club, Pasatiempo and the greatly altered Sharp Park, while also performing highly signifiant redesigns at the Claremont Country Club, the Lake Merced Golf Club and the California Golf Club.

Notably, MacKenzie often entered into architectural "partnerships" with regional designers, seldom sharing a course's actual design but guaranteeing that someone at least nominally associated with him would oversee its construction in his absence.   In Northern California, that job fell to Robert Hunter, a professor at the University of California whose input varied from project to project, but who shares credit on many of MacKenzie's top area works.

Dr. Alister MacKenzie In the San Francisco Area:	
Claremont CC – Oakland (Redesign)	1926
Meadow Club – Fairfax (w/R. Hunter)	1927
Cypress Point C – Pebble Beach (w/R. Hunter)	1928
Northwood GC – Monte Rio (9, w/R. Hunter)	1928
California GC – South San Francisco (Redesign)	1929
Lake Merced GC – Daly City (Redesign)	1929
Pasatiempo GC – Santa Cruz	1929
Green Hills CC – Millbrae (w/R. Hunter & H.C. Egan)	1930
Sharp Park GC – Pacifica	1932

Jack Nicklaus – By record the greatest golfer of all time, Jack William Nicklaus (b.1940) built a résumé which requires no amplification, his total of 18 professional Major championships (plus two U.S. Amateurs) remaining the gold standard.   The son of a Columbus, Ohio pharmacist, Nicklaus was an excellent all-around athlete as a youth, starring in basketball and giving up several other sports only when they began to conflict with golf.   But as a golfer he was uniquely special, learning the game at the Donald Ross-designed Scioto Country Club and establishing his competitive dominance early and often.   Thus some 73 PGA Tour wins later, he turned his focus to a course design business which has surely covered more ground worldwide than any other.

Indeed, Nicklaus Design (which includes all manner of family members) has completed over 400 projects in 41 countries on all six inhabited continents, and in 39 American states.   Though chided in its early years for building courses that either (A) favored long, high faders (like Jack himself) or (B) were somewhat formulaic, the company's work has seldom failed to be tactically engaging.   Indeed, one would be hard pressed to find a Nicklaus layout that doesn't regularly engender a real degree of playing interest.

Nicklaus's biggest early success came in his hometown at the Muirfield Village Golf Club, a highly thought of layout (built in partnership with Desmond Muirhead) which has hosted the PGA Tour's Memorial Tournament since 1976.   In the years to follow, courses like Alabama's Shoal

Creek (1977), Colorado's Castle Pines (1981) and Kentucky's Valhalla (1986) established themselves as big-event worthy, and if Nicklaus's San Francisco area portfolio is a relatively short one, Santa Rosa's Mayacama (2001) certainly rates among his new millennium best.

Jack Nicklaus In the San Francisco Area:	
Ruby Hill GC – Pleasanton	1996
Coyote Creek GC (Tournament) – Morgan Creek	1999
C at Pasadera – Monterey	2000
Mayacama GC – Santa Rosa	2001
Coyote Creek GC (Valley) – Morgan Creek	2002

Ted Robinson – After gaining a Masters degree in urban planning and landscape architecture from the University of Southern California, Long Beach native Ted Robinson (1923-2008) worked for a land planning firm for several years before branching out on his own in 1954. By the early 1960s, his involvement with several residential developments led him to add golf course design to his range of services, and he soon found enough success to focus on it exclusively thereafter.

All told, Robinson would lay out nearly 160 courses worldwide, the majority within California. He was particularly active in the Palm Springs area where, beginning in the 1970s, he completed more than 20 projects, and developed his reputation for frequently incorporating aesthetically incongruous man-made waterfalls. Though Robinson's work has seldom found favor among the various published rankings, his footprint upon the Northern California landscape remains one of the largest of any modern designer.

Ted Robinson In the San Francisco Area:	
Valley of the Moon C – Santa Rosa	1964
Sugarloaf GC – Santa Rosa (Executive)	1973
Crow Canyon CC – Danville	1977
Fountaingrove C – Santa Rosa	1984
Blackhawk CC (Falls) – Danville	1986
Discovery Bay CC – Discovery Bay	1986
Canyon Lakes GC & Brewery – San Ramon	1987
Silver Creek Valley CC – San Jose	1992
GC at Rio Vista – Rio Vista	1996
Brentwood GC – Brentwood (27)	2002

William Watson – A native of Kemback, a small village near St Andrews, William Watson (1860-1941) came to America in 1898 to work with his fellow Scot Robert Foulis in building the original nine holes at Minnesota's Minikahda Club, site of the 1916 U.S. Open. He then stayed on for several years as the club's pro-greenkeeper while wintering at the Hotel Green in Pasadena, California, where, during his initial season, he laid out one of the better resort nines of the period. His design career continued intermittently until after World War I, when he took up full-time residence in California and became one of that golf-crazed region's busier architects.

Watson appears to have completed more than 100 design projects within the United States – "appears" being the operative word because a number were poorly documented works dating to the World War I era, and earlier. In many cases, these represented initial layouts for well-known clubs which were later renovated by bigger-name designers, and it is rare to find one of his original creations which has not changed significantly over the decades. Given that Watson made minor (or short-lived) changes to many a Bay Area work, it can be argued that he was the most prolific Northern California architect of the Golden Age. However, in terms of original works that survived long enough to have their existences clearly recorded, his ledger weighs in more along the lines of someone like Dr. Alister MacKenzie.

Watson's most famous regional project was surely the original 36 holes of San Francisco's Olympic Club, half of which, the world-class Ocean course, landslid into oblivion less than two years after opening. Other notable area entries include the quirkily engaging Orinda Country Club and the high-profile municipal facility at San Francisco's Harding Park.

William Watson In the San Francisco Area:

Diablo CC – Diablo (w/J. Neville)	1914
Lincoln Park GC – San Francisco (Redesign)	1914
Berkeley CC – El Cerrito (w/R. Hunter)	1920
Burlingame CC – Hillsborough (Redesign) (BO)	1922
Olympic C (Lake) – San Francisco (w/S. Whiting)	1924
Olympic C (Ocean) – San Francisco (w/S. Whiting)	1924
Orinda CC – Orinda	1924
San Jose CC – San Jose (Redesign)	1925
TPC Harding Park – San Francisco (w/S. Whiting)	1925
Sonoma GC – Sonoma (w/S. Whiting)	1928

SAN FRANCISCO COUNTY

The Olympic Club (Lake) – San Francisco   ◆◆◆◆½

Sam Whiting   www.olyclub.com
599 Skyline Blvd, San Francisco, CA 94132   (415) 587-8338
              7,140 yds   Par 71   Rating: 75.8 / 141   (1927)

One of America's historic championship venues, San Francisco's Olympic Club anchors a five-course cluster (which also includes Harding Park, Lake Merced and the San Francisco Golf Club) situated near the Pacific Ocean in the city's southwestern reaches. Though initially playing second fiddle to the original version of the club's Ocean course, the Lake was better positioned to survive the late 1920s landslides that devoured much of the Ocean, and it would ultimately go on to host five U.S. Opens, three U.S. Amateurs and two PGA Tour Championships, with the 2021 U.S. Women's Open soon to be added to the docket. The Lake first came into being as a Wilfrid Reid-designed layout in 1917, but that version was torn up for a new William Watson/Sam Whiting design in 1924 – a track which was in turn substantially renovated by Whiting on his own three years later. The result was a course which, some 80 years of tree growth (and a bit of removal) later, is one of the least forgiving to be found in the United States; indeed, the trees define its playing corridors so unrelentingly that only a single fairway bunker (at the 490-yard 6th) has ever been considered necessary. Consequently, there is a body of thought which holds that the Lake is lacking in world-class holes, and it can be fairly argued that the golf here is vastly more of the penal variety than the strategic. Regardless, when set up for a U.S. Open, the opening six holes can hold their own with almost any opening six around. In part this is due to the 533-yard 1st being played as demanding par 4 during the Open (instead of as a fairly basic – though scenic – three-shotter) but there is little tricking up needed thereafter, as the 430-yard 2nd requires a dicey uphill approach to a shallow, tightly bunkered target and the 247-yard 3rd is one of the nation's most distinguished par 3s, playing steeply downhill to a very narrow green, with the definitive view of the distant Golden Gate Bridge as a backdrop. The 430-yard 4th is a thorny dogleg left in that it plays over a left-to-right-sloping fairway, and it is immediately followed by a pair of very demanding par 4s, the 498-yard dogleg right 5th and the aforementioned 6th. The action ramps down a bit thereafter but there are several well-known holes still to be encountered, namely down the stretch at the tiny 157-yard 15th, the 622-yard dogleg left 16th, and especially the 347-yard drive-and-pitch 18th, a highly distinctive finisher whose greenside bunkering resemble the letters I-O-U when viewed from the center of the fairway. The Lake also offers several points of quirk, including its recently rebuilt par-3 8th hole returning to the clubhouse (instead of the 9th) and a 2012 U.S. Open set up which, having converted the 1st to a par 4, left the field without a par 5 to attack until the long 16th. Of course, having waited this long, players then faced both of the Lake's par 5s back-to-back as the 522-yard 17th plays over a fairway whose steep pitch makes its conversion to two-shot status a shaky proposition – and yet just such a conversion was made during several previous Opens. Thus while the Lake truly does not offer a heavy dose of grand tactical design, it still succeeds in presenting one of the nation's more challenging, aesthetically beautiful, and historically rich golfing experiences. Along with the San Francisco Golf Club, it is one of two must-sees for any serious golfer visiting the Bay Area. **(G: #54 USA, #79 World   GD: #34 USA, #5 State   GW: #33 Classic)**

1	2	3	4	5	6	7	8	9	Out
533	430	247	430	498	490	294	200	449	3571
5	4	3	4	4	4	4	3	4	35
10	11	12	13	14	15	16	17	18	In
422	430	451	201	417	157	622	522	347	3569
4	4	4	3	4	3	5	5	4	36

9	Range (Grass)+	Short Game	Putting Green	On-Site Rooms	Nearby Rooms	Altitude: 192'	Middle: 6,597 yds Front: 4,698 yds

The Olympic Club (Ocean) – San Francisco   ♦♦♦

Tom Weiskopf & Jay Morrish   www.olyclub.com
599 Skyline Blvd, San Francisco, CA 94132   (415) 404-4300
              6,925 yds   Par 71   Rating: 74.3 / 133   (2000)

San Francisco's Olympic Club is best known for its celebrated Lake course but in its earliest form, the Ocean layout was actually the club's bigger drawing card as it was dramatically situated atop coastal cliffs to the west of Skyline Drive. A series of early landslides badly disfigured it, however, and in a never-ending battle with Mother Nature, the Ocean has essentially been a work-in-progress ever since. Though past attempts have been made to rebuild near the water, it is today situated entirely east of Skyline, wedged into occasionally quite hilly terrain around the southern boundary of the Lake course. Considering this enormous evolution, it is a surprisingly good layout, playing a bit less claustrophobically than its heavily tree-lined sibling and, in its modern Tom Weiskopf-designed form, featuring rather more elaborate bunkering. The hilliness is a major factor in the layout's mid-section, notably at the steeply downhill 170-yard 5th, the similarly descending 447-yard 7th and the comparably uphill 532-yard 11th. Also notable is a strong closing run that includes the 473-yard 15th (where a centerline tree defines the tee shot), the 430-yard 16th, the 206-yard tree- and sand-guarded 17th and the 426-yard dogleg right 18th. But in the end, decades worth of visitors (and the USGA) have always come to play the Lake – and while an upcoming Gil Hanse renovation might shift the balance slightly, the Ocean will surely remain a very strong number two option.

6	Range (Grass) +	Short Game	Putting Green	On-Site Rooms	Nearby Rooms	Altitude: 195'	Middle: 6,582 yds Front: 5,250 yds

San Francisco Golf Club – San Francisco   ◆◆◆◆½

A.W. Tillinghast

1310 Juniperro Serra Blvd, San Francisco, CA 94132   (415) 469-4122

6,828 yds   Par 71   Rating: 73.6 / 133   (1920)

Situated just across the southern tip of Lake Merced from the Olympic Club, the San Francisco Golf Club possesses one of the murkier design histories to be found among elite American courses. A.W. Tillinghast's initial work was actually a redesign of a lesser earlier track, and Tilly himself would be responsible for multiple further alterations, with a major bunker renovation/expansion that took place prior to World War II apparently performed to his specifications by his soon-to-be West Coast partner Billy Bell. Thus while the precise sequence of early course alterations remains somewhat jumbled, today's layout is actually quite consistent with that pre-war edition, save for the 1950 rebuild of original holes 13-15 (due to adjacent road construction), a circumstance reversed in the new millennium via some restorative work by Tom Doak. With nary a water hazard in sight, the primary feature is those Tillinghast/Bell bunkers, over 100 of which affect play from tee to green. Built at all sizes and angles, these attractive, billowy hazards often guard the preferred side of a fairway, but their wholesale presence – along with thick stands of aesthetically pleasing cypress and pine – requires constant attention, particularly with wind being a regular factor so close to the ocean. Similarly distinctive is the layout's routing, for it follows near geometric precision over a compact, squarish site, with 13 holes essentially running back and forth on an east-west axis and the remaining five being oriented nearly perpendicular, on a north-south path. The front nine occupies the west side of the east-to-west sloping acreage where, after opening with a gentle downhill 522-yard par 5, it initially features the 459-yard dogleg left 2nd (which requires a long, uphill approach), the 224-yard well-bunkered 4th and a pair of holes routed back and forth atop a narrow ridge, the 383-yard uphill 5th and the 430-yard downhill 6th. The club's most famous hole is the beautiful 189-yard 7th, which plays downhill to a two-tiered green closely guarded by sand and a grassy swale. Known as the Duel hole, it is so christened because it sits upon the site of the last legal duel in the United States, an 1859 shootout between U.S. Senator David Broderick and California Supreme Court justice David Terry (the winner). The 616-yard downhill 9th closes the stronger outward half before the back opens with the 410-yard 10th, whose green is pushed just far enough left to create various tree and bunker issues. Doak's trio of restored holes fill the loop's mid-section and help to strengthen the back nine, with golfers particularly re-welcoming "Little Tilly," the 134-yard, bunker-ringed 13th, which is a pretty fair approximation of a colorful (and much-photographed) Tillinghast original. The more compact nature of the inward half limits it to 3,221 yards, however, and only one of its par 4s extends beyond 425 yards, that being the 432-yard 17th, which doglegs sharply (and early) around some very mature trees before climbing to yet another well-bunkered green. Play then closes with the 524-yard downhill 18th, another vulnerable par 5 which would obviously make for a strong two-shotter in the inconceivable event of the club ever hosting a major men's event. There is a dissenting minority that consider San Francisco to be overrated but for most of the *cognoscenti*, this remains the Bay Area's most flavorful and desirable stop. **(G**: #21 USA, #30 World **GD**: #36 USA, #6 State **GW**: #17 Classic)

1	2	3	4	5	6	7	8	9	Out
522	459	407	224	383	430	189	377	616	3607
5	4	4	3	4	4	3	4	5	36
10	11	12	13	14	15	16	17	18	In
410	160	408	134	351	423	379	432	524	3221
4	3	4	3	4	4	4	4	5	35

6	Range (Grass)	Short Game	Putting Green	On-Site Rooms	Nearby Rooms	Altitude: 141'	Middle: 6,411 yds Front: 5,981 yds

Gleneagles Golf Course at McLaren Park – San Francisco ♦♦½

Jack Fleming   www.gleneaglesgolfsf.com
2100 Sunnydale Ave, San Francisco, CA   94134   (415) 587-2425
            3,006 yds   Par 36   Rating: 36.5 / 132   (1962)

Originally known as the McLaren Park Golf Course, today's Gleneagles Golf Course at McLaren Park is little known outside of San Francisco, but as *Golf Digest* ranked it among the 20 best nine-hole facilities in the nation early in the new millennium, it probably should be. The course was built over a typically hilly section of this large city park by Jack Fleming in 1962 and, having weathered the sort of benign neglect that was visited upon so many big city munis during the 1970s and '80s, it today remains relatively intact and decidedly challenging. Level lies are a rarity, and this is particularly true within the putting surfaces, which were rebuilt in 2010 and, beyond their heavy contours, are advertised on the course website as "San Francisco's fastest muni greens." Play opens with a pair of tricky sidehill tests (the 345-yard 1st and the 322-yard well-bunkered 2nd) before reaching a trio of solid holes: the 357-yard sharply downhill 3rd, the 162-yard 4th (where a right-side cypress tree greatly affects play) and especially the 577-yard 6th, a demanding dogleg left where trees bother any form of aggressive second. This is something of a cultish favorite, and its collectability rating should be weighed accordingly.

5	Range (Grass)	Short Game	Putting Green	On-Site Rooms	Nearby Rooms	Altitude: 265'	Middle: N/A Front: 2,854 yds

Lincoln Park Golf Course – San Francisco   ♦♦

Herbert Fowler   www.lincolnparkgolfcourse.com
300 34th Ave, San Francisco, CA   94121   (415) 221-9911
            5,146 yds   Par 68   Rating: 65.9 / 110   (1908)

Though it occupies a truly splendid site along clifftops in the city's northwestern corner, and thus offers remarkable views of the Golden Gate, there is a bit of murkiness to the design evolution of the Lincoln Park Golf Course. What's known is that three holes were built here as early as 1902, that 18 holes existed (possibly by Tom Bendelow) by 1917, and that visting British architect Herbert Fowler performed a remodel circa 1920 – though the 1924 construction of the city's Legion of Honor museum (which sits within the course's boundaries) likely mandated even more change. Today's layout is among the shorter regulation-sized facilities around and, with limited sand and no water, it poses something less than a full-sized challenge. However the hilly terrain injects some moments of difficulty, as does a closing stretch that includes nearly all of the course's strongest golf. This includes the 500-yard downhill 13th and the 383-yard tree-narrowed 18th, as well as an incongruously large trio of genuinely muscular par 3s: the 203-yard 12th, the 239-yard downhill 16th and especially the 240-yard 17th, which sits alone on the clifftop side of El Camino Del Mar and offers the jackpot view of the Golden Gate.

2	Range (Grass)	Short Game	Putting Green	On-Site Rooms	Nearby Rooms	Altitude: 344'	Middle: 4,948 yds Front: 4,732 yds

Presidio Golf Course – San Francisco   ♦♦½

Robert Johnstone & William McEwan   www.presidiogolf.com
300 Finley Rd, San Francisco, CA   94129   (415) 561-4661
6,481 yds   Par 72   Rating: 72.6 / 135   (1910)

Golf was first played within the confines of this former Army installation in the hills above the Golden Gate Bridge as early as 1895, when the original San Francisco Golf Club managed to create a private nine-hole layout on what was, quite obviously, government land. Much has changed golfwise since those ancient days with today's layout dating to 1910, but numerous architects have nipped and tucked it over the decades, most prominently Herbert Fowler in 1921. Open to the public since 1995 (following the base's deactivation), the course is located on a wooded hillside above the city's Richmond district, where its short routing is enlivened by some notably undulating fairways, with a variety of trees often pinching in at the edges. Most notable are the par 3s, a pleasant quartet led by the tightly bunkered, steeply downhill 130-yard 4th and the descending 171-yard 15th, as well as the tough 219-yard 7th and the quirky 180-yard 13th, which plays across a tree-dotted glen. Rolling holes like the 472-yard par-5 2nd and the 382-yard 16th typify the layout's rippling terrain, while the 453-yard 12th is easily the longest, toughest test. Notably, recent bunker renovations have added a dash of challenge.

5	Range (Mats)	Short Game	Putting Green	On-Site Rooms	Nearby Rooms	Altitude: 303'	Middle: 6,103 yds Front: 4,068 yds

TPC Harding Park – San Francisco   ♦♦♦♦

William Watson & Sam Whiting   www.tpc.com/hardingpark
99 Harding Rd, San Francisco, CA 94132   (415) 664-4690
            7,169 yds   Par 72   Rating: 74.1 / 128   (1925)

Long the flagship of the City of San Francisco's municipal fleet, the TPC Harding Park has been a top-shelf tournament venue almost from its inception, making its big stage debut way back in 1937 when it hosted the U.S. Amateur Public Links' first visit to the State of California. Less than a decade later, the professionals arrived for two editions of the San Francisco Open (both won by Byron Nelson) but the PGA Tour more seriously took root from 1959-1969 when the Lucky International became a centerpiece of its winter schedule, producing Hall-of-Fame champions like Gary Player, Gene Littler and Jack Burke Jr., as well as local heroes Ken Venturi and George Archer. As with so many of America's big-city municipal layouts, Harding Park suffered from budgetary neglect during the 1970s and '80s – but unlike so many others, Harding had a very important friend in former USGA President Frank "Sandy" Tatum, a prominent San Francisco attorney who spearheaded a restoration drive which, bolstered by a deal to host multiple major PGA Tour events, led to a revitalization of impressive proportion. The Tour certainly has made good on its end of the deal, first bringing the 2005 WGC-American Express Championship (where Tiger Woods beat John Daly in a playoff), then adding the 2006 Presidents Cup (a 19½-14½ American victory) and the 2015 WGC-Cadillac Match Play, which was won by Rory McIlroy. Harding Park reached a pinnacle in 2020, however, when despite the absence of spectators due to the COVID-19 pandemic, it became the rare municipal facility to host a Major when it entertained Collin Morikawa's victory at the PGA Championship. Of course, much has changed here since William Watson and Sam Whiting laid out the original 18 on a peninsula within Lake Merced in 1925, with earlier alterations being made due to the addition of a Jack Fleming-designed executive nine in 1962, and the new millennium renovation making the layout modern-tournament ready by extending it as far as 7,234 yards (with a reduced par of 70) via the use of several tees not on the everyday scorecard. Today's routing mostly makes only scenic use of the lake but is toughened by some renovated bunkering, well-contoured greens and the rows of Monterey Cypress that elegantly line its flattish fairways. The compact front nine fills the property's interior and is led by longer tests like the 449-yard 2nd and a pair of stiff dogleg lefts, the 606-yard 4th and the 473-yard 6th – though the 525-yard 9th takes on much greater relevance when shortened to a 515-yard par 4 in championship play. The more engaging back nine then makes a clockwise run around the property's perimeter and initially features the 562-yard 10th and the 494-yard 12th, the latter another par 5 which can be converted to demanding two-shot status for the pros. The homestretch is then made up of five lake-flanked holes, the strongest of which include the 467-yard 14th, the 336-yard 16th (a potentially driveable test narrowed by trees and bunkers) and especially the 468-yard 18th, a solid finisher which both crosses and flanks the water en route to a very deep, narrow putting surface. As its absence from national rankings suggests, Harding Park may not quite reach elite status on the strength of its design alone. But there is some splendid San Francisco ambience present, and precious few indeed are the municipal courses which offer anything resembling this sort of tournament pedigree.

1	2	3	4	5	6	7	8	9	Out
395	449	183	606	429	473	344	230	525	3634
4	4	3	5	4	4	4	3	5	36
10	11	12	13	14	15	16	17	18	In
562	200	494	428	467	405	336	175	468	3535
5	3	5	4	4	4	4	3	4	36

7	Range (Mats)	Short Game	Putting Green	On-Site Rooms	Nearby Rooms	Altitude: 62'	Middle: 6,405 yds Front: 5,875 yds

Golden Gate Park Golf Course – San Francisco   ◆

Jack Fleming   www.goldengateparkgolf.com
970 47th Ave, San Francisco, CA 94121   (415) 751-8987
              1,302 yds   Par 27   Rating: - / -   (1951)

Home of the First Tee of San Francisco, the Golden Gate Park Golf Course is situated in the park's west end, barely a quarter of a mile from the Pacific, where it offers a basic, lightly hazarded nine well-suited to beginners. This is full-sized par-3 golf, however (its holes average 145 yards in length), and while only six bunkers are present, there are plenty of cypress trees lining the fairways to require at least a modicum of accuracy. On the whole, basic stuff – but in a very pleasant parkland setting.

1	Range (Mats) -	Short Game	Putting Green	On-Site Rooms	Nearby Rooms	Altitude: 63'	Middle: N/A Front: N/A

The Olympic Club (Cliffs) – San Francisco   ◆◆

Tom Weiskopf & Jay Morrish   www.olyclub.com
599 Skyline Blvd, San Francisco, CA 94132   (415) 587-8338
              1,125 yds   Par 27   Rating: 26.3 / 68   (1994)

With eight of its nine holes lying on the west side of Skyline Drive, the Olympic Club's Weiskopf & Morrish-design Cliffs course occupies what remains of the clifftop acreage that long ago housed the club's spectacular Ocean course. Parts of three holes touch the edges of the cliffs and the loop is heavily bunkered, and it also includes a slightly gimmicky double green which serves holes 5 and 7. Without a doubt, this is one of the strongest, most attractively situated short courses in the region – and like the club's Ocean course, it too is set to undergo a Gil Hanse renovation in the near future.

1	Range (Grass) +	Short Game +	Putting Green	On-Site Rooms	Nearby Rooms	Altitude: 224'	Middle: N/A Front: 899 yds

TPC Harding Park (Fleming) – San Francisco   ◆½

Jack Fleming   www.tpc.com/hardingpark
99 Harding Rd, San Francisco, CA 94132   (415) 664-4690
              2,165 yds   Par 30   Rating: 30.5 / 94   (1961)

Added in 1961 as an amenity to accommodate lesser-skilled golfers at the city's flagship municipal facility, the TPC Harding Park's Fleming nine is named in honor of its designer, former Alister MacKenzie construction supervisor Jack Fleming. Though its routing is compact, this represents fairly strong executive course golf, particularly at entries like 405-yard 1st (a tree-pinched dogleg left), the 235-yard par-3 5th and the 425-yard 7th. Pilgrims to the main layout likely won't be drawn to this loop but for the lesser golfer for whom it was intended, this is a well-above-average amenity of its type.

1	Range (Mats)	Short Game	Putting Green	On-Site Rooms	Nearby Rooms	Altitude: 82'	Middle: N/A Front: 1,865 yds

MARIN
COUNTY

Marin Country Club – Novato   ♦♦

Lawrence Hughes   www.marincountryclub.com
500 Country Club Dr, Novato, CA 94949   (415) 382-6700
            6,652 yds   Par 72   Rating: 71.9 / 134   (1957)

Set attractively within the foothills south of town, the Marin Country Club dates to the late 1950s, when Lawrence Hughes routed it through several residential neighborhoods in his standard functional design style. New millennium renovations by John Harbottle and Doug Nickels have resulted in considerable bunker alteration (and a bit more playing interest) but the confined nature of the routing has limited growth potential greatly. The shorter front nine occupies the property's more elevated western side and features shortish par 4s like the 402-yard downhill 2nd, the 326-yard uphill 4th and the 367-yard 5th (a rolling, early turning dogleg left) as well as the 480-yard 7th, a short, creek-crossed par 5. The somewhat less-rustic inward half then runs out to the east, where surrounding roads and housing are a more prominent presence and a single wandering water hazard touches seven holes. Strongest here is a finishing run which includes the 412-yard water- and sand-squeezed 15th, the 212-yard 16th (where water closely flanks the right side), the 423-yard 17th (which doglegs right, around an invasive tree) and the 531-yard 18th, a reachable, downhill par 5 whose green angles beyond a another prominent tree.

4	Range (Grass)	Short Game	Putting Green	On-Site Rooms	Nearby Rooms	Altitude: 132'	Middle: 6,334 yds Front: 4,091 yds

Meadow Club – Fairfax   ♦♦♦½

Dr. Alister MacKenzie & Robert Hunter   www.meadowclub.com
1001 Bolinas Rd, Fairfax, CA 94930   (415) 462-0980
            6,718 yds   Par 71   Rating: 72.7 / 137   (1927)

Notable as Dr. Alister MacKenzie's first American design, the Meadow Club is situated, quite literally, in a mountain meadow, secluded high within the picturesque hills of Marin County. Though generally lacking the sheer strategic excellence of a Cypress Point or Crystal Downs, it is nonetheless imbued with many trademark MacKenzie touches, particularly within its bunkering and green complexes. For decades, however, the club suffered from the after-effects of the Depression and World War II, when numerous features (particularly the outer reaches of many putting surfaces) were lost to economic necessity – matters largely put right during a new millennium restoration by Mike DeVries. While MacKenzie chose not to take maximum advantage of a brook which cuts across the property, the hazard does affect a pair of strong par 4s on the outward half: the 427-yard 6th (which plays to a semi-boomerang green) and the 438-yard 7th, a dogleg left around a hillside with the brook both flanking the left side and partially crossing the fairway. The 464-yard 9th is a tactically bunkered, tree-narrowed test with out-of-bounds down its left side, and then it's off to a back nine which initially features the 544-yard 13th (where the brook angles short-right of the green) and the 200-yard 14th, which is fronted by a pond which did not exist in MacKenzie's day. Factor in the strong 429-yard 17th (played to a tricky, false-fronted putting surface) and the 363-yard 18th (where the brook menaces the favored right side) and it all adds up to one of Northern California's more enjoyable (and idyllic) golfing experiences. **(GD:** #29 State **GW:** #111 Classic)

5	Range (Grass)	Short Game	Putting Green	On-Site Rooms	Nearby Rooms	Altitude: 723'	Middle: 6,312 yds Front: 5,923 yds

Indian Valley Golf Club – Novato   ♦♦

Robert Nyberg   www.indianvalleygolfclub.com
3035 Novato Blvd, Novato, CA 94947   (415) 897-1118
6,374 yds   Par 72   Rating: 70.2 / 124   (1958)

Much like the private Marin Country Club, the Indian Valley Golf Club is built in the hills outside of Novato, but here the terrain is somewhat more undulating and the routing a bit more pastoral; indeed the layout sits upon the southern shore of Stafford Lake and its boundaries are housing-free. The course itself is somewhat polarizing; some find it lacking in design polish while others laud the challenge provided by the often-precipitous terrain, as well as the rustic surroundings and occasional panoramic view. Its outward half is fairly compact and, after opening with an uphill 528-yarder dotted with centerline trees and the 408-yard downhill, creek-fronted 2nd, its most memorable test is the 365-yard 9th, where a sharply descending tee shot can bring the green within reach for longer hitters but the banks of Stafford Lake (and a creek-like inlet) flank the left side. The back nine is more spacious and for many, its most memorable feature is the funicular that climbs up the steep 150-foot hillside that separates the 13th green from the 14th tee. At the close, the 528-yard 16th includes a great view from the tee and a pair of alternate greens (the right option being elevated and enormous), while the 491-yard 18th is a tad awkward, bending more than 90 degrees rightward around a steep hillside.

4	Range (Mats)	Short Game	Putting Green	On-Site Rooms	Nearby Rooms	Altitude: 238'	Middle: 5,931 yds Front: 5,281 yds

Peacock Gap Golf Club – San Rafael   ♦♦½

William F. Bell   www.peacockgapgolfclub.com
333 Biscayne Dr, San Rafael, CA 94901   (415) 453-4940
6,261 yds   Par 71   Rating: 69.9 / 125   (1960)

Situated close to Point San Pedro, along the northern edge of San Rafael Bay, the Peacock Gap Golf Club dates to 1960, when it was built on former wetlands by that most prolific of postwar California architects William F. Bell. Bell was a poster boy for the fairly basic design stylings of his period and Peacock was no exception, being a short, mostly flat track whose water hazards – two ponds, a wandering creek and the bordering Peacock Gap Lagoon – were all man-made. But in 2008, the club brought in Forrest Richardson to perform a renovation, a job which retained much of Bell's routing but which added lots of playing interest via significant updates in bunkering and green shaping, as well as a reconfiguring of several front nine holes. And while the 409-yard dogleg left 1st is an engagingly bunkered opener, it is two of the reconfigured entries which lead the outward half, the 176-yard pond-crossing 6th and the 297-yard 7th, whose wide, shallow green includes a deep swale dividing it into two halves. The back offers a bit of early muscle at the 435-yard 11th (played to an hourglass-shaped putting surface) and the 546-yard 12th, but its most engaging golf comes down the stretch at the 359-yard 15th (which features a boomerang green), the 155-yard 16th (played across a corner of the lagoon) and a pair of creek-bothered tests at the 329-yard 17th and the 435-yard dogleg right 18th.

3	Range (Grass)	Short Game	Putting Green	On-Site Rooms	Nearby Rooms	Altitude: 3'	Middle: 5,792 yds Front: 4,828 yds

Stone Tree Golf Club – Novato   ◆◆

Jim Summers & Sandy Tatum   www.bayclubs.com/stonetree
9 Stone Tree Ln, Novato, CA 94945   (415) 209-6090
            6,782 yds   Par 72   Rating: 73.7 / 141   (2000)

Making its debut at the dawn of the new millennium, the Stone Tree Golf Club lies just south of the mouth of the Petaluma River where it occupies rather a schizophrenic site, with 10 holes filling flat land on the property's western half and the remaining eight climbing into mountainous acreage to the east. The flat side houses the opening seven holes (the strongest of which include the 426-yard creekbed-fronted 5th and the 549-yard 6th) before the severe terrain makes its debut at holes 7-9, where the 169-yard 8th plays attractively across a chasm, and the 430-yard dogleg right 9th twists a tad awkwardly between lakes. The back also begins on low ground, but the 309-yard 13th ascends sharply along a ridgetop, setting up a trio of longer tests which draw frequent criticism: the 488-yard par-5 14th (routed through a deep valley, over a very narrow fairway), the 453-yard 15th (a downhill, bunkerless, similarly narrow dogleg right) and the 511-yard downhill 16th, whose comparably slim lay-up zone is pinched by left-side wetlands. Led by the wetlands-crossing 185-yard 17th, the par 3s find a bit more favor but in most eyes, there is too much difficulty here to rate among the area's best.

6	Range (Mats)	Short Game	Putting Green	On-Site Rooms	Nearby Rooms	Altitude: 26'	Middle: 6,325 yds Front: 5,079 yds

McInnis Park Golf Center – San Rafael   ◆½

Fred Bliss   www.mcinnisparkgolfcenter.com
350 Smith Ranch Rd, San Rafael, CA   94903   (415) 492-1800
                1,843 yds   Par 31   Rating: 29.9 / 94   (1993)

Located along both San Pablo Bay wetlands and the waters of the river-like Gallinas Creek, the McInnis Park Golf Center offers a nine-hole executive layout of distinction, as well as miniature golf and a wide range of practice facilities. Moments of regulation-type size appears early at the 343-yard 1st and the 204-yard 3rd, but more memorable are a pair of short par 4s, the 279-yard 4th (whose green is flanked by both a pond and the wetlands) and the 270-yard 6th, where a left-side pond angles into the fairway 30 yards shy of the putting surface. Also notable are the 100-yard 8th and the 270-yard 9th, which climb into some adjacent foothills, allowing play to finish on higher ground.

1	Range (Mats)	Short Game	Putting Green	On-Site Rooms	Nearby Rooms	Altitude: 17'	Middle: 1,715 yds Front: 1,526 yds

Mill Valley Golf Course – Mill Valley   ◆◆

Unknown   www.mvgolfcourse.org
280 Buena Vista Ave, Mill Valley, CA 94941   (415) 388-9982
                2,096 yds   Par 33   Rating: 30.8 / 115   (1919)

Wedged into a typically scenic (and wooded) Northern California valley, the Mill Valley Golf Course dates all the way back to 1919, and it was surely not viewed as a "short" layout at its time of construction. There are, in fact, a fair number of interesting holes here, led by the 188-yard 2nd (played downhill and across a wide creekbed), the 374-yard 4th (a tricky sidehill test requiring a sharply uphill, tree-narrowed approach) and the 317-yard 8th, another sidehill entry, this time curving rightward above the creekbed. Though obviously undersized, the 241-yard two-shot opener offers a split fairway, while the 126-yard 7th ascends to a shallow, bunker-fronted green. Quirky, old and pleasant stuff.

2	Range (Grass)	Short Game	Putting Green	On-Site Rooms	Nearby Rooms	Altitude: 126'	Middle: N/A Front: 1,904 yds

SONOMA COUNTY

The Fountaingrove Club – Santa Rosa   ◆◆½

Ted Robinson   www.thefountaingroveclub.com
1525 Fountaingrove Pkwy, Santa Rosa, CA 95403   (707) 701-3088
6,940 yds   Par 72   Rating: 73.4 / 135   (1984)

Its neighborhood now recovering from 2017 wildfires which destroyed the clubhouse and many surrounding homes, The Fountaingrove Club sports a Ted Robinson-designed layout which dates to 1984, and which had alterations made by his son Ted Jr. twelve years later. Though Robinson's work was widely known for accentuating a distinctive modern and waterfall-laden aesthetic, little of that is present here; indeed, this is surely one of his strongest designs – even with the handicap of some highly invasive power lines slashing across the front nine. This loop extends north of the clubhouse and is arguably the less-engaging half, particularly as it is led by a trio of slightly awkward closers: the 376-yard pond-guarded (and power line-crossed) 7th, the 612-yard downhill 8th (whose sliver of a lay-up zone fills the bottom of a narrow canyon) and the 173-yard 9th, where a man-made greenside creek was not a part of the original design. The inward half weighs in more strongly and opens with the 392-yard 10th, which descends sharply en route to a green angled along the edge of Fountaingrove Lake. Play also closes strongly, first with back-to-back par 4s whose fairways are tightly pinched by trees (the 394-yard 15th and the 440-yard 16th), then at the strong 215-yard 17th, a downhill, lake-crossing test.

6	Range (Both)	Short Game	Putting Green	On-Site Rooms	Nearby Rooms	Altitude: 552'	Middle: 6,439 yds Front: 5,419 yds

Mayacama Golf Club – Santa Rosa   ◆◆◆½

Jack Nicklaus   www.mayacama.com
1240 Mayacama Club Dr, Santa Rosa, CA 95403   (707) 569-2900
6,785 yds   Par 72   Rating: 73.9 / 152   (2001)

Located in scenic country north of the Bay Area, the Mayacama Golf Club is a walking-only facility that is notable as one of Jack Nicklaus's more appealing works, relying less on man-made water hazards, enormous bunkers and overshaped mounding and more on the natural flow of the often hilly terrain. The front nine offers several of its best entries early at the 525-yard 2nd (whose green is perched above a heavily bunkered hillside), the 178-yard 3rd (a pretty test played through trees, and across an old creekbed) and the 501-yard 4th, where a pseudo-boomerang green fronted by a tree provides well-delineated strategic options. While the 340-yard 7th (a potentially driveable dogleg left across another creekbed) is similarly engaging, the best remaining golf lies mostly on the back nine, which climbs into higher country south of the clubhouse. Initially, this loop features the 205-yard 11th (played downhill to a reverse Redan-like target), the 404-yard creek-fronted 13th and the 159-yard 14th, a pinpoint one-shotter played to an elevated target. The finishing run is highlighted by the 537-yard 15th (whose green lies across a deep barranca) followed by a pair of holes marked by the property's only artificial water hazards, the 298-yard 16th (where an invasive left-side pond strongly suggests laying up) and the slightly formulaic 559-yard downhill 18th. Stylistically, Mayacama was something of a departure for the Nicklaus organization circa-2001, but it continues to rank among their very best works today.   (**GD**: #114 USA, #13 State **GW**: #74 Modern)

6	Range (Grass)	Short Game	Putting Green	On-Site Rooms	Nearby Rooms	Altitude: 479'	Middle: 6,302 yds Front: 4,795 yds

Petaluma Golf & Country Club – Petaluma   ♦½

Unknown   www.petalumagolfandcountryclub.com
1500 Country Club Dr, Petaluma, CA 94952   (707) 762-7041
              2,828 yds   Par 35   Rating: 33.4 / 116   (1922)

Built in the hills just west of the Redwood Highway, the Petaluma Country Club is one of the oldest still-active courses in the northern section of the Bay Area, dating to 1922. The layout's pre-World War II routing remains intact but changes have been made, mostly by Gary Roger Baird, who added bunkering during the early 1980s. Nonetheless, this remains an old-fashioned sort of loop whose sub-3,000-yard status is due in part to the presence of a third par 3, as well as a trio of par 4s of less than 335 yards. The 401-yard downhill-then-uphill 1st opens play on a testing note, and the 282-yard 2nd has just enough bunkering to offer a dash of interest. But most engaging thereafter are a pair of one-shotters, the 196-yard 4th (whose fairway ascends steadily to a bunkerless – but very small – putting surface) and the 146-yard 6th, which plays across a right-side fallaway to a green angled among five bunkers and flanked by a right-side tree.

3	Range (Grass)	Short Game	Putting Green	On-Site Rooms	Nearby Rooms	Altitude: 323'	Middle: N/A Front: 2,711 yds

Santa Rosa Golf & Country Club – Santa Rosa   ♦♦

Jack Fleming   www.clubcorp.com
333 Country Club Dr, Santa Rosa, CA 95401   (707) 546-3485
              6,733 yds   Par 72   Rating: 72.3 / 132   (1958)

Located in flat, agricultural country on the west side of town, the Santa Rosa Golf & Country Club was built in the late 1950s by the regionally popular Jack Fleming, whose routing remains essentially intact despite considerable alteration of hazarding over the decades. Fleming's version included less than 40 bunkers (while the present layout offers nearly 75) and what little water meaningfully affects play also arrived well after him. But while today's edition thus offers greater playing interest, it remains a shortish, relatively staid facility whose challenge is limited by the fact that its par 4s average only 386-yards in length. In this light, the 436-yard 3rd and the 424-yard 8th rate among the strongest tests on size alone, though for many, the front nine's most memorable hole will be the 505-yard 2nd, where drives must find a tree-narrowed fairway en route to a green set behind in incongruously large bunker added during the 1970s. The back nine is then defined by several shorter, more heavily bunkered par 4s within its mid-section before closing strongly with the 180-yard 17th (whose greenside pond was built around the dawn of the millennium) and the 529-yard 18th, a reachable but smartly bunkered par 5.

5	Range (Grass)	Short Game	Putting Green	On-Site Rooms	Nearby Rooms	Altitude: 96'	Middle: 6,307 yds Front: 5,152 yds

Sonoma Golf Club – Sonoma   ♦♦♦

William Watson & Sam Whiting   www.sonomagolfclub.com
17700 Arnold Dr, Sonoma, CA 95476   (707) 939-4100

7,103 yds   Par 72   Rating: 74.6 / 137   (1928)

A former host of the Champions Tour's season-ending Charles Schwab Cup, the Sonoma Country Club is nominally a private facility, but it has also long been affiliated with the nearby Sonoma Mission Inn. The course was originally built by William Watson and Sam Whiting but it has been altered (and lengthened) substantially over the years, resulting in a layout with a classic sort of feel, but more of a postwar playing style. The front nine runs clockwise around the property's perimeter and finds its strongest holes in a trio of solid (if unspectacular) par 4s, the 411-yard 3rd, the 431-yard uphill 5th and the 422-yard descending 6th. Also notable here are the 204-yard out-of-bounds-flanked 4th and the 220-yard 7th, where a creekbed lurks to the right of the green. The back nine then fills the property's core and is led early by the 426-yard 10th (a downhill dogleg left) and the comparably uphill 12th, a stout 427-yard two-shotter. The 587-yard 13th runs back down the grade and can potentially have its second and/or third affected by a right-side pond, after which the action is carried home by a pair of strong dogleg right par 4s, the uphill 433-yard 15th (arguably the layout's toughest test) and the 410-yard 18th, whose fairway is pinched by bunkers en route to a creek-fronted putting surface. This is more solid than elite golf overall, but with Tom Watson, John Cook, And Bean and Jim Thorpe (thrice) having won here, there is an added dose of history thrown in for good measure.

7	Range (Both)	Short Game	Putting Green	On-Site Rooms	Nearby Rooms	Altitude: 179'	Middle: 6,679 yds Front: 5,554 yds

The Links at Bodega Harbour – Bodega Bay   ♦♦½

Robert Trent Jones II   www.bodegaharbourgolf.com
21301 Heron Dr, Bodega Bay, CA   94923   (707) 875-3538
              6,284 yds   Par 70   Rating: 71.8 / 131   (1978/1987)

Serving several nearby hostelries (including the adjacent Bodega Bay Lodge & Spa), the Robert Trent Jones II-designed Links at Bodega Harbor initially featured only today's back nine prior to the front being added in 1987, and was clearly built with housing as its top priority. With the exception of a late finishing stretch along/near the beach, the property is permeated by rows of single-family homes, leaving the majority of holes to be hemmed in on both sides. Perhaps due to such limitations, the course lacks some of the strategic bent inherent in Jones's later work, but its setting – on high ground overlooking the Pacific – remains impressive. Golf-wise, there are dashes of awkwardness, notably at the 396-yard 4th (which ascends some 70 feet and seems an odd number one stroke hole) and the 517-yard 6th, a wild, downhill double dogleg with a paved access road filling its second corner. But things improve at the 155-yard canyon-crossing 6th and the 474-yard 8th, which tumbles past another ravine to a small green. The back nine offers mostly basic golf before closing with a bang, its final three descending from the high ground to a beachfront tidal marsh, where the 319-yard 16th might be driven across the wetlands and the 197-yard 17th plays to a near-island green. The 459-yard 18th then skirts the blufftop before plunging to a putting surface set beautifully against the beach.

4	Range (Grass)	Short Game	Putting Green	On-Site Rooms	Nearby Rooms	Altitude: 107'	Middle: 5,892 yds Front: 4,887 yds

Bennett Valley Golf Course – Santa Rosa   ♦½

Ben Harmon   www.bennettvalleygolf.com
3330 Yulupa Ave, Santa Rosa, CA 95405   (707) 528-3673
                6,527 yds   Par 72   Rating: 71.1 / 118   (1969)

Located below the eponymous Bennett Peak, the Bennett Valley Golf Course dates to the late 1960s and, despite some updating of bunkering, is well representative of the blander design stylings of its period – but with a dash or two of quirk thrown in. This quirk primarily comes in the form of trees, particularly in the early going where both the 487-yard creek-crossed 1st and the 324-yard 4th play through narrow openings on approach, with the latter including a pair of oaks standing almost directly in front of the putting surface. For the most part, however, this is uneventful parkland golf, with the primary challenge being to keep one's tee shots out of the trees, particularly on the handful of longer holes, which on the front side include the 440-yard downhill 2nd and the 206-yard 8th, whose heart-shaped green is tightly bunkered. The homeward half begins and ends with straightaway, sub-500-yard par 5s and follows a mostly back-and-forth routing, with no less than six parallel holes sitting on a north-south axis. Strongest here are the arrow-straight 420-yard 12th and its neighbor, the 429-yard 17th.

4	Range (Mats)	Short Game	Putting Green	On-Site Rooms	Nearby Rooms	Altitude: 272'	Middle: 6,086 yds Front: 5,109 yds

Foxtail Golf Club (South) – Rohnert Park   ♦½

Bob Baldock   www.playfoxtail.com
100 Golf Course Dr, Rohnert Park, CA 94928   (707) 584-7766
                6,492 yds   Par 71   Rating: 71.6 / 126   (1963)

Situated five miles south of Santa Rosa, the 36-hole Foxtail Golf Club offers a pair of housing-flanked courses constructed 11 years apart on either side of the appropriately named Golf Course Drive. The older South course was designed by one of the West's most functional period designers, Bob Baldock, who was clearly instructed to fit his layout around the large residential neighborhood that defines its southern boundary. The result was a flattish track whose mid-sized stature of 1963 is short today, and which opens with a front nine that includes none-too-invasive water at the 550-yard 2nd (right of the green), the 104-yard 3rd (a modest carry) and the 376-yard 9th (along much of the right side), as well as the 403-yard 6th, which is made slightly awkward by the creek which crosses the fairway at the 230-yard mark. The significantly longer homeward half is led by a brawny (if basic) run of early holes, a group which includes the 540-yard 11th, the 443-yard 12th and the 426-yard 13th, as well as the 206-yard one-shot 14th and the 410-yard 15th. But for better golfers, the newer North course will surely be preferable.

4	Range (Mats)	Short Game	Putting Green	On-Site Rooms	Nearby Rooms	Altitude: 101'	Middle: 6,224 yds Front: 4,818 yds

Foxtail Golf Club (North) – Rohnert Park   ♦♦½

Gary Roger Baird   www.playfoxtail.com
100 Golf Course Dr, Rohnert Park, CA 94928   (707) 584-7766
6,851 yds   Par 72   Rating: 73.0 / 133   (1974)

The Foxtail Golf Club's North course arrived more than a decade after the South and is even more housing-affected, with both nines being essentially enclosed by residences and the outward half including a large hotel between the 1st and 9th fairways. The layout was designed by another popular California architect of the period, Gary Roger Baird, though Baird's occasionally heavy bunkering was significantly reduced early in the new millennium. What exists today, then, is a strong mid-sized track anchored by a collection of testing par 4s which, going out, includes a pair of sharp, soundly bunkered dogleg lefts (the 427-yard 2nd and the 460-yard 5th) as well as the water-lined 419-yard 7th (a difficult driving hole) and the 333-yard 9th, which offers multiple options off the tee. This pattern continues on a back nine that opens with the 349-yard 10th (which dares an aggressive line across right-side water) and the smartly bunkered 440-yard 11th, then eventually closes with the similarly solid 417-yard 17th and the 422-yard 18th, where water again closely flanks the right side. The strongest entry, however, may well be the 583-yard 12th, a sharp dogleg left played to a shallow, centerline-bunkered green set beyond a wide creekbed. Overall, a sturdy, fairly engaging public test.

6	Range (Mats)	Short Game	Putting Green	On-Site Rooms	Nearby Rooms	Altitude: 102'	Middle: 6,394 yds Front: 5,261 yds

Healdsburg Golf Club at Tayman Park – Healdsburg   ♦½

Unknown   www.healdsburggolfclub.com
927 S. Fitch Mountain Rd, Healdsburg, CA 95448   (707) 433-4275
2,662 yds   Par 35   Rating: 32.7 / 114   (1921)

Occupying a notably hilly, scenic and power line-crossed site half a mile east of the Redwood Highway, the Healdsburg Golf Club is another of the area's oldest – an obvious point, really, since nobody would ever build this sort of layout today. With only six bunkers present, the terrain is the primary challenge, a point especially in evidence late in the loop when the 291-yard 6th ascends a veritable mountainside, the 319-yard 7th makes the corresponding downward plunge, and the 264-yard uphill 8th and 494-yard downhill 9th have their undulations seem more manageable only by comparison. The 357-yard swale-fronted 4th is arguably the best entry while the 434-yard power line-crossed 2nd makes a sharp late ascent to a tiny hilltop green and, mercifully, is played as a par 5. Note: The course website suggests that Dr. Alister MacKenzie had a hand in its design, but as Mackenzie didn't set foot in America prior to 1926, any potential input would have been renovative – and top MacKenzie sources offer scant evidence of that.

2	Range (Mats)	Short Game	Putting Green	On-Site Rooms	Nearby Rooms	Altitude: 204'	Middle: 2,493 yds Front: 2,290 yds

Northwood Golf Course – Monte Rio   ♦♦½

Dr. Alister MacKenzie & Robert Hunter   www.northwoodgolf.com
19400 Hwy 116, Monte Rio, CA 95462   (707) 865-1116
2,893 yds   Par 36   Rating: 33.9 / 114   (1928)

Lying within a bend of Russian River, the Northwood Golf Course has quite a bit going for it, not the least of which is the fact that it was designed by Dr. Alister MacKenzie and his California partner Robert Hunter (who handled most of the on-site work). Further, its routing and putting surfaces remain intact, it offers some impressive mountain scenery and it plays through stands of towering redwoods to boot. On the down side, however, numerous bunkers are missing (their hollowed out remains staring hauntingly at the historically minded visitor) and housing today impinges on several sides, affecting what was surely one of the purer aesthetics in American golf. Playing-wise, what's left is short and only moderately challenging, with favorites including the 382-yard 2nd (whose approach must navigate a narrow path through the redwoods), the 381-yard dogleg right 7th, the 120-yard 8th (played to a tiny green whose original bunkering remains incongruously intact) and the 532-yard 9th, a rolling, natural par 5 whose left boundary is pressed dangerously by adjacent homes. Anyone expecting an inland Cypress Point will surely be disappointed but with *Golf* magazine recently rating it the #30 nine-hole layout on the planet, on both lineage and scenery, Northwood is still a very appealing stop.

3	Range	Short	Putting	On-Site	Nearby	Altitude:	Middle: 2,506 yds
	(Grass)	Game	Green	Rooms	Rooms	49'	Front: 1,983 yds

Rooster Run Golf Club – Petaluma   ♦♦

Fred Bliss   www.roosterrun.com
2301 E. Washington St, Petaluma, CA 94954   (707) 778-1211
7,001 yds   Par 72   Rating: 74.2 / 135   (1998)

Squeezed into a narrow site between farmland and the Petaluma Airport, the Rooster Run Golf Club opened just before the new millennium and has since rated among the longer and tougher public facilities in the region. A highly compact design, it is in many ways the typical modern creation of its period, but allowances were made for higher-volume public play, with little more than 40 bunkers present and the lakes or creekbeds that affect 11 holes often doing so in only moderately invasive fashion. The 3,618-yard front nine flanks the airport and follows a narrow out-and-back routing within which it features a quartet of longer entries: the 560-yard 2nd (where a creekbed crosses 20 yards shy of the green), the 460-yard bunkerless 7th, the 230-yard 8th and especially the 606-yard 9th, which twists between a pair of lakes to a putting surface angled beyond the second one. The back is far shorter and somewhat tightly dovetailed together, leaving it to be anchored by a trio of varied tests: the 420-yard dogleg left 14th, the 173-yard 15th (played to a period-predictable – but fairly forgiving – island green) and the 529-yard 18th, a straightaway par 5 with trees and another creekbed impeding the approach.

6	Range	Short	Putting	On-Site	Nearby	Altitude:	Middle: 6,464 yds
	(Grass)	Game	Green	Rooms	Rooms	98'	Front: 5,139 yds

Sea Ranch Golf Links – Sea Ranch

Robert Muir Graves   www.searanchgolf.com
42000 Hwy 1, Sea Ranch, CA 95497   (707) 785-2648
                    6,649 yds   Par 72   Rating: 72.5 / 134   (1974/1995)

Anchoring a vast coastal real estate development located in the far northwestern reaches of the county, the Sea Ranch Golf Links was designed by Robert Muir Graves in the early 1970s, but its developer elected to build nine holes initially, with the second nine added 21 years later. Only one hole (the 190-yard ravine-crossing 8th) gets anywhere near the ocean, with most of the layout sitting on higher inland ground, a location whose otherwise commanding view of the sea is often impeded by homes or trees. The design is somewhat unique in that its greens tend to be wildly shaped and loosely bunkered, while sand is a heavy presence along many fairways, usually in the form of large, grass-dotted hazards which at times have an almost geometric feel. In many eyes, the older front nine is the stronger half and after opening with a downhill 525-yarder with a pond left of its green, it features the 375-yard tree- and bunker-squeezed 4th, the 406-yard tree-narrowed 5th and the 545-yard 6th, a dogleg left upon which an invasive pond defines multiple tee shot options. The inward half opens with the 307-yard dogleg right 10th (which dares an aggressive drive across corner trees and water) and later closes with the 160-yard 17th (played over a swath of native terrain) and the 401-yard creek-crossed 18th.

5	Range	Short	Putting	On-Site	Nearby	Altitude:	Middle: 6,233 yds
	(Both)	Game	Green	Rooms	Rooms	96'	Front: 4,790 yds

Valley Of The Moon Club – Santa Rosa   ♦♦

Ted Robinson   www.playvom.com
7025 Oakmont Dr, Santa Rosa, CA 95409   (707) 539-0415
                    6,359 yds   Par 72   Rating: 70.8 / 130   (1964)

Formerly known as the Oakmont Golf Club, today's Valley Of The Moon Club sits in a typically scenic valley where it features a Ted Robinson-designed regulation-sized 18 as well as an adjacent executive track known as Sugarloaf (page 43), which operates out of a separate clubhouse. The primary 18 is a short and mostly functional layout which, with housing flanking its entire perimeter, has retained all of Robinson's routing and nearly all of his features, minus a few bunkers which have vanished over the decades. Noteworthy holes are at a premium here, with the front nine offering the 354-yard creek-crossed 4th, the 467-yard 7th (a short par 5 marked by a very wide fairway, two centerline trees and a tightly bunkered hourglass green) and the 143-yard 8th, a similarly well-bunkered test. The back opens with the somewhat awkward 485-yard 10th (where a pond impedes the fairway 265 yards out) but also includes the 381-yard tree-dotted 12th and the tricky 400-yard 17th, whose driving zone is pinched between a long right-side lake and a smaller left-side pond. There is less flash present here than on many a later Robison layout.

3	Range	Short	Putting	On-Site	Nearby	Altitude:	Middle: 6,032 yds
	(Mats)	Game	Green	Rooms	Rooms	460'	Front: 3,753 yds

Windsor Golf Club – Windsor   ♦♦½

Fred Bliss   www.windsorgolf.com
1340 19ᵗʰ Hole Dr, Windsor, CA 95492   (707) 838-7888
                6,599 yds   Par 72   Rating: 72.9 / 133   (1989)

A Korn Ferry Tour stop from 1990-1995 (with Tom Lehman and Stuart Appleby among its winners), the Windsor Golf Club is situated just north of the Sonoma County Airport and, though not overly long, offers plenty of testing golf within its 6,599 yards. The flattish layout is entirely modern in its stylings and includes several period-predictable touches, including plenty of oversized bunkering, the stone wall buttressing of putting surfaces above water hazards and a double green serving holes 1 and 17. But there is a fair amount of engaging golf as well, with the early holes including the 433-yard tree-lined (but bunkerless) 2ⁿᵈ, the 325-yard 3ʳᵈ (whose green sits beyond a large bunker) and the 501-yard 4ᵗʰ, a quirky/awkward par 5 which plays through a narrow opening in trees before turning sharply right over its last 60 yards. Both the 367-yard 8ᵗʰ and the 192-yard 13ᵗʰ require water carries to the aforementioned buttressed greens before the inward half is led by short, heavily bunkered pars 4s like the 336-yard 14ᵗʰ and the 355-yard dogleg left 16ᵗʰ, as well as the 415-yard 18ᵗʰ, a tree-pinched finisher. Also notable are a pair of par 5s crossed by Pool Creek, the 547-yard 9ᵗʰ and the 493-yard 17ᵗʰ.

5	Range (Grass)	Short Game	Putting Green	On-Site Rooms	Nearby Rooms	Altitude: 98'	Middle: 6,125 yds Front: 5,026 yds

Fairgrounds Golf Center – Santa Rosa   ♦$\frac{1}{2}$

Unknown   www.fairgroundsgolfcourse.com
1350 Bennett Valley Rd, Santa Rosa, CA 95404   (707) 284-3520
                1,500 yds   Par 29   Rating: 28.4 / 92   (2006)

Built inside of a horse racetrack within the Sonoma County Fairgrounds, the Fairgrounds
Golf Center has existed since the 1960s but was fully redesigned in 2006. As executive
courses go, there is plenty to enjoy here, with enough water and sand present to offer a
decent degree of playing interest, particularly at the 165-yard 3rd (which angles along a
right-side pond), the 320-yard 8th (a straightaway par 4 with more water right of the
green) and especially the 180-yard 9th, whose putting surface is guarded right by water
and left by bunkers and a multi-story driving range fence.

1	Range	Short	Putting	On-Site	Nearby	Altitude:	Middle: N/A
	(Mats)	Game	Green	Rooms	Rooms	168'	Front: 1,175 yds

Sebastapol Golf Course – Sebastapol   ♦

Unknown
2881 Scotts Right of Way, Sebastapol, CA 95472   (707) 823-9852
                1,617 yds   Par 31   Rating: 29.1 / 93   (1960)

Laid out on a site which slopes broadly downward from west to east, the Sebastapol Golf
Course is a short and highly basic test, with the *longest* of its four par 4s measuring 213
yards. Only four bunkers are present, though trees frequently can affect play, as do the
creek and pond that menace the 197-yard 8th hole. If one thinks of this as a par 31, it is
suitable strictly for beginners and the less skilled. But were the visitor to ignore the
scorecard and view the layout as nine par 3s, then matters get a little more interesting.

1	Range	Short	Putting	On-Site	Nearby	Altitude:	Middle: N/A
	(Grass)	Game	Green	Rooms	Rooms	87'	Front: 1,593 yds

Sugarloaf Golf Club – Santa Rosa   ♦♦

Ted Robinson   www.playvom.com
557 Oak Vista Ct, Santa Rosa, CA 95409   (707) 539-0415
                4,293 yds   Par 63   Rating: 61.8 / 103   (1973)

Officially a part of the adjacent Valley Of The Moon Club, the Sugarloaf Golf Club is a
high-quality executive layout which plays out of a separate clubhouse located a mile to
the southeast. Similarly housing-enclosed to its larger neighbor, Sugarloaf includes
several stiff (is basic) par 3s that stand out at this level of golf, including the 221-yard 4th,
the 198-yard 7th and the 203-yard 12th. It also offers several holes where trees are
primary hazards, led by the 308-yard pond-guarded 9th, the 344-yard 10th and the 171-
yard 14th. For most, however, the most engaging entry will be the 324-yard 13th, where a
right-side pond flanks both fairway and putting surface.

3	Range	Short	Putting	On-Site	Nearby	Altitude:	Middle: N/A
	(Grass)	Game	Green	Rooms	Rooms	463'	Front: 4,068 yds

NAPA COUNTY

Napa Valley Country Club – Napa   ♦♦

Unknown / Ron Fream   www.napavalleycc.com
3385 Hagen Rd, Napa, CA   94558   (707) 252-1111
           6,314 yds   Par 72   Rating: 71.4 / 129   (1915/1990)

Set in typically scenic Northern California wine country, the Napa Valley Country Club is truly a layout in two parts, with the hilly front nine dating all the way back to 1915 and the very hilly back nine arriving 75 years later. The front lies north of the clubhouse and opens with a 130-yard downhill par 3 and a 444-yard uphill par 5, but the scale of play climbs somewhat thereafter, notably at the 430-yard 4th (where left-side trees bother the second), the 424-yard 6th and the 477-yard 7th, a short par 5 whose fairway is closely flanked by a lake added in 2017. The back nine was designed by the globetrotting American Ron Fream in 1990 on some heavily undulating acreage to the south and initially features the 140-yard ridgetop 11th and the 487-yard 12th, another short par 5 featuring a tee shot which plunges steeply enough downhill that the cartpath follows a series of switchbacks, earning the rather creative nickname Lombard Street. Thereafter, the 429-yard 13th requires an uphill approach to a bunkerless green, the 219-yard 15th and 508-yard 16th both feature prominent ponds, and the 339-yard 17th is a slightly awkward dogleg right whose approach plays through a narrow gauntlet of trees.

| 5 | Range (Both) | Short Game | Putting Green | On-Site Rooms | Nearby Rooms | Altitude: 204' | Middle: 6,175 yds Front: 5,319 yds |

Silverado Country Club & Resort (North) – Napa   ◆◆◆

Robert Trent Jones   www.silveradoresort.com
1600 Atlas Peak Rd, Napa, CA 94558   (707) 257-0200
            7,190 yds   Par 72   Rating: 74.8 / 141   (1967)

Golf at the wine-rich Napa Valley's Silverado Resort dates to 1955, when Ben Harmon and 1947 U.S. Amateur runner-up Johnny Dawson built 18 holes on land which largely comprises today's North course. Several of those original holes were incorporated into Robert Trent Jones's 1967 remodel, however far more of the current layout owes directly to Trent's hand, making our modern conception of the course substantially his. The resort became famous as a PGA Tour stop from 1968-1980 and, more recently, since 2014, with Nicklaus, Casper, Miller, Watson and Crenshaw all raising trophies here – so tournament history the club possesses in spades. With Johnny Miller having made new millennium changes, today's North course is a good-sized track whose most imposing outbound holes are the 436-yard 1st and the 458-yard soundly bunkered 6th – though perhaps more engaging are the 424-yard 3rd (where a tree overhangs front-right of the green), the 407-yard 4th (whose shallow target sits behind centerline sand) and the 557-yard 9th (ditto). Back nine favorites include the 459-yard 10th (where more mature trees pinch both sides of the fairway) and a pair of water-crossing par 3s, the 182-yard all-carry 11th and the 189-yard 15th, whose green angles along a front-right pond. Though the odd creative touch does appear, this is mostly straight-ahead, strategically basic Trent Jones.

7	Range (Grass)	Short Game	Putting Green	On-Site Rooms	Nearby Rooms	Altitude: 87'	Middle: 6,793 yds Front: 5,142 yds

Silverado Country Club & Resort (South) – Napa   ◆◆½

Robert Trent Jones   www.silveradoresort.com
1600 Atlas Peak Rd, Napa, CA 94558   (707) 257-0200
            6,612 yds   Par 72   Rating: 72.3 / 133   (1967)

The Silverado Resort's South course may, in its earlier days, have been the more engaging of the club's two layouts as it offered a bit more variety (and the occasional more invasive hazard) within its shorter, and theoretically easier, design. Curiously, much of that more interesting nature has been lessened via recent renovations, with numerous bunkers being removed (including a 50-yard-long monster that fronted the entirety of the 18th green) and the impact of a prominent water hazard (the pond before the 9th green) being reduced as well. What's left, then, is a short, user-friendly track whose top outgoing tests include the 380-yard 6th (a creek-crossed dogleg right), the 426-yard dogleg right 8th (the number one stroke hole) and the 482-yard par-5 9th, which remains interesting despite its pond today lying only left of the putting surface. The back nine Is perhaps the more engaging loop overall and initially features two solid par 5s, the 565-yard 11th (a long dogleg left around water) and the 492-yard pond-fronted 13th. The 185-yard over-water 15th also merits attention as does the 500-yard dogleg left 18th – though mostly for missing its hole-defining bunker. This is clearly a "second" course now, but it's one with a bit of history, and a nice orientation towards the less-skilled.

5	Range (Grass)	Short Game	Putting Green	On-Site Rooms	Nearby Rooms	Altitude: 82'	Middle: 6,207 yds Front: 5,401 yds

Chardonnay Golf Club – American Canyon   ♦♦½

Algie Pulley   www.chardonnaygolfclub.com
2555 Jameson Canyon Rd, American Canyon, CA 94503   (707) 257-1900
                6,948 yds   Par 72   Rating: 73.6 / 137   (1989)

Originally built as a 36 hole facility by Texas-based architect Algie Pulley, the Chardonnay
Golf Club was eventually shortened to 18 in a slightly complicated process which saw 10
of its original holes become a part of the neighboring Eagle Vines (below) while others
blended back into the surrounding landscape by once again becoming vineyards. What
remains, then, is a challenging, thoroughly modern layout built around two creeks which
cross the property as well as Pulley's greens, which tend to be long, narrow and multi-
tiered. The front nine includes three par 3s and three par 5s, with two of the former
leading the way: the 159-yard 5th (played to an extremely narrow, snake-like putting
surface angled just beyond Fagan Creek) and the 198-yard 8th, whose shallow green
manages to top this by measuring 90 yards from side to side, curving around three
frontal bunkers and including at least five separate tiers. The inward half is similarly
configured, with its trio of one-shotters including a pair of creek-affected tests (the 206-
yard 12th and the 174-yard 16th) as well as the 183-yard 14th, whose "island" green is
surrounded by seemingly endless rows of grapes. Pulley's wild stylings are surely not for
everyone, but this is also a layout which is seldom accused of being dull.

6	Range	Short	Putting	On-Site	Nearby	Altitude:	Middle: 6,568 yds
	(Grass)	Game	Green	Rooms	Rooms	156'	Front: 5,219 yds

Eagle Vines Golf Club – American Canyon   ♦♦½

Algie Pulley / Jack Barry & Johnny Miller   www.eaglevinesgolfclub.com
580 S. Kelly Rd, American Canyon, CA 94503   (707) 257-4470
                7,297 yds   Par 72   Rating: 75.4 / 138   (1989/2004)

As detailed above, the Eagle Vines Golf Club lies adjacent to the Chardonnay Golf Club,
from which it appropriated eight full holes (and portions of two more) at the time of its
construction. Those holes were designed by Algie Pulley, with the remainder being laid
out by the new facility's then-manager, with apparent input from Johnny Miller. This
cobbled-together approach resulted in a somewhat disjointed routing which sees the 8th
hole return to the clubhouse, and as one might guess, there are stylistic differences
present as well, particularly within the greens, where not everyone is inclined to copy
Pulley's brand of shaping. The outward nine opens with a pair of watery holdovers (the
573-yard 1st and the 200-yard 2nd) before playing through new holes the rest of the way,
and if several of this bunch are longer on size than subtlety, the 455-yard downhill 8th is
notable, its small green squeezed between left-side sand and right-side water. The back
opens with a 499-yard dogleg left par 4 and later includes the 361-yard 12th (where the
crossing Fagan Creek creates options off the tee), a pair of holes utilizing the same lake
(the 447-yard 13th and the 165-yard island green 14th) and the 445-yard dogleg right 18th,
a strong, uphill closer. Carrying a 75.4 rating, this is one of the region's toughest tests.

8	Range	Short	Putting	On-Site	Nearby	Altitude:	Middle: 6,879 yds
	(Grass)	Game	Green	Rooms	Rooms	134'	Front: 5,587 yds

Napa Golf Course at Kennedy Park – Napa   ♦♦

Jack Fleming   www.playnapa.com
2295 Streblow Dr, Napa, CA 94558   (707) 255-4333
          6,681 yds   Par 72   Rating: 72.4 / 129   (1968)

Located just east of the Napa River and adjacent to the campus of Napa Valley College, the Napa Golf Course at Kennedy Park was built by prominent regional architect Jack Fleming and, measuring 6,500 yards in its infancy, was always intended to be a strong municipal facility. Water is a meaningful presence on 13 holes (though in most cases as a lateral hazard well removed from the main line of play) and there is a bit of muscle within the par 4s, particularly early on at the 415-yard 1st (a sharp dogleg right) and the 421-yard 3rd, where a lake parallels the left side. The water becomes a tad more invasive later in the front nine, filling the corner at the 370-yard dogleg left 6th, then more closely flanking the left side of the 487-yard par-5 8th (where a small section must be carried on the second) and the right side of the 375-yard 9th. Following a pond- and centerline tree-affected tee shot at the 392-yard 10th, the inward half is anchored by the 409-yard out-of-bounds-lined 12th and two more water-menaced tests, the 506-yard 14th (where a right-side lake pushes into the lay-up zone) and the 421-yard 15th, which is flanked down the entirety of its left side. As higher-volume munis go, this rates above the norm.

5	Range (Mats)	Short Game	Putting Green	On-Site Rooms	Nearby Rooms	Altitude: 22'	Middle: 6,081 yds Front: 5,660 yds

Vintners Golf Club – Yountville   ♦♦

Casey O'Callaghan   www.vintnersgolfclub.com
7901 Solano Ave, Yountville, CA 94599   (707) 944-1992
          2,929 yds   Par 34   Rating: 33.5 / 123   (1999)

Built around the town of Yountville's water treatment plant, the Vintner's Golf Club is a par-34 nine-hole facility which largely makes up in creative design what it lacks in pure size and challenge. The routing follows a U-shaped, out-and-back routing within which are incorporated 21 bunkers, three lakes and some wetlands, all of which create a higher level of playing interest than one might anticipate. The backbone of the loop is a collection of par 4s which includes the 357-yard 1st (whose tree-narrowed approach must cross a swath of wetlands), the 381-yard lake-flanked 3rd, the 343-yard soundly bunkered 5th (where wetlands border both sides) and the 421-yard 9th, a genuinely strong closer which bends rightward around more water. For many, however, the single strongest entry is the 188-yard 4th, which plays across a lake to a narrow green angled rightward behind a bunker, with left-side out-of-bounds lying closely at hand.

3	Range (Mats)	Short Game	Putting Green	On-Site Rooms	Nearby Rooms	Altitude: 92'	Middle: 2,611 yds Front: 2,243 yds

Meadowood Napa Valley – St. Helena   ♦½

Jack Fleming   www.meadowood.com
900 Meadowood Ln, St. Helena, CA 94574   (707) 963-3646
                 1,505 yds   Par 28   Rating: 28.7 / 94   (1965)

A recreational amenity to the eponymous resort, the Meadowood Golf Course lies in a scenic valley where it was designed by Jack Fleming in the mid-1960s. The narrowness of the sloping site mandated something of a back-and-forth routing and the loop contains a single par 4 (the 254-yard uphill 6th) along with a group of one-shotters averaging 156 yards in length. But within those one-shotters lie several solid entries, including the 148-yard 3rd (played uphill to a green set above front-right sand), the 160-yard downhill 4th, the 179-yard descending 8th and especially the 197-yard 9th, a genuinely dangerous par 3 played to a green which juts rightward into a pond. Note: For those so inclined, the club offers the option of renting hickory-shafted clubs and dialed-down golf balls as well.

1	Range (Grass)	Short Game	Putting Green	On-Site Rooms	Nearby Rooms	Altitude: 313'	Middle: N/A Front: 923 yds

SOLANO COUNTY

Green Valley Country Club – Fairfield   ♦♦

Elmer Borders   www.greenvalleycc.com
35 Country Club Dr, Fairfield, CA 94534   (707) 864-1101
                6,484 yds   Par 72   Rating: 71.3 / 136   (1949)

Situated in a somewhat secluded valley southeast of Napa, the Green Valley Country Club was the rare new golf facility to be constructed in the years just after World War II, when it was designed by little-known Elmer Borders and included a real estate component around the perimeter and, to a lesser degree, in the property's center. Renovated in the 1980s by Robert Muir Graves, it remains a short, hilly, mostly functional layout which, given Borders' decision not to make prominent use of a narrow dry wash which crosses the property, relies largely upon its terrain to provide challenge. Both nines open with short, uphill par 5s (the 451-yard 1st and the 460-yard 10th) with the front nine then being led by shortish par 4s like the 347-yard 2nd (where the dry wash crosses the fairway just over 200 yards out), the 369-yard uphill 4th (whose approach is menaced by left-side trees) and the 403-yard downhill 9th. The back encounters some undulating, heavily treed terrain early, making the 346-yard uphill 12th and the 156-yard downhill 13th among the club's more engaging entries. The loop also closes strongly with a pair of longer into-the-wind tests, the 445-yard 16th and the 199-yard 17th.

4	Range (Both)	Short Game	Putting Green	On-Site Rooms	Nearby Rooms	Altitude: 143'	Middle: 6,166 yds Front: 5,003 yds

Blue Rock Springs (West) – Vallejo   ♦½

Jack Fleming / Robert Muir Graves   www.bluerockspringsgolf.com
655 Columbus Pkwy, Vallejo, CA 94591   (707) 643-8476
                6,014 yds   Par 71   Rating: 69.1 / 125   (1949/1994)

Situated on either side of Columbus Parkway, Blue Rock Springs began life with an 18-hole Jack Fleming-designed layout which, some 45 years after its birth, was expanded to 36 holes by Robert Muir Graves. This Graves accomplished by building 18 new holes around Fleming's original work, with the resulting resequencing creating a West course that includes 13 Fleming originals (some slightly reconfigured) and an East which weighs more heavily towards Graves. As was often the case, Fleming's holes tend to be more functional than exciting, with his strongest entries on the West including a pair of terrain-oriented par 5s (the 518-yard sharply uphill 6th and the 536-yard even more sharply downhill 8th) as well as the 400-yard 18th, an ascending dogleg right which was toughened by the 2006 addition of a left-side lake along its fairway. Graves' additions, meanwhile, include two tactically engaging holes, the 314-yard lake-flanked 4th (whose steeply elevated tee brings a creek-fronted green well within reach) and the 306-yard downhill 13th, another driveable test played to a tightly bunkered putting surface.

3	Range (Both)	Short Game	Putting Green	On-Site Rooms	Nearby Rooms	Altitude: 286'	Middle: 5,661 yds Front: 4,988 yds

Blue Rock Springs (East) – Vallejo   ♦½

Robert Muir Graves   www.bluerockspringsgolf.com
655 Columbus Pkwy, Vallejo, CA 94591   (707) 643-8476
                6,162 yds   Par 70   Rating: 70.0 / 127   (1949/1994)

With more perimeter land available on the East side of Columbus Parkway at the time of Blue Rock Springs 1994 expansion, the club's East course can today be viewed as a Robert Muir Graves design, as Graves significantly altered the handful of Jack Fleming holes which remain while building 14 new ones around them. Once again there is a good deal of undulating terrain present, a point well in evidence on the front nine at the 176-yard downhill 2nd, the 488-yard 5th (a sharply uphill par 5) and the 523-yard 7th, a very sharp dogleg right which plunges off the tee before encountering a right-side fallaway flanking its lay-up zone. Perhaps the most memorable entry comes at the 141-yard downhill 8th (whose shallow green sits just beyond a swath of wetlands) before the 551-yard downhill 14th sets up a more imposing finishing run which climbs into some foothills to the northeast. This stretch includes the 413-yard uphill 15th, the 196-yard 16th (which occupies the highest ground) and especially the 412-yard 17th, a sharp, steeply downhill dogleg right which dares a bold drive across an incongruously large corner bunker.

3	Range (Both)	Short Game	Putting Green	On-Site Rooms	Nearby Rooms	Altitude: 303'	Middle: 5,776 yds Front: 4,869 yds

Hiddenbrooke Golf Club – Vallejo   ♦♦♦

Arnold Palmer & Ed Seay   www.hiddenbrookegolf.com
1095 Hiddenbrooke Pkwy, Vallejo, CA 94591   (707) 558-0330
            6,619 yds   Par 72   Rating: 73.1 / 142   (1995)

Occupying its own valley in the hills above Vallejo, the Hiddenbrooke Golf Club anchors a real estate development and features a 1995 Arnold Palmer design of only moderate length but considerable challenge. The course's routing takes it into the lower foothills and across several creeks and lakes – though it must be noted that with 14 holes at least partially flanked by housing (often at good distance), the atmosphere is far from pastoral. Given the layout's overall size, it is not surprising that several shorter holes stand out, including the 481-yard par-5 2nd (played across a creek, and to an elevated green), the 153-yard 3rd (whose stonewall buttressed target sits above a lateral hazard), the 481-yard 12th (a creek-guarded par 5) and the 149-yard 13th, whose green is benched into a small mountainside. On the longer side, favorites include the 584-yard 5th (where left-side water affects both the second and third), the tree- and creek-narrowed 434-yard 8th, the downhill 426-yard 14th and the 508-yard 16th, another descending test with a creekbed angling across the fairway and a pond lurking back-right of the green. A number of holes may push the average golfer in terms of difficulty, and the wind can blow up here, but if one can look past the housing, this is an attractive, and testing, stop.

6	Range (Grass)	Short Game	Putting Green	On-Site Rooms	Nearby Rooms	Altitude: 414'	Middle: 6,188 yds Front: 4,613 yds

Paradise Valley Golf Course – Fairfield   ♦♦

Robert Muir Graves & Damian Pascuzzo   www.fairfieldgolf.com
3950 Paradise Valley Dr, Fairfield, CA 94533   (707) 426-1600
            7,065 yds   Par 72   Rating: 73.7 / 135   (1993)

Sitting along the eastern flank of Interstate 80, the Paradise Valley Golf Course began life as a wide-open, demandingly hazarded layout which was surely one of the longest and toughest public tracks in the region. It still maintains that status today but in a slightly altered state, with trees (and housing) lining many fairways, several relevant bunkers removed and a highly invasive lake at the par-5 10th reshaped in the interest of fairness. It remains, however, a solid example of Graves' period work, being modern in its shaping, offering quirkily shaped, often large putting surfaces and a tactical component that is sporadic but not altogether absent. For most, the front nine will be the less-engaging half, its most memorable entries being a pair of par 3s with wildly shaped greens (the 192-yard 3rd and the 221-yard 8th) as well as the watery 417-yard 6th. The back, on the other hand, is a tad more interesting, offering holes like the aforementioned 542-yard 10th (where a creekbed crosses 30 yards shy of the green), the driveable 328-yard 14th (which curls rightward around a massive bunker) and the 467-yard 18th, a demanding (but bunkerless) dogleg right which turns around a pair of lakes.

6	Range (Both)	Short Game	Putting Green	On-Site Rooms	Nearby Rooms	Altitude: 132'	Middle: 6,787 yds Front: 5,386 yds

Rancho Solano Golf Course – Fairfield

Gary Roger Baird
3250 Rancho Solano Pkwy, Fairfield, CA   94533
6,688 yds   Par 72   Rating: 71.6 / 132   (1990)

www.fairfieldgolf.com
(707) 429-4653

A shortish layout that anchors a real estate development in the hills on the north side of town, the Rancho Solano Golf Course is known primarily for the size of its Gary Roger Baird-designed greens, which are of mostly normal shape but very large proportion. The housing, for its part, is a significant presence but it is not wall to wall, allowing for frequent scenic views on several of the outlying holes. Perhaps because of all the acreage committed to residences, this is a shortish track, its par 4s averaging only 380 yards and including only three in excess of 400. This becomes clear in the early going when the first four two-shotters range in length from 348-382 yards, all plentifully bunkered but lacking any real tactical component, save, perhaps, for a right-side pond threatening longer tee shots at the 382-yard 4th. The strongest action, then, lies through the turn, beginning with the outbound closers, the 217-yard downhill (and bunkerless) 8th and the 415-yard 9th. Following the 578-yard 10th (a downhill, early turning dogleg left), play then peaks at the 429-yard pond-fronted 11th and the genuinely demanding 233-yard 12th, which angles across front-right water to a massive, heavily bunkered target.

4	Range (Mats)	Short Game	Putting Green	On-Site Rooms	Nearby Rooms	Altitude: 318'	Middle: 6,269 yds Front: 5,292 yds

Golf Club at Rio Vista – Rio Vista

Ted Robinson
1000 Summerset Dr, Rio Vista, CA   94571
6,800 yds   Par 72   Rating: 73.5 / 129   (1996)

www.playriovista.com
(707) 374-2900

Emerging from a period of maintenance neglect, the Golf Club at Rio Vista is located a mile northwest of the Sacramento River and features a mid-1990s Ted Robinson design routed through a real estate development dense enough that houses closely flank most fairways. At 6,800 yards it is long enough to offer a representative degree of challenge and the layout includes the standard modern Robinson stylings highlighted by the man-made waterfalls that flank both the 9th and 18th greens. Water is the driving factor on most of the stronger entries with the outward half being led by the 363-yard 1st (where a right-side pond threatens the opening tee shot), the 502-yard 2nd (which dares a long, water-carrying second) and especially the 443-yard 9th, which bends gently leftward to a green flanked closely by terraced/waterfalled ponds. The back then opens with the 321-yard pond-fronted 10th before closing with a pair of more muscular entries (the stiff 222-yard 15th and the 428-yard 16th) as well as the 372-yard 18th, whose stonewall-buttressed green is fronted by a pond and bordered right by more waterfalls. New ownership is cited as a positive factor by many, so the future may be brighter here.

6	Range (Grass)	Short Game	Putting Green	On-Site Rooms	Nearby Rooms	Altitude: 43'	Middle: 6,393 yds Front: 5,330 yds

Cypress Lakes Golf Course – Vacaville   ♦♦

Joe Finger   www.travisfss.com
5601 Meridian Rd, Vacaville, CA   95687   (707) 448-7186
                6,873 yds   Par 72   Rating: 73.0 / 124   (1960)

Owned and operated by Travis Air Force Base, the Cypress Lakes Golf Course is the rare military layout to have a significant design pedigree, having been built by popular Texas architect Joe Finger in 1960. Though never intended to be on par with Finger's best work, this is, unquestionably, one of the stronger military tracks around, offering length and plenty of strong holes before peaking over an exciting three-hole finish. The front nine occupies the flat property's eastern half and is more functional than exhilarating, with its strongest entries including the 506-yard 1st, the 176-yard pond-guarded 3rd and the 402-yard 4th, a sharp dogleg right. The longer homeward half then kicks the action up several notches, beginning with the 437-yard 12th and the 428-yard 13th, an early turning dogleg right. But the fun really starts at 409-yard 16th, a 90-degree dogleg right which offers multiple aggressive lines across a corner lake, as well as a second lake short-left of the green to keep big hitters honest. It is followed in turn by the 557-yard dogleg left 17th (where trees and more water fill the corner) and the 451-yard 18th, which doglegs right and crosses both water and sand on approach. Notably, several water hazards have gone dry in recent years, making their holes less visually appealing – but no less difficult.

5	Range (Grass)	Short Game	Putting Green	On-Site Rooms	Nearby Rooms	Altitude: 80′	Middle: 6,505 yds Front: 5,535 yds

CONTRA COSTA COUNTY

Berkeley Country Club – El Cerrito   ♦♦½

William Watson & Robert Hunter   www.berkeleycountryclub.com
7901 Cutting Blvd, El Cerrito, CA   94530   (510) 233-7550
              6,503 yds   Par 72   Rating: 72.6 / 133   (1920)

Known for many years as the Mira Vista Country Club before reverting back to its original name, the Berkeley Country Club was designed in 1920 by a one-time pairing of William Watson with Robert Hunter, design partner of Dr. Alister MacKenzie and professor at the nearby University of California. The short, undulating layout is situated in the Berkeley Hills and thus features plentiful panoramic views, but also a fair amount of fun, old-fashioned lay-of-the-land course design. The layout's backbone is a collection of strong mid-sized par 4s, which on the front side includes the 407-yard 3rd (played uphill to a green set above a deep front-left bunker), the 414-yard 5th, the steeply downhill (and scenic) 433-yard 7th and the 364-yard aggressively bunkered 9th. The back then offers the strong, tumbling 427-yard 13th, the 421-yard 14th (where longer hitters must be mindful of a left-side fairway pond) and the 344-yard 18th, which climbs past three crossbunkers to a large, elevated green that cannot be missed right. Also notable is a collection of par 3s that includes tricky sidehill tests like the 142-yard 2nd and the 201-yard 12th, as well as the 254-yard 7th, an uphill brute played across more crossbunkers to an elevated target.

5	Range (Both)	Short Game	Putting Green	On-Site Rooms	Nearby Rooms	Altitude: 687'	Middle: 6,106 yds Front: 5,125 yds

Blackhawk Country Club (Lakeside) – Danville   ♦♦½

Robert von Hagge & Bruce Devlin   www.blackhawkcc.org
599 Blackhawk Club Dr, Danville, CA   94506   (925) 736-6500
              6,769 yds   Par 72   Rating: 73.4 / 140   (1981)

Built in the foothills of the Diablo Mountains, the Blackhawk Country Club is a 36-hole facility whose courses play out of separate clubhouses, each routed over hilly terrain and among a range of residential neighborhoods. The older Lakeside course dates to 1981, when it was designed by the colorful team of Robert von Hagge and Bruce Devlin, with subsequent bunker and green renovations made by Robert Muir Graves' firm 20 years later. The Lakeside enjoyed a run as an LPGA stop from 2006-2010 (counting Karrie Webb and Suzanne Pettersen among its winners) and follows an expansive carts-only routing that actually plays shorter than its 6,769-yard total, this because with four of its five par 5s averaging 577 yards, there is limited room left for muscle among the two-shotters. The much longer front nine runs out to the south and, after providing a taste of the terrain at the plunging 585-yard 3rd, is led by the 206-yard pond-guarded 7th and 407-yard uphill 8th. The often tumultuous back then runs northward where it is led by a closing run which includes the 380-yard creek-fronted 14th, the 620-yard 15th (whose green is backed by a 200-foot hillside), the 224-yard 16th (which drops steeply off of that hillside) and the 394-yard 18th, which features both a plummeting tee shot and a huge island green.

6	Range (Both)	Short Game	Putting Green	On-Site Rooms	Nearby Rooms	Altitude: 737'	Middle: 6,310 yds Front: 5,339 yds

Blackhawk Country Club (Falls) – Danville   ♦♦

Ted Robinson   www.blackhawkcc.org
599 Blackhawk Club Dr, Danville, CA 94506   (925) 736-6500
              6,759 yds   Par 72   Rating: 72.9 / 136   (1986)

Its clubhouse lying just over a mile southeast of the Lakeside, the Blackhawk Country Club's newer Falls course dates to 1986, when it was laid out over similarly severe terrain (and on a comparable scale) by Ted Robinson. The undulating nature of the site is on full display at the 480-yard opener, a dogleg right par 4 that drops over 200 feet from tee to green. The descent then continues at the 363-yard 2nd (where longer hitters might have a go at the green across a lake – as well as several adjacent houses) with the remainder of the outward half being led by the 537-yard creek-fronted 3rd and the 205-yard 9th, a gently descending test played to a pond-flanked green. After one of several huge cart rides to return to the clubhouse, the 561-yard -10th mirrors the precipitous descent of the 1st en route to a green tucked behind front-left water, and the 173-yard 11th plays to one more pond-guarded target. Following the attractive 183-yard 13th, a bit of awkwardness is encountered at the 394-yard 14th (where tee shots must be laid up ahead of a plunging approach) before a pair of challenging uphill par 4s – the 421-yard barranca-fronted 15th and the 417-yard dogleg right 18th – close out play on a strong note.

5	Range	Short	Putting	On-Site	Nearby	Altitude:	Middle: 6,314 yds
	(Grass)	Game	Green	Rooms	Rooms	1,028'	Front: 5,289 yds

Crow Canyon Country Club – Danville   ♦♦

Ted Robinson   www.clubcorp.com
711 Silver Lake Dr, Danville, CA 94526   (925) 735-5700
              6,052 yds   Par 69   Rating: 70.0 / 129   (1977)

Another facility set in the Mount Diablo foothills, the Crow Canyon Country Club was a relatively early entry in the portfolio of the prolific Ted Robinson and serves as the anchor of a somewhat compact real estate development. That housing took priority is evident in the limited acreage allotted for golf, a circumstance which manifests itself both in a layout measuring 6,052 yards and in the fact that nearly every fairway is closely flanked by residences. Robinson was not much for strategic design at this stage of his career, leaving this as a fairly basic layout whose front nine is led by the 570-yard 2nd (a long par 5 made slightly awkward by its fairway ending 75 yards shy of the green), the 200-yard pondside 6th and the very narrow uphill 403-yard 9th. The inward half initially offers another watery par 3 at the 148-yard 12th, as well as a tricky two-shotter at the 340-yard dogleg right 15th, whose fairway is pinched by sand, a pond...and a cart path. The 401-yard 18th is a watery finisher but again a bit of awkwardness is introduced, as a large lake (and another cart path) mandate a laid-up tee shot of no more than 235 yards.

3	Range	Short	Putting	On-Site	Nearby	Altitude:	Middle: 5,535 yds
	(Grass)	Game	Green	Rooms	Rooms	506'	Front: 5,023 yds

Contra Costa Country Club – Pleasant Hill   ◆◆½

Vernon Macan   www.contracostacc.org
801 Golf Club Rd, Pleasant Hill, CA   94523   (925) 798-7135
              6,528 yds   Par 72   Rating: 71.4 / 127   (1925)

The Contra Costa Country Club does indeed date to the mid-1920s but the design credit for Irish/Canadian architect Vernon Macan carries little validity today, in part because he was only responsible for an initial nine holes, but also because the current course retains precious little of his handiwork. More in evidence now are the stylings of Robert Trent Jones II, whose firm performed a significant renovation in 2015, a job with introduced lots of classically flavored bunkering and green shaping, adding playing interest to a layout which has little room to expand beyond its 6,528-yards. For many, the front nine is the stronger half due in large part to a mid-section which includes the 487-yard 3rd (an uphill, centerline-bunkered par 5), the 137-yard pinpoint 5th and the 534-yard dogleg left 6th, which sweeps around a steep hillside en route to a green angled leftward above sand and a barranca. Following the muscular 242-yard 8th and another short, centerline bunkered par 5 at the 481-yard 9th, the back nine features the 408-yard 11th (which plays to a deep, extremely narrow green) and two more short-but-engaging par 5s, the 539-yard dogleg left 15th (which descends to a target angled behind multiple bunkers) and the 505-yard 17th, another dogleg left, this one turning around invasive left-side sand.

4	Range (Both)	Short Game	Putting Green	On-Site Rooms	Nearby Rooms	Altitude: 151'	Middle: 6,183 yds Front: 4,989 yds

Diablo Country Club – Diablo   ◆◆◆

William Watson & Jack Neville   www.diablocc.org
1700 Clubhouse Rd, Diablo, CA   94528   (925) 837-4221
              6,761 yds   Par 71   Rating: 73.4 / 135   (1914)

Considering its early date of establishment, the Diablo Country Club is situated surprisingly far out in the East Bay, though given its proximity to, and scenic views of, 3,849-foot Mt. Diablo, being close to San Francisco likely wasn't the club's top priority. While the great majority of William Watson and Jack Neville's 1914 routing still exists, the course underwent a 2020 restoration/renovation at the hands of Todd Eckenrode, a job which removed lots of modern-era bunkering (as well as a postwar pond from the 164-yard 3rd) while establishing a more classic feel within the hazarding that remains. The layout follows a non-returning routing amidst some very well-established housing and, despite its limited overall size, finds room for several longer par 4s including the 460-yard 9th (where a creek lines much of the left side), the 440-yard pond-flanked 12th, the newly lengthened 480-yard 15th and the 428-yard 17th – as well as the 471-yard 18th, a quirky, tree-dotted par 5 that would readily convert to two-shot status for tournament play. Including the 18th, there are five par 5s within the reconfigured layout (including a back-to-back pair at the 536-yard 10th and the 506-yard 11th) while among the one-shotters, the 220-yard 12th (whose green angles beyond left-side bunkers) weighs in the heaviest. Overall, a pleasant, very scenic test which has surely benefitted from its re-fitting.

6	Range (Grass)	Short Game	Putting Green	On-Site Rooms	Nearby Rooms	Altitude: 546'	Middle: 6,517 yds Front: 5,066 yds

Discovery Bay Country Club – Discovery Bay   ♦♦

Ted Robinson   www.dbgcc.com
1475 Clubhouse Dr, Discovery Bay, CA   94505   (925) 634-0700
6,518 yds   Par 71   Rating: 72.0 / 129   (1986)

The centerpiece of a large real estate development carved from former wetlands and farms in the eastern reaches of the county, the Discovery Bay Country Club was built by Ted Robinson and features rows of housing and man-made water hazards in roughly equal measure. The water meaningfully affects 14 holes and provide the great majority of the layout's playing interest, in part because Robinson's bunkering, while plentiful, is seldom central to ideal lines of play. The front nine opens with a 499-yard par 5 played to a forgiving island green complex and is subsequently led by similarly watery tests like the 160-yard 2nd, the 314-yard 8th (where a left-side hazard – and right-side trees – threaten aggressive drives) and the 376-yard 9th. Left-side water menaces the second and/or third at the 516-yard 10th, while the 332-yard 11th is a water-lined dogleg left which was originally a drive-and-pitch, but which today may tempt longer hitters to aim at or near the green off the tee. The round eventually closes with the 180-yard pondside 17th (which features a dangerous front-right pin) and the 448-yard 18th, a surprisingly dry dogleg left and comfortably the layout's longest par 4.

4	Range	Short	Putting	On-Site	Nearby	Altitude:	Middle: 6,224 yds
	(Grass)	Game	Green	Rooms	Rooms	0'	Front: 5,279 yds

Moraga Country Club – Moraga   ♦½

Robert Muir Graves / Algie Pulley   www.moragacc.com
1600 St. Andrews Dr, Moraga, CA   94556   (925) 376-2200
6,103 yds   Par 71   Rating: 71.1 / 127   (1973/1992)

Situated a mile west of St. Mary's College, the Moraga Country Club offers a short, quirky, somewhat disjointed layout whose oddness can largely be explained by its genesis. Specifically, it began life as a short Robert Muir Graves-designed nine squeezed into limited, housing-lined acreage, then had several of those holes redesigned by Algie Pulley when he added nine more on some tumultuous terrain to the northwest in 1992. This redesign allowed the old loop (today's front nine) to begin with two full-sized pr 4s (the 407-yard 1st and 426-yard 3rd). though the 265-yard yard creek-fronted 8th is more emblematic of the layout's beginnings. After the 8th green returns to the clubhouse, the back nine climbs nearly 250 feet, then makes the return descent, with its strongest entries including a pair of sharply downhill par 3s (the 223-yard 15th and the 182-yard 17th) as well as the 550-yard 18th, a dangerous, creek-fronted dogleg right whose driving zone is squeezed rather too tightly between lakes. Style-wise, this is not everyone's cup of tea.

4	Range	Short	Putting	On-Site	Nearby	Altitude:	Middle: 5,709 yds
	(Grass)	Game	Green	Rooms	Rooms	504'	Front: 5,068 yds

Oakhurst Country Club – Clayton   ♦♦½

Ron Fream   www.oakhurstcc.com
1001 Peacock Creek Dr, Clayton, CA 94517   (925) 672-9737
                6,746 yds   Par 72   Rating: 72.9 / 142   (1990)

Another facility situated in the Mount Diablo foothills, the Oakhurst Country Club drew a measure of regional attention upon its 1990 opening, primarily because within designer Ron Fream's period-standard modern stylings, a fair number of interesting holes appear. The course follows an expansive, non-returning routing which begins and ends at the base of a towering hillside, with the remainder running adjacent to (or being enclosed by) residential neighborhoods. Although the 419-yard uphill 2nd is a strong early test (as it curves along the base of the hillside), the most engaging stretch of golf begins at the 397-yard 5th (played uphill to a barranca-fronted green), then includes a pair of descending pond-guarded entries (the 513-yard 7th and the 154-yard 8th) as well as the 383-yard 9th, which plunges downhill to a green which extends forward into a large bunker. The inward half then begins on lower, residence-flanked ground and features two of its best at the 154-yard 13th (whose green is fronted by a huge, grass-dotted bunker and backed by out-of-bounds) and the 372-yard barranca-fronted 14th. Among the closers, tops (easily) is the 435-yard downhill 18th, a tough dogleg left whose second angles across a wide ravine to a putting surface situated beneath the hilltop clubhouse.

5	Range (Both)	Short Game	Putting Green	On-Site Rooms	Nearby Rooms	Altitude: 463'	Middle: 6,293 yds Front: 5,323 yds

Orinda Country Club – Orinda   ♦♦♦

William Watson   www.orindacc.org
315 Camino Sobrante, Orinda, CA 94563   (925) 254-4313
                6,290 yds   Par 72   Rating: 71.2 / 133   (1924)

One of Northern California's more overlooked courses, the Orinda Country Club is an attractive, quirky William Watson layout located three miles east of the Caldecott Tunnel in the closest of Oakland's affluent East Bay communities. Mostly routed across a broad, housing-dotted hillside, the course's generally modest beginning is broken only by the 251-yard 3rd, a demanding (if fairly basic) downhill par 3. But the action picks up quickly thereafter over a run of highly original holes kicked off by the 354-yard 5th, which climbs to a wild, V-shaped green and is the first of several entries to flank a road-bottomed canyon (out-of-bounds). Subsequent favorites include the downhill 118-yard 8th (played to a suitably tiny, tightly bunkered plateau putting surface), the descending 442-yard 9th (where the canyon lies right of the green), the narrow, driveable 301-yard 10th (ditto) and the 435-yard creek-crossing 11th, which features a bunkerless, hourglass-shaped target. More noteworthy golf follows at a pair of holes routed along San Pablo Creek, the potentially driveable 285-yard 14th (which features an extremely narrow green) and the 178-yard 15th, which found a dash of period fame in Robert Hunter's classic 1926 volume *The Links*. Power lines make an unfortunate incursion across several holes and the scorecard is palpably light by modern standards, but with so many unique entries dotting the attractive Northern California landscape, this a worthwhile Bay Area stop.

4	Range (Grass)	Short Game	Putting Green	On-Site Rooms	Nearby Rooms	Altitude: 437'	Middle: 6,070 yds Front: 5,504 yds

Richmond Country Club – Richmond   ♦♦

Ed Sawyer   www.myrichmondcc.org
1 Markovich Ln, Richmond, CA 94806   (510) 232-1080
            6,512 yds   Par 72   Rating: 72.0 / 127   (1924)

On its sloping site above San Pablo Bay, the Richmond Country Club has witnessed its share of history, hosting four playings of the PGA Tour's Richmond Open between 1944-1948 and the LPGA thrice between 1951-1955 – but also an ignominious moment when the PGA of America banned three African-American golfers from the 1948 Richmond Open, sparking a groundbreaking lawsuit. Design-wise, the golf course has always been more functional than flashy, and it hasn't changed tremendously since those early years – but after nearly a century of tree growth, today's version is purely a parkland test, with a number of fairways hemmed in tightly down both sides. The lone water hazard is a lake along the right side of the 343-yard 1st, with remaining outbound favorites including the 165-yard tightly bunkered 3rd, the muscular 231-yard 7th and the 507-yard 9th, which climbs off the tee before descending back to the clubhouse. The back initially includes the club's two longest par 4s (the 417-yard 10th and the 419-yard 12th) before offering the 336-yard 14th (which plays to a narrow light bulb-shaped green) and the 504-yard 18th, where a small fronting bunker defines the approach.

4	Range (Grass)	Short Game	Putting Green	On-Site Rooms	Nearby Rooms	Altitude: 116'	Middle: 6,260 yds Front: 5,005 yds

Rossmoor – Walnut Creek   ♦½

Harry Rainville / Desmond Muirhead / Robert Muir Graves   www.rossmoor.com
1001 Golden Rain Rd, Walnut Creek, CA 94595   (925) 988-7700
        Dollar Ranch: 6,162 yds   Par 72   Rating: 70.0 / 123   (1964/1977)
        Creekside: 2,997 yds   Par 36   Rating: 33.7 / 117   (1965)

A retirement community set in a valley two miles west of Interstate 680, Rossmoor offers 27 holes of golf, with its primary 18 (Dollar Ranch) including nines built by Harry Rainville and Robert Muir Graves, while its third nine (Creekside) is the handiwork of Desmond Muirhead. The routing of the Dollar Ranch layout intermingles the work of Rainville and Graves and is power line crossed, but it offers a decent degree of playing interest despite its limited size. This is often due to tactically relevant fairway bunkering, which defines holes like the 300-yard 1st, the 377-yard 3rd, the 389-yard 6th and the 369-yard 9th – and with 57 bunkers present, sand is a significant presence overall. Also notable are the 169-yard 4th and the 526-yard 5th (which sit flush along the base of some foothills) as well as the 171-yard downhill 10th (played to a creek-fronted green) and the 506-yard descending 18th, where a well-placed right-side bunker menaces the second. Muirhead's Creekside loop, meanwhile, has been slightly reconfigured (and heavily rebunkered) over the years, and aside from the double green serving the 3rd and 5th holes, is most memorable for the 310-yard pondside 1st and the 347-yard creek- and tree-flanked 6th. Note: There are some incredibly invasive cart paths here, frequently offering the possibility of gigantic bounces off paths running literally right up the center of fairways.

3	Range (Mats)	Short Game	Putting Green	On-Site Rooms	Nearby Rooms	Altitude: 342'	Middle: 5,822 yds Front: 4,704 yds

Round Hill Country Club – Alamo   ♦♦½

Lawrence Hughes   www.rhcountryclub.com
3169 Round Hill Rd, Alamo, CA 94507   (925) 934-8211
                6,483 yds   Par 72   Rating: 72.3 / 140   (1960)

One more layout set in the Mount Diablo foothills, the Round Hill Country Club was laid out by Lawrence Hughes in 1960 and found a place in the national spotlight by decade's end, hosting seven playings of the LPGA Tour's Lincoln-Mercury Open between 1969-1978. The course later had more than 30 bunkers added during a 2004 renovation by John Steidel, resulting in today's short but often-challenging track, which continues to follow its original housing-lined routing. The front nine forms a wide clockwise loop around the property's northern half and initially offers a bit of muscle in its mid-section in the form of the 434-yard 3rd (where a left-side tree can impede the second), the 203-yard 5th and especially the 446-yard 6th, a bunker-narrowed par 4 that ascends more than 100 feet from tee to green. For many, however, its most memorable entry is the 137-yard downhill 6th, which is played to a green set above two deep fronting bunkers. The back offers two more tough uphill par 4s of its own, first at the 424-yard 12th (whose early – and sharp – rightward turn mandates a long fade off the tee), then at the 417-yard 17th, which climbs nearly 60 feet through a canyon. Also notable are two short par 5s, the 483-yard pond-guarded 14th and the downhill 489-yard creek-fronted 18th.

5	Range (Both)	Short Game	Putting Green	On-Site Rooms	Nearby Rooms	Altitude: 398'	Middle: 6,136 yds Front: 5,152 yds

Boundary Oak Golf Course – Walnut Creek

Robert Muir Graves   www.playboundaryoak.com
3800 Valley Vista Rd, Walnut Creek, CA 94598   (925) 934-4775
               7,100 yds   Par 72   Rating: 73.8 / 134   (1969)

Set in the foothills on the northwestern side of Mount Diablo, the Boundary Oak Golf Course is a muscular Robert Muir Graves-designed municipal layout which at least partially offsets the architectural blandness of its period by offering some impressive panoramic views. The site slopes significantly from east to west (dropping roughly 150 feet from high point to low point) and this terrain exerts a major influence on play, as demonstrated by a trio of early entries: the 172-yard 2nd (which drops sharply to a very wide, centerline-bunkered green), the 555-yard downhill 3rd (a dogleg left marked by invasive corner bunkers and right-side water on approach) and the 407-yard uphill 4th. The layout's remaining water hazards then affect the 356-yard pond-flanked 8th, the 405-yard 9th (which climbs to a partially creek-fronted green) and especially the 432-yard 11th, a sharp and demanding downhill dogleg right with a pond filling the corner. Thereafter, the action is more basic than tactically engaging, but this is "basic" on a larger scale, as holes 12-17 measure 209, 435, 577, 437, 416 and 222 yards – fairly broad-shouldered stuff for a municipal layout. Without a doubt, one of the region's stronger public tracks.

6	Range (Mats)	Short Game	Putting Green	On-Site Rooms	Nearby Rooms	Altitude: 328'	Middle: 6,739 yds Front: 5,699 yds

Brentwood Golf Club – Brentwood

Ted Robinson   www.brentwoodgolf.com
100 Summerset Dr, Brentwood, CA 94513   (925) 516-3400
        Creekside/Hillside: 6,828 yds   Par 72   Rating: 72.9 / 131   (2002)
        Diablo: 3,144 yds   Par 36   Rating: 34.7 / 122   (2002)

Anchoring a real estate development built on a vast alluvial plain east of Mount Diablo, the Brentwood Golf Club offers 27 holes of Ted Robinson-designed, housing-enclosed golf – and rates among the most power line-affected layouts one will ever encounter. All three loops represent standard period Robinson, with water being the primary hazard and tactical questions popping up infrequently enough to perhaps be accidental. Notably, the power lines were in place before the course's construction, a point which at least explains why a number of holes run neatly parallel to them or, on occasion, directly beneath them. The Creekside and Hillside nines combine to form a non-returning 18 holes and thus represent the primary layout, with the Creekside offering longer par 4s like the 454-yard power line-flanked 2nd and the 422-yard 4th, as well as the 162-yard lakeside 6th. The Hillside then opens with power lines crossing right over the green at the 386-yard 10th, and directly over the heart of the 221-yard 11th. The 518-yard pond-fronted 13th is a strong enough test before the wires return above the 552-yard 15th and alongside the 178-yard 17th. The Diablo nine lies mostly north of Balfour Road and, after offering engaging water holes at the 297-yard 2nd and the 166-yard 5th, closes with two more power line-flanked tests, the 529-yard 8th and the 354-yard 9th.

5	Range (Grass)	Short Game	Putting Green	On-Site Rooms	Nearby Rooms	Altitude: 114'	Middle: 6,424 yds Front: 5,363 yds

Bridges Golf Club – San Ramon   ♦♦½

Damian Pascuzzo & Johnny Miller   www.thebridgesgolf.com
9000 S. Gale Ridge Rd, San Ramon, CA 94582   (925) 735-4253
                6,861 yds   Par 72   Rating: 73.6 / 141   (1999)

Located on rugged but scenic terrain a mile and a half east of Interstate 680, the Bridges Golf Club is a demanding Damian Pascuzzo and Johnny Miller-designed facility built in the era when "upscale daily fee" was all the rage. While the layout's 73.6 rating is hardly eye-popping, the residence-lined course is widely viewed as one of the region's toughest – though its canyon-dotted routing does offer a fair amount of tactical golf within its difficulty. The opening four holes (plus the 17th and 18th) sit south of Bollinger Canyon Road and are canyon-riddled, with favorites including the 363-yard dogleg right 3rd (allowing an aggressive diagonal drive across a wide arroyo) and the 514-yard 4th, where the arroyo flanks the left side. Holes 5-16 lie north of the road in three separate canyons, with the front nine featuring the downhill 558-yard 8th and the back offering the 223-yard 11th (whose green angles above another fallaway) and the 148-yard 13th, a mere pitch to a V-shaped target. Following the wild, arroyo-crossed 402-yard 14th, play closes with the 564-yard arroyo-menaced 15th, the 463-yard 16th (which flanks a left-side canyon all the way to a deep, wildly shaped putting surface) and, back across the road, the 232-yard 17th (whose green teeters above an abyss) and the 557-yard ravine-fronted 18th. This sort of toughness is definitely not for everyone, but if it's your cup of tea...

7	Range (Mats)	Short Game	Putting Green	On-Site Rooms	Nearby Rooms	Altitude: 553'	Middle: 6,561 yds Front: 5,111 yds

Canyon Lakes Golf Course & Brewery – San Ramon   ♦♦

Ted Robinson   www.canyonlakesgolfbrew.com
640 Bollinger Canyon Way, San Ramon, CA 94582   (925) 735-6511
                6,373 yds   Par 71   Rating: 71.4 / 130   (1987)

The Bridges Golf Club's immediate neighbor to the west, the Canyon Lakes Golf Course and Brewery offers a short but occasionally engaging Ted Robinson design routed over similarly rugged terrain and through several residential neighborhoods. As with many a Robinson creation, the most memorable holes inevitably involve water or, on a property like this, some imposing aspect of the terrain; where both are absent, play tends to be more functional than exciting. The front nine extends northward from the clubhouse and is driven by a pair of short, watery par 4s, the 340-yard downhill 1st (whose green is perched above a left-side pond) and the 292-yard 4th, a driveable test, but to a putting surface situated upon an island within a lake. The back nine plays along and around a housing-topped ridge, initially following an ascending, counter-clockwise route around the base of the ridge before climbing on approach to the 523-yard dogleg left 14th and at the 163-yard bunker-fronted 15th. The 365-yard 16th then plunges downhill (with a centerline fairway bunker forcing a decision off the tee) before the 548-yard 17th and 433-yard 18th return atop the ridge, with a long, steep fallaway lining their left sides.

4	Range (Grass)	Short Game	Putting Green	On-Site Rooms	Nearby Rooms	Altitude: 596'	Middle: 5,970 yds Front: 5,191 yds

Diablo Creek Golf Course – Concord   ♦½

Bob Baldock   www.diablocreekgc.com
4050 Port Chicago Hwy, Concord, CA   94520   (925) 686-6262
                  6,896 yds   Par 71   Rating: 73.2 / 125   (1963)

Occupying a flattish triangular site on the northeastern side of town, the Diablo Creek Golf Course was laid out by Bob Baldock in 1963 – though the front nine was substantially reconfigured during the 1970s when additional acreage became available. Now a good-sized test which features putting surfaces large enough to accommodate higher volumes of public play (several by a wide margin), it makes limited use of the crossing waters of Mount Diablo Creek, and thus offers mostly functional golf throughout. The far longer outward half includes plenty of brawn, beginning with the 632-yard 3rd (which bends leftward around a pond) and the 234-yard 4th, then adding a trio of muscular par 4s at the 437-yard 5th and the back-and-forth 418-yard 8th and 443-yard 9th. The back opens with the lone hole to meaningfully utilize the creek, the 392-yard 10th, where the hazard crosses 30 yards shy of the green before flanking its left side, and several prominent trees also pinch the approach. The 450-yard 15th and 454-yard 16th offer plenty of late muscle, offsetting the tiny 110-yard 17th, which plays to a gigantic putting surface.

5	Range (Mats)	Short Game	Putting Green	On-Site Rooms	Nearby Rooms	Altitude: 36'	Middle: 6,441 yds Front: 5,333 yds

Diablo Hills Golf Course – Walnut Creek   ♦½

Robert Muir Graves   www.diablohillsgolfcourse.com
1551 Marchbanks Dr, Walnut Creek, CA   94598   (925) 939-7372
                  2,302 yds   Par 34   Rating: 31.1 / 104   (1968)

Only narrowly rising above executive status, the Diablo Hills Golf Course is a short Robert Muir Graves-designed nine built upon a broadly sloping site, and wedged in among all manner of housing. As the 88-yard 4th and 323-yard power line-crossed 5th suggest, this may not have been an ideal site for golf, but Graves at least attempted to enliven things with some prominent bunkering, providing dashes of playing interest along the way. Most notable on a short list are the 254-yard 6th (a heavily bunkered par 4 with trees impeding the green's left side), the 489-yard uphill 8th and the 310-yard 9th, a downhill closer made awkward by the cluster of bunkers which consume the last 80 yards before the green, mandating that tee shots be laid up with little more than a mid-iron.

2	Range (Grass)	Short Game	Putting Green	On-Site Rooms	Nearby Rooms	Altitude: 171'	Middle: N/A Front: 2,173 yds

Franklin Canyon Golf Course – Hercules   ♦½

Robert Muir Graves   www.franklincanyongolf.com
Hwy 4, Hercules, CA 94547   (510) 799-6191
          6,550 yds   Par 72   Rating: 71.8 / 132   (1968)

Situated just off the south side of the John Muir Parkway (aka Highway 4), the Robert Muir Graves-designed Franklin Canyon Golf Course occupies rolling terrain which twice climbs into attractive foothills, making for a pleasantly pastoral round of golf. The course is short and mostly functional in design, with little in the way of tactically deep challenges present. However, it sets a tone early by opening with a four-hole up-and-back excursion into elevated terrain, a run which includes a pair of solid par 3s at the 186-yard uphill 2nd and the 179-yard descending 4th. The outward half also offers a pair of par 5s of some note, the 521-yard 7th (whose green is defended by a large front-left tree) and the 518-yard 9th, which bends leftward around a lake. The slightly longer homeward nine includes bigger tests like the 212-yard 11th, the 519-yard uphill 13th and the 456-yard downhill 15th. More engaging, however, are the 363-yard 14th (a downhill dogleg right daring a shortcut over a bunker-lined corner) and the 150-yard 17th, which plays across a small, creekbed-bottomed valley to a platform green set above a left-side fallaway.

4	Range (Mats)	Short Game	Putting Green	On-Site Rooms	Nearby Rooms	Altitude: 208'	Middle: 6,145 yds Front: 5,373 yds

Lone Tree Golf & Event Center – Antioch   ♦½

Bob Baldock   www.lonetreegolfcourse.com
4800 Golf Course Rd, Antioch, CA 94531   (925) 706-4220
          6,427 yds   Par 71   Rating: 68.8 / 123   (1957)

Built upon the southern and western shorelines of the Antioch Municipal Reservoir, the Lone Tree Golf & Event Center began life with nine holes in 1934, but that early loop was reconfigured and expanded to 18 by Bob Baldock in 1957. Save for tee shots blasted over the green at the 117-yard 5th, or snap hooked at the 362-yard 6th, the reservoir serves mostly as a scenic backdrop, and the overall design is fairly short and mostly functional in scope. The par-37 front nine does open strongly, first at the 407-yard 1st (which requires a tough approach to a small, elevated target), then at the 518-yard out-of-bounds-lined 3rd, where aggressive seconds must carry a swale 80 yards shy of the green. The back also begins with a testing par 4, though the 434-yard 10th is probably most memorable for offering dual putting surfaces, with the right-side option including a tough, sand-guarded back-right pin. The 180-yard 11th then drops 50 feet to a narrow green wedged among trees, sand and out-of-bounds, with remaining favorites including the 389-yard 14th (played to a very wide, tightly bunkered target) and the 422-yard downhill 17th.

3	Range (Mats)	Short Game	Putting Green	On-Site Rooms	Nearby Rooms	Altitude: 197'	Middle: 6,102 yds Front: 5,493 yds

San Ramon Golf Club – San Ramon   ♦½

Clark Glasson   www.golfsanramon.com
9430 Fircrest Ln, San Ramon, CA 94583   (925) 828-6100
           6,459 yds   Par 72   Rating: 71.4 / 128   (1962)

Located half a mile east of Interstate 680, the San Ramon Golf Club dates to the early 1960s, when designer Clark Glasson built it within a then fledgling/now fully built out residential development. Its routing thus locked firmly into place, the mostly functional layout has seen considerable alteration of its bunkering over the decades (there are only 34 hazards in play today) but its one really major change took place at the 339-yard 9th, where a small island within a left-side lake was converted into a large island green during the 1990s. The 9th shares top billing with the adjacent 385-yard 18th (a gentle dogleg left played to a pond-fronted target), with the remaining 16 holes being quite a bit more staid in their stylings. Many of the more engaging entries lie on the front nine, where the 341-yard 1st (a creek-crossed dogleg right) requires a bit of thought off the tee, the 293-yard 3rd is defined by crossbunkers at the 225-yard mark, and the stiff 218-yard 7th angles across a short-right creek. The inward half is more basic still, with its strongest entry besides the 18th being the 415-yard 16th, an early turning dogleg right.

4	Range	Short	Putting	On-Site	Nearby	Altitude:	Middle: 6,076 yds
	(Mats)	Game	Green	Rooms	Rooms	355'	Front: 4,748 yds

Tilden Park Golf Course – Berkeley   ♦♦

William P. Bell   www.tildenparkgc.com
10 Golf Course Dr, Berkeley, CA 94708   (510) 848-7373
           6,294 yds   Par 70   Rating: 71.3 / 128   (1937)

Wonderfully secluded within a wooded 2,079-acre park in the Berkeley Hills, the Tilden Park Golf Course was constructed with Depression-era WPA funding and laid out by Billy Bell, co-designer (with George Thomas) of Southern California standouts Riviera, Bel-Air and the Los Angeles Country Club, among others. The caliber of Bell's solo projects varied widely, and if Tilden Park was somewhat limited by its hilly terrain, Bell at least succeeded is building a fair number of engaging holes here. This is apparent immediately at the 411-yard 1st, which climbs 100 feet from tee to very small green, and thus requires a skillful uphill second. The front nine later closes with another delicate uphill approach at the 334-yard 9th, but in between it features the 464-yard 3rd (a steeply downhill par 4), the 143-yard 4th (whose green is perched above a grassy slope) and the 221-yard 7th, a stiff (though gently downhill) par 3. The back nine includes two more muscular one-shotters, first at the 234-yard downhill 11th, then at the 206-yard 16th, a demanding test played across a small valley. Tilden Park may not be for long-hitting modern golfers but its pastoral atmosphere and old-fashioned stylings will certainly still appeal to many.

4	Range	Short	Putting	On-Site	Nearby	Altitude:	Middle: 5,823 yds
	(Mats)	Game	Green	Rooms	Rooms	1,082'	Front: 5,399 yds

Buchanan Fields Golf Course – Concord   ♦

Robert Muir Graves
1091 Concord Ave, Concord, CA 94520   (925) 682-1846
                1,911 yds   Par 31   Rating: 29.5 / 91   (DU)

Lying just off the southern end of the runways of Buchanan Airport, the Buchanan Fields Golf Course dates to the 1960s, but it came into its present form via a Robert Muir Graves redesign circa 1990. The loop contains five par 3s as well as a quartet of par 4s ranging in length from 281-330 yards, and while there is little in the way of grand playing interest present, Graves did create a pair of more engaging entries at the 149-yard well-bunkered 2nd and the 150-yard 3rd, whose green sits beyond a drainage ditch. With a large practice range adjacent, this is well-suited to newcomers and the less-skilled.

1	Range (Mats)	Short Game	Putting Green	On-Site Rooms	Nearby Rooms	Altitude: 21'	Middle: 1,731 yds Front: 1,500 yds

ALAMEDA
COUNTY

Club at Castlewood (Hill) – Pleasanton   ♦♦½

William P. Bell   www.castlewoodcc.org
707 Country Club Circle, Pleasanton, CA 94566   (925) 846-2871
                 6,219 yds   Par 70   Rating: 71.6 / 131   (1926)

Located just west of Interstate 680, in the foothills beneath Pleasanton Ridge, the Club at Castlewood was built upon land formerly owned by the Hearst family and debuted the first of its two golf courses, known as the Hill, in 1926. Billy Bell was the layout's original designer but that credit is more than a little attenuated today, owing to the significant reconfigurations necessary to accommodate the trio of residential neighborhoods which now mark the course's interior. Nonetheless, the layout retains a classic Golden Age feel within its often-hilly routing, and the terrain particularly influences a strong quartet of front nine par 4s: the 426-yard downhill 1st, the 418-yard uphill 5th, the 483-yard 7th (which drops nearly 150 feet as it angles along a right-side fallaway) and the 404-yard 8th, whose green is closely protected by left-side trees. The inward half offers a pair of strong two-shotters of its own at the 400-yard 15th (which requires an uphill, tree-narrowed approach) and the 400-yard downhill 18th, though the Hill is equally well thought of for its varied group of par 3s, a foursome led by the 181-yard uphill 4th, the 138-yard 6th (whose green sits above a left-side fallaway) and the 210-yard sharply descending 17th. This may not quite be vintage stuff, but its better holes represent a pretty good facsimile thereof.

4	Range (Mats)	Short Game	Putting Green	On-Site Rooms	Nearby Rooms	Altitude: 546'	Middle: 5,957 yds
							Front: 5,206 yds

Club at Castlewood (Valley) – Pleasanton   ♦♦

William F. Bell   www.castlewoodcc.org
707 Country Club Circle, Pleasanton, CA 94566   (925) 846-2871
                 6,756 yds   Par 72   Rating: 73.6 / 133   (1956)

The Club at Castlewood's Valley course was built three decades after its older sibling but its creation was kept in the family, as Billy Bell's son William F. was retained to design it. The Valley lies on lower (and much flatter) acreage closer to the freeway and is arranged largely in a back-and-forth manner, yet this compact configuration still allows it to easily be the longer of the two courses. Though Bell's original routing remains, a fair amount has changed over the decades, with bunkering evolving considerably and multiple lakes being added. The front nine lies on the west side of a single track of the Western Pacific railroad and after opening with a strong 429-yard par 4, is led by a pair of par 3s which border the same lake, the 167-yard 4th and the 205-yard 6th. The challenge picks up noticeably on the back nine, however, where a densely packed section includes the 561-yard pond-guarded 10th, the 447-yard bunkerless 13th, the 443-yard 15th and the 544-yard 16th, where a left-side lake threatens the second and third. Also notable are the 125-yard 14th (whose slim green angles along more water) and the 426-yard 18th, which bends gently leftward and is defined off the tee by a prominent centerline tree.

6	Range (Grass)	Short Game+	Putting Green	On-Site Rooms	Nearby Rooms	Altitude: 305'	Middle: 6,330 yds
							Front: 5,206 yds

Claremont Country Club – Oakland ♦♦♦½

Dr. Alister MacKenzie
5925 Broadway Terrace, Oakland, CA 94618
www.claremontcountryclub.com
(510) 653-6789
5,536 yds   Par 68   Rating: 67.6 / 123   (1926)

Occupying scarcely 100 acres in the affluent hills east of Oakland, the Claremont Country Club stands virtually unique among American golf courses, measuring only 5,536 yards and barely reaching its par of 68, yet remaining a quirky, challenging layout of distinction. Dr. Alister MacKenzie's work was actually a redesign of a rudimentary early 18 and resulted in a routing which crosses a public road (Broadway Terrace) for a sequence of five front nine holes, two of which (the 4th and 5th) are actually crossed by the fairway of the 386-yard 7th. But while this section of the property is enormously compact, it also includes two tiny gems, the 140-yard bunker-ringed 3rd and the 256-yard par-4 6th, which makes a late climb to a tightly bunkered target. The remaining 11 holes traverse stately columns of trees as they march up and down a steady grade, and are first led by the 167-yard 8th (which itself crosses the 18th fairway), the attractive 164-yard 10th and both the 394-yard 11th and the 399-yard 12th, a tightly bunkered pair running gently uphill. The stout 223-yard 13th then kicks of a set of mostly downhill finishers that are anchored by the 133-yard 17th (played to another small, closely bunkered target) and the downhill 501-yard 18th, a short par 5 complicated by a bunker placed precisely where a run-up second would like to land. It is quite remarkable how much engaging golf MacKenzie was able to build into so small a site, and there is a bit of history present as well, as Sam Snead claimed his first official victory here – at the old Oakland Open – way back in 1937.

3	Range (Grass)	Short Game+	Putting Green	On-Site Rooms	Nearby Rooms	Altitude: 223'	Middle: 5,428 yds Front: 5,287 yds

Ruby Hill Golf Club – Pleasanton ♦♦♦

Jack Nicklaus
3404 W. Ruby Hill Dr, Pleasanton, CA 94566
www.rubyhill.com
(925) 417-5850
7,459 yds   Par 72   Rating: 75.8 / 137   (1996)

Located halfway between Pleasanton and Livermore, the Ruby Hill Golf Club is a real estate-oriented Jack Nicklaus-designed layout capable of presenting a notably strong challenge to anyone choosing to step back to the tips. Though little new architectural ground is broken here, much of Nicklaus's usual high degree of playing interest is present – a point quickly in evidence at the demanding 450-yard 2nd (where a drive flirting with/ carrying a left-side bunker cluster yields the best angle to a pond-guarded green) as well as over a pair of smartly bunkered (but surprisingly short) front nine par 5s, the 520-yard 4th and the 529-yard 8th. After opening with stout par 4s measuring 473, 464 and 456 yards (the latter a dogleg right daring a drive across a large corner bunker), the inward half offers a trio of holes whose centerpiece is a meandering creekbed: the 549-yard 13th, the 193-yard bunkerless 14th (upon which two front-left trees must also be dealt with) and the 436-yard uphill 15th, where the tee shot angles across the creekbed and the green's right side is closely flanked by it. Toss in one more creekbed-flanked hole at the 414-yard 16th as well as the 583-yard downhill 18th (where a left-side pond affects the second and third) and you have a strong, if mostly unspectacular, overall test. Notably, while every hole is housing-flanked (many on both sides), there is generally a wide buffering area of native terrain, allowing things seldom to feel overly claustrophobic.

8	Range (Grass)	Short Game	Putting Green	On-Site Rooms	Nearby Rooms	Altitude: 545'	Middle: 6,547 yds Front: 5,279 yds

Sequoyah Country Club – Oakland   ◆◆½

Unknown   www.sequoyahcc.com
4550 Heafey Rd, Oakland, CA 94605   (510) 632-2900
          6,149 yds   Par 70   Rating: 70.2 / 135   (1913)

The design history of Oakland's Sequoyah Country Club is a muddled one as the layout's original designer is unknown, with varying degrees of evidence existing (some quite flimsy) to suggest later involvement from men like Fowler, Egan, MacKenzie and Raynor. What is clear is that a set of long-unused Egan renovation plans were the base of a new millennium overhaul by Douglas Nickels, making today's layout a modern interpretation of a circa 1930 design. Typical of the region's older facilities, there is lots of hilly terrain present here, as well as a bit of quirk, such as the crossing fairways of the 328-yard uphill 15th and the 484-yard par-5 16th. But there is also plenty of interesting (if often short) golf, with the outward half including entries like the 374-yard 4th (where a wooded depression pushes into the right side of the fairway), the 137-yard downhill 5th, the 532-yard 6th (an uphill dogleg right routed along a steep hillside) and the 410-yard downhill 8th, whose second is played across a wide swale. The back nine includes dashes of muscle at the 453-yard sharply downhill 11th and the 235-yard 14th before eventually closing with a 450-yard uphill par 5 marked by an invasive centerline bunker. The club also possesses a bit of tournament history as the PGA Tour's Oakland Open was played here from 1938-1944, with Nelson, Demaret, Cooper and Ferrier among its champions.

3	Range (Both) -	Short Game +	Putting Green	On-Site Rooms	Nearby Rooms	Altitude: 567'	Middle: 5,837 yds Front: 4,852 yds

TPC Stonebrae – Hayward   ◆◆◆

David McLay Kidd   www.tpcstonebrae.com
202 Country Club Dr, Hayward, CA 94542   (510) 728-7878
          7,188 yds   Par 72   Rating: 74.8 / 138   (2007)

A patently ambitious undertaking, the TPC Stonebrae lies high in the hills above Oakland, affording the property some dazzling westward views of the Bay Area, from San Mateo northward to Mount Tamalpais. Carved into frequently rugged terrain by Scottish designer David McLay Kidd, it required some significant earthmoving simply to establish enough playable golfing ground, yet usually manages to appear reasonably natural nonetheless. A Korn Ferry Tour stop since 2009 (Kevin Chappell, Tony Finau and Si Woo Kim have all won here), the layout opens with a front nine which circumnavigates a large residential neighborhood, and which features several strong par 4s including the 461-yard downhill 2nd (bordered by a steep right-side fallaway) and the 466-yard 8th. But the really memorable golf is reserved for the start of the back nine, where the steeply downhill 437-yard 10th and the 240-yard, Redan-like 11th set the stage for the 625-yard dogleg left 12th, a plunging epic offering daring players a chance to get home in two. The 377-yard 14th requires an uphill, ravine-crossing drive and kicks off a muscular closing stretch that concludes with the downhill 465-yard 17th and the 598-yard 18th. Several imposing cart rides are required, but few American courses located in major markets succeed in blending this type of setting with interesting design. Note: Tough though it may be, Stephan Jaeger shot a 58 here during the Korn Ferry's 2016 Ellie Mae Classic, with his final total of 250 breaking the circuit's 72-hole scoring record by five shots.

7	Range (Grass)	Short Game	Putting Green	On-Site Rooms	Nearby Rooms	Altitude: 1,433'	Middle: 6,515 yds Front: 4,774 yds

Calippe Preserve Golf Course – Pleasanton   ♦♦½

Brian Costello   www.playcalippe.com
8500 Clubhouse Dr, Pleasanton, CA 94566   (925) 426-6666
                6,748 yds   Par 72   Rating: 73.0 / 136   (2005)

Built across Interstate 680 (as well as some shielding hills) from the Club at Castlewood, the Calippe Preserve Golf Course offers a well thought of public facility situated in scenic, mostly undeveloped country – though low-density housing does flank the property on three sides. The Brian Costello-designed layout offers enough challenge and playing interest for skilled golfers (hence a 73.0 rating on a 6,748-yard course) but it also suits the mid-range player by providing mostly wide fairways as well as larger greens – the latter also being a maintenance plus relative to a higher-volume of play. Despite the relatively modest total yardage, a number of longer holes are present, with the front nine featuring the 433-yard downhill opener, the 550-yard uphill (and soundly bunkered) 3rd and the 568-yard 9th, where a prominent centerline bunker can affect the second. The back counters with the 446-yard 10th (played downhill and across a large creekbed) as well as a pair of creekbed-bothered closers, the 447-yard 17th and the 573-yard 18th. For many, however, equally memorable may be a trio of shorter tests: the 348-yard 11th (played to an elevated, bunkerless green), the 322-yard downhill 12th and the 346-yard 14th, a dogleg left which gently ascends along a left-side creekbed.

5	Range (Mats)	Short Game	Putting Green	On-Site Rooms	Nearby Rooms	Altitude: 498'	Middle: 6,409 yds Front: 4,788 yds

Corica Park (South) – Alameda   ♦♦½

Rees Jones   www.coricapark.com
1 Clubhouse Memorial Dr, Alameda, CA 94502   (510) 747-7800
                6,874 yds   Par 70   Rating: 73.2 / 129   (2018)

Formerly known as the Chuck Corica Golf Complex, Corica Park lies on a peninsula in San Francisco Bay, immediately adjacent to Oakland International Airport, where it began life with a Billy Bell-designed 18 in 1927 before having Bell's son add a second 18 exactly 30 years later. This latter layout, the South course, underwent a multi-year renovation at the hands of Rees Jones, reopening in 2018 as a facility rather curiously styled after the heavily bunkered courses of the Australian sandbelt. Following a very compact routing, it fills the flat property's east side and initially features a trio of varied par 4s: the 394-yard centerline-bunkered 2nd, the 388-yard 3rd and the 469-yard 4th, whose narrow green angles rightward beyond a line of bunkers. The outward half also includes the 297-yard tightly bunkered 8th before heading off to a much longer back nine which immediately flexes its muscle at the 448-yard 10th (where a right-side pond threatens longer drives), the 248-yard 11th and the 474-yard 12th, a tough dogleg right marked by a centerline tree and eight right-side fairway bunkers. The 579-yard 17th (whose narrow green is guarded left by its cart path) and the 418-yard 18th later close a layout which may not quite transport one to Melbourne, but which is among the region's stronger public tracks.

6	Range (Mats)	Short Game	Putting Green	On-Site Rooms	Nearby Rooms	Altitude: 2'	Middle: 6,303 yds Front: 4,767 yds

Corica Park (North) – Alameda   N/A

William P. Bell   www.coricapark.com
1 Clubhouse Memorial Dr, Alameda, CA   94502   (510) 747-7800

Corica Park's North course was the popular municipal facility's first, having been laid out
by Billy Bell all the way back in 1927. Though much of Bell's routing remains in place, the
course had witnessed numerous alterations (including some late 1960s work by Desmond
Muirhead) prior to being closed in 2018 for another significant renovation. This redesign
is being performed by Greenway Golf (the company which handled construction of Rees
Jones' South course makeover) and was, inevitably, delayed by the COVID-19 pandemic.
The transition here will apparently be far less dramatic than that which overtook the
South course, with the layout scheduled to reopen before the end of 2021.

NA	Range (Mats)	Short Game	Putting Green	On-Site Rooms	Nearby Rooms	Altitude: 1'	Middle: N/A Front: N/A

Lake Chabot Golf Course – Oakland   ♦½

William Locke   www.lakechabotgolf.com
11450 Golf Links Rd,, Oakland, CA   94605   (510) 351-5812
                6,004 yds   Par 70   Rating: 69.3 / 119   (1921)

The golf spawning ground of 1964 British Open champion Tony Lema, the Lake Chabot
Golf Course occupies a somewhat secluded site in the San Leandro Hills, making it highly
pastoral in nature – and one of the more undulating golf courses to be found so close to a
major American city. All evidence points towards William Locke as the course's designer
(though the better-known William Watson may have had some input) and this credit still
holds relevance today because on terrain so hilly, not a tremendous amount has been
changeable over the course of a century. With the hills dictating so much of the layout's
character (there are only five bunkers present overall), one expects the par 3s to rate
among the strongest entries, and the 188-yard uphill 7th and the 182-yard downhill 9th
measure up accordingly. Also noteworthy are the demanding 420-yard 11th and the
potentially driveable 306-yard 16th – but the layout's calling card remains the 673-yard
par-6 18th, which drops more than 250 feet over a fairway steep enough to require
switchbacks for its cart path before making a late climb to a tiny, bunkerless green.

3	Range (Mats)	Short Game	Putting Green	On-Site Rooms	Nearby Rooms	Altitude: 448'	Middle: 5,676 yds Front: 5,194 yds

Las Positas Golf Course – Livermore

Robert Muir Graves   www.alpinebaygolf.com
917 Clubhouse Dr, Livermore, CA 94551   (925) 455-7820
                 6,707 yds   Par 72   Rating: 72.9 / 131   (1967)

Built on a gently sloping site between Interstate 580 and Livermore Municipal Airport, the Las Positas Golf Course was initially laid out by Robert Muir Graves in 1967, but Graves would return in 1990 to significantly expand his original layout while also adding an executive nine (page 81). Today's layout retains most of that 1990 configuration and is a moderately difficult, heavily bunkered facility with water meaningfully affecting play on seven holes. There are also several awkward moments present (e.g., the water hazards which mandate laid-up tee shots at the 391-yard 1st and the 338-yard 10th, and the early turning dogleg at the 431-yard 9th) but there is still enough engaging golf to lift the overall facility above the mundane. Outbound favorites include the 365-yard pond-menaced 3rd, the 401-yard 5th and the 170-yard 8th, whose shallow green sits beyond a long, narrow pond. Coming home, there is a bit of muscle in the two holes which parallel the freeway (the 586-yard 13th and the 432-yard 14th) before play closes with the 526-yard 18th, a reachable dogleg left par 5 which bends around a wide creekbed, the tree-lined nature of which makes aggressive seconds a testing proposition.

5	Range (Both)	Short Game	Putting Green	On-Site Rooms	Nearby Rooms	Altitude: 383'	Middle: 6,323 yds Front: 5,313 yds

Metropolitan Golf Links – Oakland

Fred Bliss & Johnny Miller   www.playmetro.com
10051 Doolittle Dr, Oakland, CA 94603   (510) 569-5555
                 6,959 yds   Par 72   Rating: 73.5 / 129   (2003)

Situated at the opposite end of the Oakland International Airport runways from Corica Park, the Metropolitan Golf Links were built in 2003 by Fred Bliss and Bay Area native Johnny Miller on the site of the former (and rather less-imposing) Lew Galbraith municipal layout. As the site lies close to an inlet off San Francisco Bay, it is naturally flat and open, leaving mounding, a moderate level of bunkering and, of course, wind as primary hazards on a track marketed as an "American links." For many, the front nine represents the less interesting half, with favorites including the 469-yard bunkerless 4th (which borders the airport entrance road), the 191-yard lake-crossing 5th and the 503-yard 6th, whose right side is flanked by a swath of wetlands. But the menu runs a bit deeper on the homeward nine, which initially features a pair of creek-bothered tests at the 569-yard double dogleg 10th and the 428-yard 14th, as well as the 437-yard bunkerless 11th. The homestretch is then capped by the 552-yard 17th (which dares an aggressive second across a greenside pond) and the 413-yard 18th, where ideal drives flirt with a large left-side bunker. Though this may not quite rank among the nation's municipal elite, it is strong enough to serve as the primary home course for the powerful University of California golf team.

6	Range (Both)	Short Game+	Putting Green	On-Site Rooms	Nearby Rooms	Altitude: 14'	Middle: 6,529 yds Front: 5,099 yds

Monarch Bay Golf Club (Lema) – San Leandro   ♦♦

William F. Bell   www.monarchbaygc.com
13800 Neptune Dr, San Leandro, CA 94577   (510) 895-2162
                7,015 yds   Par 71   Rating: 73.8 / 132   (1983)

Despite a prime location along the eastern shore of San Francisco Bay, the Monarch Bay Golf Club took a circuitous route into its present state, beginning life during the 1960s as a William F. Bell-designed executive course (part of which still remains – page 82) before being expanded into 18 regulation-sized holes in 1983. That layout was renovated by John Harbottle in 2001 and renamed in honor of Oakland native (and 1964 British Open champion) Tony Lema, with today's track boasting impressive cross-bay views of the San Francisco skyline while providing a mix of functional and more engaging golf. The course is crossed by a wide flood control channel, with five holes lying on the clubhouse side and the remaining 13 marching out to the south. The outward half plays to a par of 35 and includes brawny entries like the 443-yard 3rd, the 244-yard tightly bunkered 7th and the 437-yard 9th, though slightly more subtle in their challenge are a pair of holes defined by centerline bunkers, the 198-yard 4th and the 514-yard 5th. The back offers Mutt-and-Jeff par 4s at the robust 497-yard 13th and the 315-yard 14th before eventually closing big with the 598-yard 16th, the 213-yard 17th and the 407-yard channel-crossing 18th.

6	Range	Short	Putting	On-Site	Nearby	Altitude:	Middle: 6,567 yds
	(Mats)	Game	Green	Rooms	Rooms	7'	Front: 5,140 yds

Poppy Ridge Golf Course – Livermore   ♦♦½

Rees Jones   www.poppyridgegolf.com
4280 Greenville Rd, Livermore, CA 94550   (925) 447-6779
        Merlot/Chardonnay: 7,106 yds   Par 72   Rating: 74.8 / 135   (1996)
        Zinfandel: 3,535 yds   Par 36   Rating: 37.0 / 138   (1996)

Owned and operated by the Northern California Golf Association, the Poppy Ridge Golf Course is a 27-hole Rees Jones-designed facility built on open, rolling land two miles southeast of the famed Lawrence Livermore National Laboratory. Among the club's three loops, the highest-rated combination pairs the Merlot and Chardonnay nines, with the former beginning on the property's southwest side before being led by a trio strong par 4s in its mid-section (the 444-yard uphill 4th, the 454-yard downhill 6th and the 442-yard ascending 7th), then closing with the 524-yard 9th, a downhill par 5 whose second half bends leftward along a lake. The slightly shorter Chardonnay loop wends its way between its sister nines and, after the heavily bunkered 305-yard 2nd, eventually closes strongly with the 452-yard 6th, the 470-yard downhill 8th (whose green angles between bunkers and an intrusive left-side cart path) and the 526-yard pond-guarded 9th. The Zinfandel nine covers terrain north and east of the clubhouse, where it is led by a pair of lake-guarded par 3s, the downhill 198-yard 2nd and the 171-yard 7th. Among its longer tests, favorites include the downhill 425-yard 6th and the 452-yard 9th, where drives flirting with left-side sand leave the ideal second to a pond-flanked green. Though there is little that qualifies as highly memorable here, Poppy Ridge nonetheless represents strong public golf – and Jones' fans in particular won't feel let down by the challenge.

7	Range	Short	Putting	On-Site	Nearby	Altitude:	Middle: 6,686 yds
	(Grass)	Game	Green	Rooms	Rooms	827'	Front: 5,240 yds

Redwood Canyon Golf Course – Castro Valley   ◆½

Bob Baldock   www.redwoodcanyongolf.com
17007 Redwood Rd, Castro Valley, CA 94546   (510) 537-8001
                5,801 yds   Par 71   Rating: 68.2 / 118   (1966)

Located at the eastern tip of the Lake Chabot reservoir, the Redwood Canyon Golf Course is a short 1966 Robert Baldock design which occupies an admirably secluded mountain site unspoiled by adjacent development. The layout forms a large V around a central ridge, with each nine following an out-and-back routing through a narrow valley crossed by the waters of San Leandro Creek. The creek is a far more central presence on the outward half, particularly at the 411-yard 1st (where it flanks the right side), the 366-yard dogleg right 2nd (bothering aggressive drives), the 161-yard 7th (paralleling the green's right edge) and the incongruously large 564-yard 9th, which bends gently rightward along its banks. Though a visual presence on the back, the creek seldom meaningfully affects play, leaving favorites here to include a pair of tree-squeezed par 4s (the 264-yard 11th and the 296-yard 14th) as well as the 346-yard 17th, whose tiny putting surface has trees overhanging its right side and the creek passing several paces to its left.

3	Range	Short	Putting	On-Site	Nearby	Altitude:	Middle: 5,429 yds
	(Grass) -	Game +	Green	Rooms	Rooms	235'	Front: 5,188 yds

The Course at Wente Vineyards – Livermore   ◆◆◆

Greg Norman   www.wentevineyards.com
5050 Arroyo Rd, Livermore, CA 94550   (925) 456-2475
                7,181 yds   Par 72   Rating: 74.7 / 144   (1998)

A rather unique amenity to this eponymous Livermore Valley winemaker's facility, the Course at Wente Vineyards was among the first of Greg Norman's American designs and is an engaging, testing track routed among the grapes and, more pressingly, over some heavily undulating terrain. Play opens on an elevated ridgetop behind the winery, where the 474-yard par-4 1st is a sharply downhill, bunkerless opener, and it is followed by two small but heavily bunkered tests, the 307-yard 2nd and the 138-yard 3rd. The action begins to pick up as the routing descends northward at the sharply downhill 228-yard 7th and the 602-yard creek-crossed 8th before peaking following a climb to another mesa via a switchback-laden cart path named for San Francisco's famed Lombard Street. The 304-yard 10th (a tauntingly driveable test which confers the death penalty upon slices) and the 564-yard 12th both angle daringly along the mesa's edge before the 420-yard dogleg left 13th and the 173-yard 14th descend back to the valley. This sets up a demanding finish composed of a trio of muscular par 4s whose fairways are lined by endless rows of grapes: the 454-yard creek-crossed 16th, the 453-yard 17th (whose fairway is flanked closely on its right by this same hazard) and the 472-yard 18th, where the creek first divides the fairway, then widens into a greenside pond. Toss in some appealing wine country scenery and this certainly rates among the region's very best public facilities.

7	Range	Short	Putting	On-Site	Nearby	Altitude:	Middle: 6,840 yds
	(Grass)	Game	Green	Rooms	Rooms	528'	Front: 4,865 yds

Corica Park (Mif Albright Par 3) – Alameda   ♦

Unknown   www.coricapark.com
1 Clubhouse Memorial Dr, Alameda, CA 94502   (510) 747-7800
             1,245 yds   Par 27   Rating: 26.4 / 88   (2014)

A nice amenity to go along with two adjacent regulation-sized 18-hole courses, Corica
Park's Mif Albright Par 3 layout began life in the early 1980s, reaching its present form via
a 2014 renovation. With holes averaging 138 yards, this is well above the pitch-and-putt
level, but with only six bunkers present (affecting three holes), it remains relatively basic
of its type. Occasionally relevant are the grassy man-made mounds which separate a
number of fairways but overall, this is mostly functional, novice-oriented stuff.

1	Range (Mats)	Short Game	Putting Green	On-Site Rooms	Nearby Rooms	Altitude: 4'	Middle: N/A Front: 980 yds

Dublin Ranch Golf Course – Dublin   ♦♦

Robert Trent Jones II   www.dublinranchgolf.com
5900 Signal Hill Dr, Dublin, CA 94568   (925) 556-7040
             5,079 yds   Par 63   Rating: 64.6 / 108   (2004)

Routed amidst a large real estate development in the far northern reaches of the county,
the Dublin Ranch Golf Course qualifies as a short layout solely because it includes 11 par
3s; designed by Robert Trent Jones II, it is filled with regulation-sized holes that are quite
testing in nature – but with an overall par of 63. Though housing-flanked at every turn, it
also offers numerous panoramic views as it marches over hilly terrain, with the majority
of its strongest offerings lying among the par 3s. Shorter entries like the 155-yard 6th
(played uphill to a very shallow green) and the 158-yard downhill 7th are solid enough,
but stronger still are more muscular entries like the 200-yard 8th, the 214-yard downhill
11th, the 193-yard 14th and the 224-yard 15th, which drops 50 feet from tee to green.

2	Range (Grass)	Short Game	Putting Green	On-Site Rooms	Nearby Rooms	Altitude: 634'	Middle: 4,505 yds Front: 3,455 yds

Fremont Park Golf Club – Fremont   ♦½

Unknown   www.fremontparkgc.com
39751 Stevenson Pl, Fremont, CA 94539   (510) 320-5333
             1,989 yds   Par 32   Rating: 30.9 / 105   (2000)

Wedged into narrow acreage adjacent to some tracks of the Southern Pacific Railway, the
Fremont Park Golf Club opened in 2000 and offers considerably more challenge than one
might guess given its logistical limitations and circumstances. This is because its site is
dotted with wetlands and man-made lakes, allowing water to have a significant effect on
five holes. Thus while several entries (including a pair of sub-100-yard par 3s) are fairly
basic, holes like the 253-yard 2nd (whose green angles rightward into a pond), the 152-
yard all-carry 3rd, the 257-yard wetlands-lined 4th and the 288-yard dogleg right 5th (which
dares a tee shot across the same wetlands) rise well above standard short course fare.

2	Range (Mats)	Short Game	Putting Green	On-Site Rooms	Nearby Rooms	Altitude: 63'	Middle: N/A Front: 1,355 yds

Lake Chabot Golf Course (Short) – Oakland   ♦

Robert Dean Putman   www.lakechabotgolf.com
11450 Golf Links Rd,, Oakland, CA 94605   (510) 351-5812
                1,023 yds   Par 27   Rating: - / -   (c1965)

Occupying lower ground than much of the adjacent regulation-sized 18 (page 76), the Lake Chabot Golf Course's par-3 nine is routed over mostly wooded terrain to the south, and thus affords the facility's best views of the eponymous reservoir. Holes range in length from 66-162 yards and are hazard-free, making this an attractive option ambience-wise, but one suited to beginners or the less-skilled in strictly golfing terms.

1	Range	Short	Putting	On-Site	Nearby	Altitude:	Middle: N/A
	(Mats)	Game	Green	Rooms	Rooms	456'	Front: N/A

Las Positas Golf Course (Executive) – Livermore   ♦½

Robert Muir Graves   www.alpinebaygolf.com
917 Clubhouse Dr, Livermore, CA 94551   (925) 455-7820
                1,133 yds   Par 27   Rating: 27.5 / 95   (1990)

Built by Robert Muir Graves in conjunction with an expansion of the club's adjacent 18-hole regulation facility (page 77), the Las Positas Golf Course's Executive layout is wedged between the main course and Livermore Municipal Airport, where it offers an above-the-median facility of its type. Holes range in length from 72-197 yards, and with 29 bunkers present, there is a fair degree of playing interest to be found. Among the more engaging tests are the 92-yard 5th (played to a heart-shaped, tightly bunkered green), the 154-yard pondside 8th and the 197-yard 9th, a testing par 3 played to a very narrow target.

1	Range	Short	Putting	On-Site	Nearby	Altitude:	Middle: 991 yds
	(Both)	Game	Green	Rooms	Rooms	374'	Front: 882 yds

Mission Hills of Hayward Golf Course – Hayward   ♦½

David Rainville   www.haywardrec.com
275 Industrial Pkwy, Hayward, CA 94544   (510) 888-0200
                1,720 yds   Par 30   Rating: 29.3 / 93   (1999)

A nine-hole executive facility routed around a large residential neighborhood, the Mission Hills of Hayward Golf Course offers above-the-median golf of its type, its mix of six par 3s and three par 4s including 25 bunkers and two man-made ponds. The ponds affect two of the most engaging holes, the 320-yard 6th (along the fairway's left side) and the 271-yard 8th, where any sliced tee shot will splash down. Putting surfaces tend to be on the larger side, allowing for a wide range of pin positions, and an added variety of challenge.

1	Range	Short	Putting	On-Site	Nearby	Altitude:	Middle: N/A
	(Mats)	Game	Green	Rooms	Rooms	18'	Front: 1,343 yds

Monarch Bay Golf Club (Marina) – San Leandro   ♦½

William F. Bell   www.monarchbaygc.com
13800 Neptune Dr, San Leandro, CA   94577   (510) 895-2162
                    1,734 yds   Par 30   Rating: 29.4 / 89   (1963)

Today's Marina course at the Monarch Bay Golf Club began life in something resembling its present nine-hole form, with the second executive nine that was added across Fairway Drive to the south during the 1970s later being absorbed into a new regulation-sized 18 (page 78) in 1983. This, the original nine, has witnessed minor modifications over the years but retains its original routing, and offers a pleasant short-course experience – but also fewer direct bayside views than its sister 18. Though water realistically affects three holes, most engaging are the 249-yard par-4 3rd (where a centerline bunker bothers aggressive drives) and the 111-yard 9th, where another center hazard fronts the green.

1	Range (Mats)	Short Game	Putting Green	On-Site Rooms	Nearby Rooms	Altitude: 6'	Middle: N/A Front: 1,484 yds

Pleasanton Golf Center – Pleasanton   ♦

Ron Curtola   www.pleasantongolfcenter.com
4501 Pleasanton Ave, Pleasanton, CA   94566   (925) 462-4653
                    1,681 yds   Par 30   Rating: 28.9 / 87   (1974)

A nine-hole executive course located inside of a horse racing track within the Alameda County Fairgrounds, the Pleasanton Golf Center has been around since the mid-1970s and provides a somewhat unique golfing ambience along with its strictly recreational level of challenge. Play opens with a sharp 269-yard dogleg left which turns little beyond its halfway mark, a slightly awkward opener which sets something of a tone. However, it is subsequently bettered by the 174-yard tightly bunkered 2nd and the 298-yard 7th, a gentle dogleg right which bends around the layout's lone water hazard.

1	Range (Both) -	Short Game	Putting Green	On-Site Rooms	Nearby Rooms	Altitude: 339'	Middle: N/A Front: 1,586 yds

SANTA CLARA COUNTY

Almaden Golf & Country Club – San Jose   ♦♦½

Jack Fleming   www.almadengcc.org
6663 Hampton Dr, San Jose, CA 95120   (408) 268-3959
            6,900 yds   Par 72   Rating: 73.7 / 131   (1956)

Set against the foothills of the Santa Cruz Mountains, the Almaden Golf & Country Club was designed by Jack Fleming in 1956 and soon found a place in the national spotlight, hosting the PGA Tour's mostly official Almaden Open from 1960-1965, with winners including Ken Venturi, Jim Ferrier and Billy Casper. The club would later serve as an LPGA Tour stop from 1983-1989 and today stands as a good-sized, moderately altered layout routed through extensive residential development. Among the stronger entries are the layout's quartet of par 5s, with the 521-yard 1st and the 533-yard 18th flanking either side of a lake constructed in 2008, the 506-yard 8th playing to a green tucked beyond sand and a front-right tree, and the 539-yard 10th doglegging right around a large modern bunker en route to another tree- and sand-guarded putting surface. Beyond its three-shotters, the front nine is anchored by a pair of back-to-back longer par 4s (the 424-yard 4th and the 435-yard 5th) and well as another hole enlivened by a water hazard added long after Fleming's day, the 201-yard pond-guarded 8th. The back follows suit with the 423-yard bunkerless 12th and the 442-yard 16th, but even allowing for this relatively high degree of challenge, tournament history definitely carries some collectability weight here.

6	Range (Grass)	Short Game	Putting Green	On-Site Rooms	Nearby Rooms	Altitude: 301'	Middle: 6,530 yds Front: 5,536 yds

The Golf Club at Boulder Ridge – San Jose   ♦♦♦

Bradford Benz   www.bayclubs.com/boulderridge
1000 Old Quarry Rd, San Jose, CA 95120   (408) 323-9900
            6,923 yds   Par 72   Rating: 73.2 / 138   (2001)

Located surprisingly close to downtown for so modern a facility, San Jose's Golf Club at Boulder Ridge managed this geographic coup by squeezing itself atop a V-shaped, 450-foot-high hilltop wrapped around an abandoned quarry from which, it is reported, much of the rock utilized in the building of Stanford University was drawn. Architect Brad Benz's distinctly modern layout places each nine upon one leg of the V, with the 10th and 11th holes (the latter an attractive downhill 232-yard par 3) actually dipping into the quarry itself. The outward half (which, unfortunately, is crossed by power lines) offers a pair of distinctive entries routed among huge rocks at the 205-yard 2nd and the narrow 397-yard 8th, as well as two shorter par 4s marked by imposing left-side fallaways, the 381-yard 5th and the 400-yard 6th. Following the strikingly demanding 11th, the inward half largely continues this death-on-the-left motif, particularly over a trio of holes seemingly perched at the end of the earth: the 372-yard uphill 13th, the spectacular 162-yard 14th (played across a steep hillside to a green angled above three very deep bunkers) and the 401-yard ascending 15th. Splendid views of Silicon Valley and the Santa Cruz Mountains abound, making for something of a unique golfing experience – and one which, slicers will happily note, always finds the precipice falling on the left.

6	Range (Both)	Short Game	Putting Green	On-Site Rooms	Nearby Rooms	Altitude: 468'	Middle: 6,530 yds Front: 5,005 yds

The Institute – Morgan Hill

Damian Pascuzzo & Neal Meagher
14830 Foothill Ave, Morgan Hill, CA 95037   (408) 782-7101
          7,952 yds   Par 72   Rating: - / -   (2002)

Among the most secretive golf courses in the United States, The Institute was the creation of electronics store magnate John Fry, who intended the property to also be the home of The American Institute of Mathematics, a nonprofit organization which he co-founded. Fry hired Robert Muir Graves' firm (primarily in the form of Damian Pascuzzo and Neal Meagher) to convert a nondescript layout known as the Flying Lady Golf Course, with the result being a 7,952-yard behemoth which includes a number of holes bearing the influence of more famous tests, such as the 12th, 13th and 15th at Augusta National, among others. In a sense, the "club" doesn't even exist; in order to get around initial environmental and permitting issues, the facility was reportedly designated as private property (i.e., Fry's back yard) as opposed to any sort of organized golfing entity, with the City of Morgan Hill retroactively granting temporary usage in 2004, with a 36 player per day limit. By most accounts, that number has never been reached, and no published scorecard numbers currently exist. The layout is widely considered among the toughest in California and was several times rumored to be in line to host the PGA Tour's Frys.com Open prior to the event switching sponsorship. Today it sits quietly, representing a great "get" collectability-wise based mostly on the fact that nobody ever gets to play it.

10	Range (Grass)	Short Game	Putting Green	On-Site Rooms	Nearby Rooms	Altitude: 424'	Middle: N/A Front: N/A

La Rinconada Country Club – Los Gatos

Unknown   www.larinconadacc.com
14595 Clearview Dr, Los Gatos, CA 95032   (408) 395-4181
          6,105 yds   Par 70   Rating: 70.4 / 134   (1929)

Dating to the onset of the Depression, the La Rinconada Country Club lies just south of Route 85 on a residence-surrounded site at the base of the Santa Cruz Mountains, where its routing has remained essentially unchanged since the early days. Nearly everything else has been altered, however, as a succession of architects have added sand and (a little) water over the decades, with tree growth also meaningfully affecting several holes. On so small a layout, the presence of numerous short par 4s is inevitable, though only two are particularly memorable, with the 275-yard 3rd ascending steadily through a very narrow corridor among trees and the much-altered 303-yard 14th playing to a green guarded by a front-left pond added during the 1960s. Among the more demanding entries are a pair of long, uphill par 4s that anchor the front nine, the 431-yard 4th (whose smallish green angles behind front-right sand) and the 421-yard 9th, which ascends roughly 50 feet from tee to putting surface. With considerable acreage consumed by a strong practice facility, this is a layout consigned to permanent undersized status.

3	Range (Grass) +	Short Game	Putting Green	On-Site Rooms	Nearby Rooms	Altitude: 357'	Middle: 5,786 yds Front: 5,019 yds

Los Altos Golf & Country Club – Los Altos   ♦♦

Tom Nicoll   www.lagcc.com
1560 Country Club Dr, Los Altos, CA 94024   (650) 947-3100
          6,505 yds   Par 71   Rating: 72.3 / 136   (1923)

One of the area's earlier golfing entities, the Los Altos Country Club was designed in 1923 by Scottish transplant Tom Nicoll, but owing to surrounding residential development and, eventually, the construction of Interstate 280, very little of that original layout remains today. The present routing has been in place since the early 1950s but numerous hands have affected changes since, with today's short but often-engaging layout moving across rolling terrain and among affluent neighborhoods. With the exception of the downhill/ sidehill 237-yard 3rd and the 545-yard 17th (where a left-side pond threatens the second), the compact nature of the property mandates that play remain mostly on the shorter side. Thus front nine favorites include the 330-yard pond-guarded 4th (the first of three holes to be routed through a residence-lined canyon near the freeway), the 418-yard 8th (a gentle but early turning dogleg right) and the 414-yard uphill 9th. The back then features a trio of shortish two-shotters of its own: the 390-yard downhill 10th (whose green angles along a front-left pond), the 360-yard uphill 11th and especially the 411-yard 14th, a sharp dogleg left which bends around an invasive lake.

5	Range (Both) -	Short Game	Putting Green	On-Site Rooms	Nearby Rooms	Altitude: 283'	Middle: 6,139 yds Front: 5,372 yds

Palo Alto Hills Golf & Country Club – Palo Alto   N/A

Clark Glasson   www.pahgcc.com
3000 Alexis Dr, Palo Alto, CA 94304   (650) 948-1800
          6,278 yds   Par 72   Rating: 71.6 / 129   (1958)

Built in elevated country south of town, on a site which slopes significantly downward from south to north, the Palo Alto Hills Golf & Country Club dates to the late 1950s, when the regionally semi-prominent Clark Glasson designed it with reported input from Ken Venturi. Their creation was a short, hilly track which experienced a number of nips and tucks over the decades (including the addition of multiple water hazards and some often-invasive cart paths) before finally undergoing a major modernization by architect Brian Costello that is partially completed at the time of this writing. Costello's plan includes lengthening the layout to beyond 6,600 yards, considerable tree removal, the removal of the 120-yard 2nd hole (to be replaced with a new par-3 7th), lengthening all four opening and closing holes and a bit of bunker renovation. Early indications suggest a significant improvement of the overall layout, though some of its original quirky features (such as the boomerang green at the short par-4 4th) are being retained. Note: The below specs are taken from the layout's pre-renovation configuration.

4	Range (Both)	Short Game	Putting Green	On-Site Rooms	Nearby Rooms	Altitude: 624'	Middle: 6,005 yds Front: 4,766 yds

San Jose Country Club – San Jose   ♦♦½

Tom Nicoll   www.sanjosecountryclub.org
15571 Alum Rock Ave, San Jose, CA 95127   (408) 258-3636
            6,225 yds   Par 70   Rating: 71.2 / 132   (1912)

Another very early entry on the area golfing scene, the San Jose Country Club was laid out by Tom Nicoll in 1912, though with William Watson and A.W. Tillinghast both known to have made early changes, it is safe to assume that this design credit is a bit attenuated today. The course has retained nearly all of its pre-World War II routing, however, so while multiple architects have altered bunkering over the years, this remains a short, hilly, old-style test with moments of flavor. The opening three holes work their way up a large ridge (with the 174-yard 3rd offering a panoramic westward view) before the 444-yard 4th tumbles its way downward nearly 80 feet to a small, tightly bunkered green. The remainder of the non-returning front nine features a pair of downhill tests (the 159-yard bunker-fronted 7th and the 436-yard descending 8th) before the back offers the 477-yard 11th (a downhill par 5 flanked by a greenside pond) and the 439-yard uphill 12th, the number one stroke hole. Most memorable, however, are a pair of barranca-crossed closers, the 516-yard 17th (where the hazard appears 335 yards off the tee) and the 370-yard 18th, where portions of it are crossed on both shots. Once upon a time, Wild Bill Mehlhorn won the 1926 Santa Clara Valley Open here, there is a bit of history as well.

4	Range (Both)	Short Game	Putting Green	On-Site Rooms	Nearby Rooms	Altitude: 398'	Middle: 5,933 yds Front: 5,492 yds

Saratoga Country Club – Saratoga   ♦½

Robert Muir Graves   www.saratogacc.com
21990 Prospect Rd, Saratoga, CA 95070   (408) 253-0340
            2,441 yds   Par 34   Rating: 33.4 / 123   (1960)

Built in a semi-secluded valley in the Santa Cruz Mountain foothills, the Saratoga Country Club is a short nine-hole layout which made its debut in 1960 before being moderately redesigned by Robert Muir Graves in 1966. Rebunkered a bit along the way, the loop has little room to expand and thus remains palpably short, with no par 5s present and its longest par 4 being the 336-yard 8th. There are moments of interest among these short two-shotters, however, with the 289-yard 2nd climbing to a tightly bunkered green, the 3rd and 4th (which both measure 271 yards) doing an out-and-back into higher terrain to the west, and the 300-yard 7th ascending to a narrow, elevated putting surface built into a hillside. The aforementioned 8th is a dogleg left which also plays to a (more sharply) elevated target but as its fairway turns at about 150 yards, it is rather awkward as well.

2	Range (Both)	Short Game	Putting Green	On-Site Rooms	Nearby Rooms	Altitude: 618'	Middle: N/A Front: N/A

Silver Creek Valley Country Club – San Jose   ♦♦♦½

Ted Robinson   www.scvcc.com
5460 Country Club Pkwy, San Jose, CA   95138   (408) 239-5888
        7,000 yds   Par 72   Rating: 74.0 / 139   (1992)

Built in elevated country southeast of town, the Silver Creek Valley Country Club features what is actually a 2002 Mike Strantz redesign of a Ted Robinson-designed layout – but those expecting the sort of larger-than-life stylings that soon made Strantz famous may come away slightly disappointed. In addition to being surrounded by housing, the site is a hilly one, a point quickly reflected in a pair of plunging par-4 openers (the 452-yard 1st and the 446-yard 10th) as well as at especially undulating entries like the 507-yard uphill 8th, the downhill 446-yard 9th (which descends to a lakeside green), the climbing 500-yard 11th and the 237-yard 12th, which runs downhill to a tightly bunkered putting surface. Though seldom is a flat hole encountered, less tumultuous favorites include the 195-yard 4th (played across a massive Strantz-made waste bunker), the 511-yard creek-crossed 6th, and the 184-yard tightly bunkered 15th, whose right side is perched above a steep hillside. Also notable are a pair of pond-guarded closers, the 414-yard 17th and the 404-yard 18th – the latter bearing the quirky option of also being played as a 174-yard water-crossing par 3. In most eyes, Strantz improved things significantly; indeed, it might strike just the right balance for those who find his subsequent high-octane style slightly over the top.

6	Range (Both)	Short Game	Putting Green	On-Site Rooms	Nearby Rooms	Altitude: 605'	Middle: 6,540 yds Front: 5,197 yds

Stanford University Golf Course – Stanford   ♦♦♦♦½

William P. Bell & George Thomas   www.stanfordgolfcourse.com
91 Links Rd, Stanford, CA 94305   (650) 323-0944
        6,742 yds   Par 70   Rating: 73.7 / 138   (1930)

Seemingly forever in danger of obliteration by one campus project or another, the Stanford University Golf Course is built into the foothills along the southwest side of "The Farm" and remains alive and kicking – for now. Having helped nurture the games of Tiger Woods, Tom Watson, Mickey Wright and Michelle Wie, it remains a fun and fairly challenging test, and one which bears a unique design pedigree; indeed, unlike several Billy Bell projects upon which George Thomas is known to have consulted, Stanford was actually a case of Bell building the golf course, with his work being significantly affected by Thomas who, due to illness, was in Los Angeles during its construction. Save for recent changes which created back-to-back par 3s at the 3rd and 4th, their work still stands fairly intact, and begins with a front nine powered by two very strong par 4s, the 478-yard 2nd and the 426-yard 6th, a tree-narrowed, slightly uphill test which serves as the number one stroke hole. The back nine offers several more imposing two-shotters, and if the 474-yard 12th (where centerline trees can impede the second) is the class of the crowd, the 430-yard 10th, the 437-yard 13th and the 454-yard 18th (a downhill, panoramic closer) all measure up quite nicely. Also notable are a pair of shortish par 3s which cross the waters of San Francisquito Creek, the attractive 186-yard 8th and the 188-yard 14th, which plays over both the creek and a steep fronting slope. Despite continued threats to its existence, among Golden Age American collegiate layouts, only The Course at Yale can truly be rated its better – and *much* bigger golfing footsteps have trod these fairways!

6	Range (Both)	Short Game +	Putting Green	On-Site Rooms	Nearby Rooms	Altitude: 218'	Middle: 6,213 yds Front: 5,363 yds

Villages Golf & Country Club – San Jose

Robert Muir Graves

5000 Cribari Ln, San Jose, CA 95135

www.thevillagesgcc.com

(408) 223-4643

6,630 yds   Par 71   Rating: 72.2 / 125   (1968)

Located less than a mile northeast of the Silver Creek Valley Country Club, the Villages Golf & Country Club is the recreational anchor of a 55-and-over retirement community and features a shortish Robert Muir Graves-designed layout that began with nine holes in 1968 before expanding to 18 soon thereafter. The site climbs significantly as play moves eastward away from the clubhouse and while bits and pieces of Graves' bunkering have faded with time, his routing remains intact, resulting in a layout whose housing is fairly well-removed from lines of play, and whose descending westward holes offer some fine views of the city. The design is rather more functional than engaging, though exceptions appear at the two finishing holes, the 518-yard 9th (which descends past a right-side pond to a green closely fronted by a creek) and the 421-yard 18th, a similarly downhill test whose putting surface is fronted by the same meandering water hazard. Most of the par 4s are of a short and basic variety but longer entries pop up at the 444-yard 3rd and the 430-yard 8th (a downhill dogleg right), while the 474-yard 16th is a reachable par 5 with water down its right side. A nine-hole par-3 course adjoins (page 101).

5	Range (Mats)	Short Game	Putting Green	On-Site Rooms	Nearby Rooms	Altitude: 517'	Middle: 6,306 yds Front: 4,031 yds

CordeValle – San Martin

♦♦♦½

Robert Trent Jones II

www.cordevallegolf.com

1 CordeValle Club Dr, San Martin, CA 95046

(408) 695-4590

7,360 yds   Par 72   Rating: 76.3 / 146   (1999)

Set in a secluded valley within the scenic Santa Cruz Mountains, 30 minutes southeast of San Jose, the CordeValle resort offers a strategically interesting Robert Trent Jones II-designed layout which holds impressive tournament bonafides, having hosted the PGA Tour from 2010-2013, as well as Brittany Lang's playoff victory at the U.S. Women's Open in 2016. Well-stocked with appealing holes, the front nine in particular shows few weak links and is championed by a trio of creek-affected tests: the 605-yard 3rd (where the hazard first crosses the fairway, then splits the lay-up zone), the 540-yard 6th (which ascends gently over another divided lay-up area) and the 425-yard 9th, where the driving zone is split, with the easier left side option leaving a tree-bothered approach. The inward half poses fewer strategic questions but provides a long run of sound, attractively bunkered holes. Initially these include the 434-yard uphill 11th (where three diagonal bunkers affect the drive) and the 230-yard 12th, which descends over three more angled hazards. The 413-yard uphill 13th favors drives that carry a right-side swale and sets up a varied and interesting trio of closers: the tightly bunkered 166-yard 16th, the 478-yard par-4 17th (which doglegs right past some mature trees) and the 555-yard 18th, a downhill, par 5 whose green is tucked behind a left-side lake. Though sometimes rather heavily shaped, CordeValle weighs in as a fine modern test and one of the region's top public-access stops. **(GD: #27 State, #46 Public GW: #192 Modern, #53 Resort)**

9	Range (Both) +	Short Game	Putting Green	On-Site Rooms	Nearby Rooms	Altitude: 326'	Middle: 6,810 yds Front: 5,385 yds

Baylands Golf Links – Palo Alto   ◆◆◆

Forrest Richardson
1875 Embarcadero Rd, Palo Alto, CA   94303
6,680 yds   Par 72   Rating: 72.2 / 125   (2018)

www.baylandsgolflinks.com
(650) 856-0881

The Baylands Golf Links began life in 1956 as the William F. Bell-designed Palo Alto Municipal Golf Course, a name it retained for more than 50 years before the layout was completely rebuilt by Forrest Richardson in 2018. The property sits adjacent to Palo Alto Airport and close to the shoreline of San Francisco Bay, and while it is hardly a links per se, the open, windblown terrain, (man-made) rumpled fairways and frequent range of shotmaking options at least add up to a fair approximation. While fairways are generally wide (and on several occasions interconnected), most offer more advantageous lines of play, and it is thus no surprise that two of the best-received holes are short, tactical par 4s, the 335-yard 7th (driveable, but across a swath of rugged native terrain) and the 377-yard 16th, where tee shots carried aggressively across right-side sand open the ideal angle of approach. Also popular is a collection of five par 3s, a varied bunch led by the 233-yard 8th (played downwind to a deep, tiered putting surface fronted by sand), the 153-yard 12th (whose green is guarded by left-side native terrain and a deep centerline bunker) and the 231-yard punchbowl-like 17th. Also notable among the multi-shot holes are the 392-yard 14th (which plays along a left-side creek and includes alternate greens) and the 511-yard 18th, a readily reachable par 5 whose lay-up zone is dotted by five rather invasive trees. Without a doubt, one of the Bay Area's most distinctive public layouts.

5	Range (Mats)	Short Game	Putting Green	On-Site Rooms	Nearby Rooms	Altitude: 5'	Middle: 6,110 yds Front: 4,821 yds

Bay View Golf Club – Milpitas   ◆½

Unknown
1500 Country Club Dr, Milpitas, CA 95035
6,331 yds   Par 72   Rating: 71.8 / 136   (1978)

www.playbayview.com
(408) 262-8813

Known originally as the Tularecitos Golf Club, then later as Summitpointe, today's Bay View Golf Club resides in some decidedly undulating country just east of Interstate 680, where it was built around (and very much upon) a large, residence-covered ridgetop. As a result, it rates among the hilliest courses in the region, particularly on a front nine whose lack of architectural pedigree is evident in a number of fairways which include steep sidehill slopes in addition to their sharp climbs or descents; indeed, popular holes are few and far between on the outward half. The back nine then wanders up a narrow canyon where wind is an issue but the terrain is at least somewhat better-suited to golf, and the loop begins with two of the layout's more engaging tests, the 358-yard 10th (which bends rightward around a lake and dares an aggressive line) and the 329-yard pond-fronted 11th. Also noteworthy are pair of back-to-back outlying par 5s (the 488-yard uphill 14th and the 498-yard downhill 15th) as well as the 199-yard 16th, an engaging one-shotter which plunges from a hillside tee to a pond-fronted green.

4	Range (Both)	Short Game	Putting Green	On-Site Rooms	Nearby Rooms	Altitude: 437'	Middle: 6,063 yds Front: 3,767 yds

Cinnabar Hills Golf Club – San Jose   ♦♦♦

John Harbottle III   www.cinnabarhills.com
23600 McKean Rd, San Jose, CA 95141   (408) 323-7814
    Lake/Mountain: 6,854 yds   Par 72   Rating: 73.7 / 142   (1998)
    Canyon: 3,238 yds   Par 36   Rating: 36.0 / 140   (1998)

Set in the hills overlooking Silicon Valley, 15 miles southeast of downtown San Jose, the Cinnabar Hills Golf Club is a 27-hole John Harbottle-designed facility built over typically rolling, oak-dotted Bay Area terrain. Its highest-rated 18 pairs the Lake and Mountain nines, with the former opening with two of the club's best holes, the 523-yard uphill 1st (which bends leftward around a wide ravine) and the 175-yard Redan-like 2nd. The Lake also closes strongly, first with the 567-yard downhill 7th (whose green extends leftward into a lake, then with the 172-yard 8th (played across rough native country) and the uphill 439-yard 9th. The Mountain opens with a pair of shorter holes (the 496-yard par-5 1st and the uphill 157-yard 2nd) before stretching out at the 437-yard 3rd and the 409-yard 4th, the latter a dogleg right requiring longer drives to carry a low-lying out-of-bounds area. For many, however, the Mountain's most engaging hole is the 196-yard 6th, an attractively bunkered uphill par 3. Though nearly 200 yards shorter than its siblings, the Canyon course more than holds its own in terms of playing interest, with favorites including the downhill, pond-fronted 400-yard 2nd, the 307-yard barranca-fronted 3rd, the 222-yard ridgetop 8th and the 555-yard 9th, a plunging, heavily bunkered dogleg left. With three strong 18-hole combinations, this is one of the region's top public facilities – with the added bonus of having the Brandenburg Historical Golf Museum on site as well.

6	Range (Both)	Short Game	Putting Green	On-Site Rooms	Nearby Rooms	Altitude: 573'	Middle: 6,349 yds Front: 5,030 yds

Coyote Creek Golf Club (Tournament) – Morgan Creek   ♦♦♦

Jack Nicklaus   www.coyotecreekgolf.com
1 Coyote Creek Golf Dr, Morgan Hill, CA 95037   (408) 463-1400
    7,027 yds   Par 72   Rating: 74.8 / 144   (1999)

Another multi-course Silicon Valley facility, the Coyote Creek Golf Club straddles the South Valley Freeway and features a pair of strong Jack Nicklaus-designed courses dating to 1999 and 2001. The Tournament course is the older and tougher of the pair, and it enjoyed a brief run in the limelight upon hosting the PGA Tour Champions in 2001 and 2002, with Hale Irwin claiming the maiden edition. Though opening south of the freeway, the great majority of the layout's front nine lies on more elevated, rugged (and power line-crossed) acreage to the north, where the action is highlighted by the four holes occupying the highest ground: the 512-yard downhill 4th (whose green is fronted by small creekbed), the 163-yard 5th (ditto), the 437-yard 6th (where trees and a central bunker complicate the ascending approach) and the 167-yard downhill 7th. After the routing returns across the freeway at the 9th, the inward loop sits on the flatter land around the clubhouse where it initially features the 320-yard 11th, a driveable but heavily bunkered test which moves gently uphill. Longer par 4s like the 425-yard 15th and the 432-yard 16th then begin a homeward run which is dominated by a pair of watery closers that are an aesthetic mismatch for their 16 brethren, the 533-yard 17th (played to a near-island green) and the 431-yard 18th, a sweeping dogleg right around a lake.

7	Range (Grass)	Short Game	Putting Green	On-Site Rooms	Nearby Rooms	Altitude: 324'	Middle: 6,633 yds Front: 5,184 yds

Coyote Creek Golf Club (Valley) – Morgan Creek   ♦♦½

Jack Nicklaus
1 Coyote Creek Golf Dr, Morgan Hill, CA 95037
7,066 yds   Par 72   Rating: 74.4 / 135   (2002)

www.coyotecreekgolf.com
(408) 463-1400

The Coyote Creek Golf Club's newer Valley course remains entirely on the clubhouse side of the South Valley Freeway and, despite being of similar size, is somewhat easier and less engaging than its more established sister. Indeed, the Valley includes far fewer tactical considerations than are generally central to any Nicklaus design – but it is worth noting in this context that the Golden Bear may not have had an entirely free hand in its construction, as the Valley is actually a rebuild of the old Riverside Golf Course, which had existed on the site since the 1950s. Play opens solidly enough, with the 439-yard 1st featuring a creek angling rightward before its green and the 529-yard 2nd being a short but soundly bunkered par 5. The front nine also ends in style, offering what is arguably the layout's best three-hole stretch at the 209-yard pond-crossing 7th, the 408-yard 8th (where tee shots must carry a pair of left-side bunkers in order to open the ideal angle of approach) and the 441-yard 9th, which rewards drives placed between a centerline bunker and a right-side creek. The back offers a slightly shorter menu of favorites, with the 456-yard straightaway 12th being the Valley's longest par 4 and the 582-yard dogleg left 14th having its driving zone divided by a cluster of centerline trees.

7	Range (Grass)	Short Game	Putting Green	On-Site Rooms	Nearby Rooms	Altitude: 326'	Middle: 6,558 yds Front: 5,187 yds

Eagle Ridge Golf Club – Gilroy   ♦♦½

Ron Fream & David Dale
2951 Club Dr, Gilroy, CA 95020
7,005 yds   Par 72   Rating: 74.5 / 145   (2000)

www.eagleridgegc.com
(408) 846-4531

Built in scenic foothills on the west side of Gilroy, the Eagle Ridge Golf Club is a tough, housing-oriented layout which serves as a fine representative of the "Everything But The Kitchen Sink" school of hazarding – though this was lessened a bit by the removal of incongruously huge bunkers on the 2nd and 3rd holes a decade after opening. Ron Fream and David Dale were responsible for the course's initial design and if their approach strikes many as overkill, there are, at least, a number of interesting holes present. The 457-yard 5th (whose green sits above a dried-out pond) may be the front nine's toughest test, but also notable going out are the 513-yard 7th (which dares the carry of a large left-side bunker off the tee) and the 452-yard 9th, a tree-narrowed, downhill closer. The longer inward half is a bit more imposing, first at the 438-yard pond-flanked 12th and the 228-yard Redan 13th, then at the Mutt-and-Jeff-like 600-yard 14th and 330-yard creek-fronted 15th. Play later closes in style with the 411-yard 18th, a tricky par 4 whose approach must cross a barranca through a narrow opening among oak trees. Eagle Ridge surely isn't for the classically minded, but it will seldom be accused of being dull.

7	Range (Both)	Short Game	Putting Green	On-Site Rooms	Nearby Rooms	Altitude: 311'	Middle: 6,640 yds Front: 5,186 yds

Gilroy Golf Course – Gilroy   ♦½

Unknown   www.gilroygolfcourse.com
2695 Hecker Pass Rd, Gilroy, CA 95020   (408) 848-0490
            3,009 yds   Par 35   Rating: 34.4 / 111   (1923)

Built by local businessmen in 1923, the Gilroy Golf Course is widely characterized as an 11-hole facility, though in reality it is a fairly basic nine which offers one extra hole (an alternative to the par-4 7th) and a widely different angle of play on the short par 4 to follow. The layout is partially routed around the local Elks Lodge (the shorter tee of the 8th hole sits nearly within its parking lot) and is entirely basic in its stylings, with only five bunkers and zero water hazards present. Notably, two of the bunkers serve as centerline hazards before the typically small greens of the 375-yard uphill 1st and the 342-yard downhill 2nd. The loop's lone par 5, the 520-yard 4th, bends rightward along a 200-foot hillside and after this, the big question is which side of the Elks Lodge to play past at the 7th, with the 432-yard right side option representing the facility's longest par 4.

2	Range (Grass)	Short Game	Putting Green	On-Site Rooms	Nearby Rooms	Altitude: 283'	Middle: N/A Front: 2,751 yds

Los Lagos Golf Course – San Jose   ♦½

Mike Poellot & Brian Costello   www.playloslagos.com
2995 Tuers Rd, San Jose, CA 95113   (408) 361-0250
            5,393 yds   Par 68   Rating: 65.9 / 116   (2002)

A new millennium addition to the San Jose golfing scene, the Los Lagos Golf Course is the *extremely* rare layout to actually include more par 5s than par 4s – a circumstance made even more remarkable by the fact that the course measures less than 5,400 yards in total. In some eyes, this is considered an executive track, but that seems a hard case to make when holes measuring 500, 523, 567 and 583 yards are present. Of course, also present are nine par 3s averaging 155 yards, so the short course idea is hardly without merit. The standard of design is frequently high, with the front nine featuring a trio of water-influenced entries: the 291-yard 4th, the 567-yard pond-guarded 6th and the 485-yard 9th, where a left-side lake can affect the second or third. The inward half includes a pair of watery par 3s (the 177-yard 12th and the 148-yard 16th) but also a pair of decently sized, well-bunkered par 4s, the 340-yard 11th and the 389-yard 17th.

3	Range (Mats)	Short Game	Putting Green	On-Site Rooms	Nearby Rooms	Altitude: 136'	Middle: 4,922 yds Front: 3,903 yds

San Jose Municipal Golf Course – San Jose   ♦½

Robert Muir Graves
1560 Oakland Rd, San Jose, CA 95131
6,700 yds   Par 72   Rating: 71.5 / 121   (1968)

www.sjmuni.com
(408) 441-4653

A late 1960s creation by period star Robert Muir Graves, the San Jose Municipal Golf Course is a prototypical functional design of its period, being of relatively modest size and playing interest but offering just enough beyond the basic to keep the more experienced golfer engaged if they are visiting with a novice. Nearly 60 bunkers are present, though for the skilled player a good many will not be relevant to primary lines of play. There are, however, a handful of solid par 4s to be found, with the front nine including the 417-yard 2nd (a genuinely testing dogleg right which turns sharply around trees and a marginally invasive pond), the 411-yard 3rd and the 375-yard 6th, another dogleg right, this time with three bunkers lining the corner. The inward half then includes a pair of two-shotters set on opposite banks of another none-too-threatening lake, the 424-yard dogleg left 15th and the 394-yard 16th. The bunkering on Graves' original layout was made up mostly of clusters of small, circular hazards, a style that was gone from the landscape by 1980.

4	Range	Short	Putting	On-Site	Nearby	Altitude:	Middle: 6,304 yds
	(Mats)	Game	Green	Rooms	Rooms	58'	Front: 4,200 yds

Santa Teresa Golf Club – San Jose   ♦½

George Santana
260 Bernal Rd, San Jose, CA 95119
6,744 yds   Par 71   Rating: 72.1 / 122   (1963)

www.santateresagolf.com
(408) 225-2650

Despite being designed by a relative unknown, the Santa Teresa Golf Club is, in its raw form, an occasionally interesting layout which includes dashes of muscle and a handful of more engaging holes – a package which, unfortunately, is weighed down by the major presence of power lines running directly through the heart of the property. Sadly, their impact is felt nowhere more than on two of what might otherwise be the layout's best holes, the 500-yard 11th (a sharp, creek-crossed dogleg right whose approach ascends into the foothills) and the 417-yard downhill 12th, another sharp dogleg right with trees and the creek filling its corner; one imagines the local free-replay rule comes into play on the latter more than anywhere else. The front nine, meanwhile opens with a pair of strong dogleg par 4s of its own (the 416-yard 1st and the 412-yard 2nd) and later features the 190-yard 7th, whose green angles along a steep right-side fallaway. Play also finishes strongly at the 220-yard 16th, the 571-yard 17th and the 421-yard 18th, a muscular (if largely basic) closing stretch. A nine-hole par-3 course (page 100) adjoins.

5	Range	Short	Putting	On-Site	Nearby	Altitude:	Middle: 6,434 yds
	(Mats)	Game	Green	Rooms	Rooms	221'	Front: 5,460 yds

Shoreline Golf Links – Mountain View   ♦♦

Robert Trent Jones II   www.shorelinelinks.com
2940 N. Shoreline Blvd, Mountain View, CA 94043   (650) 903-4653
            6,996 yds   Par 72   Rating: 74.2 / 129   (1983)

Built as part of a coastal redevelopment project which included the famed Shoreline Amphitheatre, the Shoreline Golf Links sits near the southern tip of San Francisco Bay, where it was designed by Robert Trent Jones II on a then-treeless expanse in 1983. With a long and challenging layout and a location conducive to breezy conditions, this was an ambitious undertaking in the municipal golf world, but having long suffered the sort of budgetary neglect inherent therein, it is far less highly regarded today than the project once surely looked like on paper. The front nine follows a compact routing east of the clubhouse where in addition to the 186-yard pond-crossing 4th, it is anchored by a trio of strong dogleg par 4s: the 413-yard 3rd, the 429-yard 6th and especially the 403-yard 7th, which dares a drive across invasive corner bunkers. The back nine lies to the west and southwest and features several water holes of note, including the 525-yard dogleg right 10th (whose green flanks Shoreline Lake) and a trio of entries that involved wetlands: the 173-yard 11th, the 401-yard dogleg left 12th and the 207-yard 17th. The skeleton still remains but for far too many, this is a facility which clearly failed to maximize its potential.

7	Range (Both)	Short Game	Putting Green	On-Site Rooms	Nearby Rooms	Altitude: 15'	Middle: 6,608 yds Front: 5,437 yds

Spring Valley Golf Course – Milpitas   ♦

Ray Anderson   www.springvalleygolfcourse.com
3441 Calaveras Rd, Milpitas, CA 95035   (408) 262-1722
            6,139 yds   Par 70   Rating: 68.5 / 115   (1956)

Located in a relatively undeveloped valley a mile and a half east of Interstate 680, the Spring Valley Golf Course dates to the mid-1950s and represents a very basic form of functional golf, albeit on a half-decently sized frame. There is, in fact, a run of somewhat brawny golf that appears through the turn, with the 515-yard uphill 6th and the 190-yard 7th paving the way for a pair of longer par 4s at the 439-yard 8th and the 417-yard 9th, and these, in turn, are followed by the 512-yard dogleg right 10th and the 192-yard pond-crossing 11th. Unfortunately, this stretch includes all of two bunkers (both guarding the back of the 10th green) and of the five additional bunkers that mark the remaining 12 holes, three protect the putting surface of the 403-yard 18th. The rest of the track is considerably shorter and, for the most part, hazard-free, so this is perhaps an ideal layout for those who've moved beyond the beginner phase and are just learning how to score.

3	Range (Both)	Short Game	Putting Green	On-Site Rooms	Nearby Rooms	Altitude: 564'	Middle: 5,860 yds Front: 5,453 yds

Sunnyvale Municipal Golf Course – Sunnyvale   ♦½

David Kent   www.sunnyvalegolfcourses.com
605 Macara Ave, Sunnyvalle, CA 94085   (408) 738-3666
              6,248 yds   Par 70   Rating: 70.1 / 117   (1968)

Located just off the end of the runways of Moffett Airfield, the Sunnyvale Municipal Golf Course occupies a small, oddly shaped tract crossed by the Southbay Freeway, which was constructed at the same time as the golf course. The layout is thus quite short and compact, with holes 1, 2 and 14-18 located on the clubhouse side of the freeway and the other 11 residing across it to the north, and in this light it is commendable that the only truly awkward hole is the 297-yard 5th, a sharp dogleg right which turns at about 160 yards. A bit of size pops up through the layout's mid-section, particularly at the 433-yard 9th, the 549-yard heavily bunkered 10th and the 414-yard 11th, as well as the 194-yard 13th, whose green sits beyond a huge front-left bunker added during the late 1980s. A number of man-made ponds also appear (several currently dry), adding interest to holes like the 381-yard dogleg right 1st, the 159-yard 7th, the 343-yard 8th and the 358-yard 18th, where a large left-side hazard can affect both drive and approach.

3	Range (Grass)	Short Game	Putting Green	On-Site Rooms	Nearby Rooms	Altitude: 49'	Middle: 5,742 yds Front: 5,170 yds

Golf Club at Moffett Field – Sunnyvale   ♦½

Bob Baldock   www.moffettgolf.com
934 Macon Rd, Sunnyvale, CA 94043   (650) 386-0720

6,572 yds   Par 72   Rating: 71.6 / 122   (1959)

As with many a Western military golfing facility, the Golf Club at Moffett Field was designed by Bob Baldock, who laid out an initial nine in 1959, then added a second loop in the years immediately to follow. The course occupies flattish land between the runways and wetlands adjacent to the southern tip of San Francisco Bay, and it offers the sort of basic, fundamental sort of golf so common to period military courses. The par-37 front nine includes a trio of par 5s, with the 540-yard 2nd playing through a heavily bunkered lay-up zone and the 3rd and 9th – which both measure 547 yards – relying more on size than anything else. The back nine's lone three-shotter, the 517-yard 11th, turns sharply leftward around and invasive pond and is followed by the 404-yard 12th, a solid, early turning dogleg left. The finishing run is then led by the 446-yard 17th (a sweeping dogleg right and the layout's strongest par 4) and the 358-yard 18th, whose fairway is squeezed by a pair of bunkers – but well shy of the better golfer's driving zone.

4	Range (Both)	Short Game	Putting Green	On-Site Rooms	Nearby Rooms	Altitude: 9'	Middle: 6,338 yds Front: 5,386 yds

Blackberry Farm Golf Course – Cupertino   ◆

Robert Muir Graves   www.blackberryfarmgolfcourse.com
22100 Stevens Creek Blvd, Cupertino, CA 95014   (408) 253-9200
                1,544 yds   Par 29   Rating: 28.5 / 93   (1962)

Occupying a narrow, gently sloping site less than a mile west of Route 85, the Blackberry Farm Golf Course offers a tree-lined Robert Muir Graves-designed executive nine that includes a pair of short par 4s along with seven par 3s. While the design is essentially pretty basic, there is enough bunkering present to add at least a dash of playing interest, particularly at the 272-yard 4th (whose putting surface sits behind a pair of frontal hazards) and the 189-yard 9th, one of four full-sized one-shotters present.

1	Range (Grass)	Short Game	Putting Green	On-Site Rooms	Nearby Rooms	Altitude: 298'	Middle: N/A Front: 1,410 yds

Deep Cliff Golf Course – Cupertino   ◆

Clark Glasson   www.playdeepcliff.com
10700 Clubhouse Ln, Cupertino, CA 95014   (408) 253-5357
                3,305 yds   Par 60   Rating: 58.9 / 94   (1961)

Located half a mile south of Blackberry Farm, the Deep Cliff Golf Course is an 18-hole executive layout which rises modestly above the short course norm, its tree-lined holes including six short par 4s along with a dozen par 3s averaging 142 yards in length. While the design standard is largely basic, bunkering is frequent and a pair of man-made ponds also help to define play, notably at the slightly awkward 284-yard 11th, a sharp dogleg left. The tree-lined waters of Stevens Creek wend their way across the property as well but for whatever reason, Glasson opted to use this potentially frequent hazard mostly for scenery.

1	Range (Mats)	Short Game	Putting Green	On-Site Rooms	Nearby Rooms	Altitude: 346'	Middle: 3,051 yds Front: 2,501 yds

Gavilan Golf Course – Gilroy   ◆

Unknown   www.gavilangolfcourse.com
5055 Santa Teresa Blvd, Gilroy, CA 95020   (408) 846-4920
                1,818 yds   Par 31   Rating: 29.6 / 92   (1967)

Situated on the campus of Gavilan College, the Gavilan Golf Course is a fairly basic nine-hole executive track that includes a quartet of par 4s – though the 226-yard 4th (whose green angles behind front-right sand) really out to be a par 3. Eight bunkers are present to provide brief dashes of playing interest and the loop's shortest hole, the 92-yard 8th, has its putting surface flanked by a small pond. A wide, creek-bottomed swale that bisects the property might well have made for an engaging hazard but instead it comes into play only at the 281-yard 2nd (just off the tee) and the 138-yard 9th.

1	Range (Both)	Short Game	Putting Green	On-Site Rooms	Nearby Rooms	Altitude: 227'	Middle: N/A Front: 1,776 yds

Pruneridge Golf Course – Santa Clara   ◆

Jack Fleming   www.pruneridgegolfclub.com
400 N. Saratoga Ave, Santa Clara, CA 95050   (408) 248-4424
                1,770 yds   Par 30   Rating: 29.3 / 98   (1967)

Built on the site of a former citrus grove, the Pruneridge Golf Course was initially laid out
by Jack Fleming in 1967, but today's course owes mostly to a 1978 Mark Rathert redesign
which reconfigured the layout around a small residential neighborhood. A dozen bunkers
are present, all positioned greenside, so a genuine element of accuracy is often required.
This is especially true at the 292-yard 4th (which plays to a narrow, wildly shaped target
wedged among three bunkers), the 168-yard tree-narrowed 5th, the 131-yard 7th (whose
green bends around a front-left hazard) and the 125-yard tightly bunkered 8th.

1	Range (Both)	Short Game	Putting Green	On-Site Rooms	Nearby Rooms	Altitude: 112'	Middle: N/A Front: 1,504 yds

Rancho Del Pueblo Golf Course – San Jose   ◆

Robert Muir Graves & Damian Pascuzzo   www.ranchodelpueblo.com
1649 Hermocilla Way, San Jose, CA 95116   (408) 347-0990
                1,338 yds   Par 28   Rating: - / -   (2000)

Built on roughly half the acreage of the former Thunderbird Golf Course (the other half
being sold off for residential development), the Rancho Del Pueblo Golf Course was one
of the later projects in the long portfolio of Robert Muir Graves and represents solid golf
of this type. While only nine bunkers are present, all are central to the line of play, lifting
holes like the 168-yard 3rd, the 142-yard 7th and the 123-yard 9th somewhat above the
short-course mundane. A trio of ponds only marginally affect play, though shots missed
right at the 250-yard par-4 4th and the 194-yard 6th might well end up wet.

1	Range (Both)	Short Game	Putting Green	On-Site Rooms	Nearby Rooms	Altitude: 90'	Middle: N/A Front: 1,072 yds

Santa Teresa Golf Club (Par 3) – San Jose   ◆

Gene Bates   www.santateresagolf.com
260 Bernal Rd, San Jose, CA 95119   (408) 225-2650
                922 yds   Par 27   Rating: - / -   (1996)

Set adjacent to the Santa Teresa Golf Club's regulation-sized 18 (page 95), the club's
nine-hole Gene Bates-designed par-3 layout lies at the base of the Santa Cruz Mountains
and, though short enough nearly to qualify as pitch-and-putt, is strong of this type. Sand
is used sparingly (but meaningfully) while a trio of ponds enliven play considerably, first
at the 98-yard 3rd (whose green sits between water and a backing hillside) and the 124-
yard downhill 4th (where ponds flank either side), then at both the 74-yard 6th and the
116-yard 9th, whose putting surfaces lie along right-side hazards. A very nice amenity.

1	Range (Mats)	Short Game	Putting Green	On-Site Rooms	Nearby Rooms	Altitude: 214'	Middle: N/A Front: N/A

Sunken Gardens Golf Course – Sunnyvale   ♦

Clark Glasson   www.sunnyvalegolfcourses.com
1010 S. Wolfe Rd, Sunnyvale, CA 94086   (408) 739-6588
                1,502 yds   Par 29   Rating: 28.2 / 87   (1955)

Dating all the way back to the mid-1950s, the Sunken Gardens Golf Course is a fairly basic executive nine which pairs two short par 4s with a collection of seven par 3s averaging 138 yards in length. As it happens, these two-shotters are arguably the most engaging holes as the 267-yard 2nd is a soundly bunkered, out-of-bounds-flanked test and the 267-yard 6th twists its way to a tiny green. The one-shotters are a bit more straightforward, save for the 128-yard 5th, where a line of left-side trees which serves to buffer adjacent housing actually extends somewhat into the line of play.

1	Range (Mats)	Short Game	Putting Green	On-Site Rooms	Nearby Rooms	Altitude: 97'	Middle: N/A Front: N/A

Villages Golf & Country Club (Short) – San Jose   ♦

Robert Muir Graves   www.thevillagesgcc.com
5000 Cribari Ln, San Jose, CA 95135   (408) 223-4643
                723 yds   Par 27   Rating: - / -   (1968)

Built within the regulation-sized 18 (page 89) of the private Villages Golf & Country Club, the club's Short course is a mostly basic pitch-and-putt layout which serves more as a pleasant golfing amenity than as a serious practice ground. Only three bunkers are present as well as two mostly scenic ponds, all of which adds up to a limited challenge on a loop whose holes average only 80 yards in length.

1	Range (Mats)	Short Game	Putting Green	On-Site Rooms	Nearby Rooms	Altitude: 531'	Middle: N/A Front: N/A

SAN MATEO COUNTY

Burlingame Country Club – Hillsborough   ◆◆½

Unknown   www.burlingamecc.org
80 New Place Rd, Hillsborough, CA 94010   (650) 342-0750
           6,283 yds   Par 70   Rating: 71.4 / 125   (1922)

By most reports, the Burlingame Country Club first played golf (over three basic holes) in 1893 which, if correct, would make the club the first recorded golf facility to exist west of the Mississippi. Evidence suggests that both Herbert Fowler and William Watson helped expand the course to 18 holes early in the 1920s, but their work was buried beneath a 1950s renovation widely credited to Robert Trent Jones – though neither Cornish & Whitten nor the Robert Trent Jones Society support this credit. What remains today is a short layout but one which offers the occasional flavorful moment within a somewhat disjointed routing. For many, the most memorable hole will be the 123-yard 9th, a mere pitch but one played across a barranca and through a narrow opening among trees. Also present, however, is a varied collection of engaging par 4s which, on the front side, include the 401-yard downhill 1st (where trees overhang the green's right side) and the 414-yard 4th, a tree-pinched dogleg left. The back then offers three more noteworthy two-shotters in rapid succession: the 426-yard downhill 10th (a sharp, early turning dogleg left), the 292-yard 11th (which plays to one of the narrowest greens on the planet) and the 438-yard 12th, which features another tiny putting surface. To be sure, dating to the 19th century adds significantly to the collectability here.

4	Range (Both) -	Short Game	Putting Green	On-Site Rooms	Nearby Rooms	Altitude: 209'	Middle: 6,155 yds Front: 5,578 yds

Green Hills Country Club – Millbrae   ◆◆½

Dr. Alister MacKenie, Robert Hunter & Chandler Egan   www.greenhillscc.com
500 Ludeman Ln, Millbrae, CA 94030   (650) 588-4616
           6,351 yds   Par 71   Rating: 70.7 / 138   (1930)

Built on a wooded hillside overlooking San Francisco International Airport, the Green Hills Country Club will never rank among the very best of Dr. Alister MacKenzie's vaunted portfolio. However, its lushly landscaped 6,351 yards do offer enough challenge that one can reasonably suggest that the Good Doctor (with help from Robert Hunter and former U.S. Amateur champ Chandler Egan) surely got the most out of the compact, undulating site. Relying mostly on the hilly terrain and some well-contoured greens to provide challenge, MacKenzie created few standout holes here, and with the 11 par 4s averaging 375 yards, very little in the way of muscle is required. Among the favorites are the uphill 178-yard 4th (played to a tiny, two-tiered green), the 364-yard 9th (whose ascending approach must carry a deep front-left bunker), the attractive 166-yard 13th and the 432-yard 18th, which descends sharply off the tee before climbing to a final well-bunkered target. The par-5 16th, which offers a splendid view towards the bay before tumbling 540 downhill yards, is also notable – though the pond which flanks its green arrived long after Dr. MacKenzie's day. Not quite Cypress Point, certainly, but for MacKenzie fans in particular, this represents a quirky, pleasant Bay Area option.

3	Range (Grass)	Short Game	Putting Green	On-Site Rooms	Nearby Rooms	Altitude: 151'	Middle: 6,033 yds Front: 4,243 yds

California Golf Club – South San Francisco   ◆◆◆◆

William Locke   www.calclub.org
844 W. Orange Ave, South San Francisco, CA 94080   (650) 589-0144
        7,216 yds   Par 72   Rating: 74.7 / 135   (1926)

The California Golf Club of San Francisco was first planned by little-known Scotsman William Locke, but by the time construction began, he'd been replaced by the popular Pacific Northwest designer A. Vernon Macan who, it is generally believed, retained the original routing but built green complexes pretty much as he saw fit. But for reasons unrecorded, Macan apparently constructed no fairway bunkers, an omission that was put right soon after opening when the club hired the legendary Dr. Alister MacKenzie to complete the job. Thus imbued with a good measure of MacKenzie styling on a layout which he did not actually create, the club spent the next four decades playing a well-thought-of track whose front nine routing was eventually somewhat altered to make room for the late-1960s construction of the adjacent Westborough Boulevard. Handling those changes was the ubiquitous Robert Trent Jones, who further left his mark by building a trio of ponds near the greens of holes 3, 16 and 18. By the new millennium, however, Jones' work no longer held the cachet it once did and the club saw the need for major change, hiring Kyle Phillips to perform as 2007 renovation which fully restored 13 holes to their prewar specs while also building five entirely new ones, all on the formerly weaker front nine. Particularly after the removal of Jones' ponds, this "new" layout emerged as a stylish blend of strategic MacKenzie-esque bunkering and impressively contoured greens, all supported by picturesque cypress trees and numerous panoramic views across the gorgeous Bay Area landscape. The front nine begins in a narrow corner of the property north of the clubhouse before doubling back to the southwest and after an attractive par-5 opener, initially features a pair of Phillips par 4s, the uphill 448-yard 2nd and the downhill 437-yard 3rd, a soundly bunkered gentle dogleg right. Another favorite is one of the loop's original holes, the 195-yard 6th, whose typically small green is fronted by a deep front-left bunker and backed by both a sharp fallaway and a panoramic view northeastward, towards the bay. But the front's most memorable entry is surely the 411-yard dogleg right 7th, another Phillips creation which occupies previously unused land and bends nearly 90 degrees around a deep depression, daring the better ball striker to try the most aggressive route. Following the long (but downhill) par-3 8th and the blind tee shot of the dogleg left 9th, the back nine follows a compact, back-and-forth routing south of the clubhouse and initially features the 412-yard uphill 10th and the 232-yard 12th, which angles across a restored line of MacKenzie bunkers and plays from an elevated championship tee set flush against the clubhouse. The back-and-forth nature of things is readily apparent over the next four holes as the 433-yard 13th and 513-yard par-5 15th climb significantly, while the palpably strong 479-yard 14th and 567-yard 17th each descend correspondingly. But squeezed in between is a tiny chestnut, the 133-yard 16th, which plays downhill to a shallow, very tightly bunkered green benched into a hillside; there is no good place to miss here. Rather like Cypress Point, the nicely bunkered 416-yard 18th may strike some as a modest letdown, but this does little to change the fact that in its renovated state, this is certainly one of California's most enjoyable and engaging stops. **(G:** #27 USA, #50 World **GD:** #101 USA, #15 State **GW:** #34 Classic**)**

1	2	3	4	5	6	7	8	9	Out
535	448	437	592	346	195	411	241	419	3624
5	4	4	5	4	3	4	3	4	36
10	11	12	13	14	15	16	17	18	In
412	407	232	433	479	513	133	567	416	3592
4	4	3	4	4	5	3	5	4	36

7	Range (Grass)	Short Game	Putting Green	On-Site Rooms	Nearby Rooms	Altitude: 118'	Middle: 6,797 yds Front: 5,401 yds

Lake Merced Golf Club – Daly City   ◆◆◆

Robert Muir Graves   www.lmgc.org
2300 Juniperro Sierra Blvd, Daly City, CA   94015   (650) 755-2233
                6,960 yds   Par 72   Rating: 73.6 / 134   (1964)

The Lake Merced Golf Club was originally built by Bay Area architect William Locke in 1922, but quickly rose to far greater fame upon being redesigned in 1929 by Dr. Alister MacKenzie, whose rolling, aesthetically attractive version hosted several PGA Tour events of the 1930s. The early 1960s construction of the 280 Freeway impinged upon the layout's eastern flank, however, prompting the club to bring in Robert Muir Graves to perform a comprehensive redesign which, with its uninspiring style and flat greens, lowered MacKenzie's colors for posterity. However, in 1996, Rees Jones rebuilt all the greens and bunkers, re-injecting a bit of life and giving the course a far more appealing look. Now essentially a modern, cypress-lined layout that manages something of a classic feel, Lake Merced features a solid front nine anchored by several long par 4s, including the 434-yard opener, the downhill 419-yard 2nd, the 447-yard 4th (an uphill dogleg right) and the 457-yard 7th. Measuring 250 shorter, the inward half lacks this sort of muscle but does provide an engaging finish via the 221-yard 15th, the 335-yard 16th (which makes a late drop to a suitably small target) and the 547-yard dogleg right 18th. An LPGA stop since 2014, Lake Merced represents a solid Bay Area option – but only if near neighbors Olympic and the San Francisco Golf Club are off the table.

6	Range (Both) +	Short Game	Putting Green	On-Site Rooms	Nearby Rooms	Altitude: 181'	Middle: 6,324 yds Front: 5,096 yds

Menlo Country Club – Woodside   ◆◆◆

Tom Nicoll   www.menlocc.com
2300 Woodside Rd, Woodside, CA   94062   (650) 366-5751
                6,802 yds   Par 71   Rating: 72.2 / 130   (1912)

The Menlo Country Club has been around for a while, having begun life with a short-but-tricky 18-hole layout designed on a sloping site by Tom Nicoll in 1912. That track was materially altered by Robert Trent Jones during the 1960s, however, leaving it as a short but attractive test which drew little beyond local Bay Area attention. But in 2014, Kyle Phillips performed a major renovation, retaining some corridors of play but essentially creating an entirely new golf course – one with considerably greater size and no shortage of playing interest. Phillips' outward half is first led by a pair of short par 4s, the 376-yard downhill 3rd (whose green sits beyond an ancient creekbed) and the driveable 307-yard 6th. The layout's mid-section is then carried by a quartet of longer two-shotters: the 444-yard sharply uphill 8th, the 414-yard dogleg right 9th, the 447-yard 10th (whose tee shot is squeezed by some very mature trees) and the gently ascending 475-yard 11th. For many, the most engaging entry will be the 326-yard downhill (but neatly bunkered) 13th, but also measuring up nicely is a closing run that starts with the 417-yard 15th (where the creekbed lies left of the green) and the 141-yard 16th, whose very small putting surface is fronted by it. The 514-yard 17th is defined by imposing right-side trees on both drive and second, setting up the demanding 436-yard 18th, which climbs nearly 50 feet from tee to green. Fairly engaging stuff, and one of the most improved layouts in the region

5	Range (Grass)	Short Game	Putting Green	On-Site Rooms	Nearby Rooms	Altitude: 178'	Middle: 6,300 yds Front: 5,842 yds

Peninsula Golf & Country Club – San Mateo   ♦♦½

Donald Ross
701 Madera Dr, San Mateo, CA 94403
6,571 yds   Par 71   Rating: 72.2 / 130   (1922)

www.thepgcc.com
(650) 638-2200

Originally known as the Beresford Country Club, today's Peninsula Golf & Country Club boasts the significant distinction of being the only course ever laid out by Donald Ross west of the Rockies. Ross's work was actually a redesign and expansion of a prehistoric nine-holer, and was later altered frequently enough to require a large new millennium restoration by classicist Ron Forse. What exists today, then, is a blend of original Ross holes and some newer ones bearing a bit of Ross style – not quite the real deal but a fairly decent mix just the same. Standouts on the front side include the 440-yard downhill 2nd, the 201-yard 4th (a strong one-shotter played across a wide swale), the 460-yard sharply downhill 5th and the 448-yard downhill 9th, a Ross original which long ago served as the 18th. While the back nine follows Ross's routing (though not his sequence) almost completely, its best-known hole, the downhill, heavily bunkered 155-yard 15th was actually built by Robert Trent Jones as a replacement for a Ross par 3 cleared to make room for the club parking lot. Thus despite older par 4s like the downhill 452-yard 13th and the 285-yard 17th (a driveable but heavily bunkered test), Peninsula can hardly be considered vintage Donald Ross - but it's certainly not bad.

5	Range (Both)	Short Game	Putting Green	On-Site Rooms	Nearby Rooms	Altitude: 153'	Middle: 6,243 yds Front: 5,375 yds

Sharon Heights Golf & Country Club – Menlo Park   ♦♦½

Jack Fleming
2900 Sand Hill Rd, Menlo Park, CA 94025
6,863 yds   Par 72   Rating: 73.6 / 136   (1962)

www.sharonheightscc.com
(650) 854-6422

Built on a sloping site just north of Interstate 280, the Sharon Heights Golf & Country Club is routed around/through a residential development and is widely considered one of the stronger original designs of ex-Alister MacKenzie construction foreman (and San Francisco city parks greenkeeper) Jack Fleming. The layout is of fairly good size and while nearly water-free, its use of plentiful bunkering and the native terrain adds up to a solid challenge. The front nine is perhaps the less-engaging half with favorites including the 425-yard downhill opener as well as a pair of downhill-then-uphill, dovetailed par 5s, the 502-yard 3rd and the 590-yard 5th. Though its first couple of holes flank the freeway, the longer inward half then lifts the challenge noticeably, first at the 540-yard downhill 10th, then via a quartet of strong par 4s that includes the 430-yard 11th (where a long, downhill approach is required), the 450-yard dogleg right 12th, the 432-yard 15th (which descends to a shallow, tightly bunkered target) and the 401-yard uphill 16th. Much of Fleming's Bay Area work was more functional than highly engaging, so one might assume that the bunker renovations which have taken place here were difference-makers – but this was actually a testing, heavily bunkered layout right from the start.

6	Range (Grass)	Short Game	Putting Green	On-Site Rooms	Nearby Rooms	Altitude: 304'	Middle: 6,490 yds Front: 5,058 yds

Half Moon Bay Golf Links (Old) – Half Moon Bay   ♦♦½

Arnold Palmer & Frank Duane   www.halfmoonbaygolf.com
2 Miramontes Point Rd, Half Moon Bay, CA 94019   (650) 726-1800
              7,001 yds   Par 72   Rating: 74.3 / 135   (1973)

Built on prime oceanfront real estate 45 minutes south of San Francisco, Half Moon Bay is a resort developed in two distinct parts, over nearly a quarter-century. The Old course drew much attention back in 1973 for its seaside location, though in truth this Arnold Palmer & Frank Duane-designed track is virtually all inland in nature. Touched up by Arthur Hills in 1999, it retains its original routing (wall-to-wall housing provided no alternative) but also offers a tad more playing interest than many courses of the period. The less-engaging front nine offers mostly steady, functional golf, though the 225-yard 3rd is a challenging lake-flanked par 3, the 499-yard downhill 5th is a tempting par 5 whose green angles along a front-right pond, and the 449-yard descending 8th is a more heavily bunkered entry. The back nine begins in a similar vein, and having seen slightly awkward doglegs (to accommodate housing) at the 376-yard 4th and the par-5 10th, discerning golfers may at this point begin to wonder what all of that early publicity was about. But the action does pick up noticeably down the homestretch, where the pond-guarded 571-yard 15th and the 410-yard 16th (whose green is fronted by an overgrown creekbed) set the table for the 405-yard 18th, a spectacularly situated closer which bends gently rightward along the Pacific clifftops to a green set directly below a Ritz-Carlton hotel.

7	Range (Grass)	Short Game	Putting Green	On-Site Rooms	Nearby Rooms	Altitude: 55'	Middle: 6,610 yds Front: 5,319 yds

Half Moon Bay Golf Links (Ocean) – Half Moon Bay   ♦♦♦

Arthur Hills   www.halfmoonbaygolf.com
2 Miramontes Point Rd, Half Moon Bay, CA 94019   (650) 726-1800
              6,854 yds   Par 72   Rating: 72.5 / 132   (1997)

The Half Moon Bay resort added the Arthur Hills-designed Ocean course in 1997, its arrival coinciding with the construction of the Ritz-Carlton hotel which separates its 18th hole from the Old course's celebrated finisher. The site of the LPGA's Samsung World Championship in 2008 (won by regional native Paula Creamer), the Ocean occupies a tumbling, treeless expanse to the south which had somehow managed to remain undeveloped nearly into the new millennium. The site is not large, however, resulting in a shortish layout by modern standards as well as a pronounced compactness to Hills' largely back-and-forth routing. On the plus side, however, a complete lack of housing gives the Ocean a far more natural feel – in spots actually resembling the links of the Old Country. The front nine features the 332-yard 2nd (whose drive carries a wide ravine), the 465-yard into-the-wind 5th (which shares a bunker-dotted double fairway with the par-5 4th), the 155-yard 7th (the layout's lone true water hole) and the 526-yard 8th, where a centerline bunker and a small tree impede the lay-up zone. The inward half then offers a pair of scenic tests (the sidehill 220-yard 12th and the 431-yard 13th) before peaking with a trio of attention-getting, wind-exposed clifftop closers: the 381-yard 16th, the 184-yard 17th and the 533-yard 18th, which bears a passing similarity to the 18th at Pebble Beach as its elevated fairway skirts the bluffs all the way home. (GW: #197 Resort)

5	Range (Grass)	Short Game	Putting Green	On-Site Rooms	Nearby Rooms	Altitude: 57'	Middle: 6,470 yds Front: 4,872 yds

Crystal Springs Golf Course – Burlingame   ◆◆

Herbert Fowler   www.playcrystalsprings.com
6650 Golf Course Dr, Burlingame, CA 94010   (650) 342-4188
            6,550 yds   Par 72   Rating: 72.3 / 131   (1924)

The Crystal Springs Golf Course occupies an enviable location, being laid out on high ground above the Lower Crystal Springs Reservoir, with westward views across the water towards the northern spur of the Santa Cruz Mountains. Sadly, this once pastoral setting has, since the 1950s, also abutted Interstate 280, whose construction forced considerable changes to a layout originally built by the fine British architect Herbert Fowler. The result is that very little of Fowler's work remains, with today's track owing mostly to alterations made by two generations of Billy Bells (among others) and offering moments of stylistic variance that underscores a disjointed design history. The front nine extends to the southeast and offers several of the most memorable holes, including the 386-yard 5th (which climbs steadily to a shallow, centerline-bunkered green), the 420-yard 6th (a steeply downhill dogleg left) and a pair of solid closers at the 203-yard 8th and the 421-yard tree-pinched 9th. The back nine then runs out to the northwest and offers the 150-yard 13th (played downhill to a wildly shaped green) and the descending 417-yard 14th before closing with a trio of holes which run adjacent to the freeway.

5	Range (Mats)	Short Game	Putting Green	On-Site Rooms	Nearby Rooms	Altitude: 646'	Middle: 6,183 yds Front: 5,296 yds

Poplar Creek Golf Course – San Mateo   ◆½

Stephen Halsey   www.poplarcreekgolf.com
1700 Coyote Point Dr, San Mateo, CA 94401   (650) 522-4653
            6,035 yds   Par 70   Rating: 69.7 / 117   (2000)

Originally built in 1933 as the San Mateo Municipal Golf Course, today's Poplar Creek was redesigned in 2000 by Stephen Halsey, who retained much of the original routing but also added several completely new holes in addition to altering greens and bunkering. The limited size of the power line-crossed site has consigned the course to measuring little beyond 6,000 yards, so a major challenge this is not. There are, however, a fair number of good-sized holes present, led by the demanding/awkward 421-yard 2nd (an early turning dogleg right with water lining the outside corner), the 403-yard 4th, the 455-yard 10th (a gentle dogleg right) and the 537-yard 14th, where a creek crosses 60 yards before a narrow green which angles rightward between bunkers. Also notable is a collection of six par 3s which includes the 188-yard pond-guarded 3rd and the 158-yard 15th, as well as a pair of shorter, watery par 4s, the 321-yard 11th (where an invasive pond must be carried off the tee) and the 382-yard 18th, whose large green sits along a right-side lake.

3	Range (Mats)	Short Game	Putting Green	On-Site Rooms	Nearby Rooms	Altitude: 6'	Middle: 5,631 yds Front: 4,726 yds

Sharp Park Golf Course – Pacifica

♦♦½

Dr. Alister MacKenzie

www.sfrecpark.org

2600 Francisco Blvd, Pacifica, CA 35014

(650) 359-3380

6,432 yds   Par 72   Rating: 71.4 / 126   (1932)

Owned by the City of San Francisco despite lying 10 miles south of its borders, Sharp Park Golf Course was certainly one of the nation's elite municipal layouts in its early days, having been designed by Dr. Alister MacKenzie on a seaside site that included two oceanfront holes and several more highly strategic tests routed around a large central lake. But damaged by World War II-era coastal storms and subsequent mismanagement, today's layout retains only a fraction of MacKenzie's work, with 13 holes still following original corridors of play, but often lacking most of their original MacKenzie features. Present holes 4-7 (which lie east of the Pacific Coast Highway) were added in the 1940s to replace those that were lost along the ocean, while entries like the 89-yard 8th and the 207-yard 12th are much shorter holes than those which originally occupied their acreage. But stronger (resequenced) entries do remain, led by the 423-yard dogleg left 10th (originally the 18th), the 391-yard 14th (which curves along the central lake/wetlands but is missing an original alternate fairway), the 354-yard 16th (the lone remaining seaside hole) and the 348-yard 17th, which approximates the original 5th but, once again, minus an alternate fairway. With recent minor restorative steps underway, Sharp Park's future now looks rosier than much of its past, but many MacKenzie features cannot be restored, and much of its collectability hinges on history...and an optimistic future.

4	Range (Grass)	Short Game	Putting Green	On-Site Rooms	Nearby Rooms	Altitude: 22'	Middle: 6,195 yds Front: 5,693 yds

Emerald Hills Golf Course – Redwood City   ♦

Ellis Van Gorder   www.emeraldhillsgolfcourse.com
938 Wilmington Way, Redwood City, CA 94061   (650) 368-7820
                1,156 yds   Par 27   Rating: - / -   (1959)

Lying just north of both Interstate 280 and the campus of Cañada College, the Emerald Hills Golf Course dates to the late 1950s and offers a hilly, but fairly basic, nine-hole par-3 layout routed around the Redwood City Elks Club. Though hazarding is light (only five bunkers are present), holes average 128 yards in length, so this does rise comfortably above pitch-and-putt level. The three longest tests come right out of the box, with the 172-yard 3rd leading the way by virtue of playing to a tiny green tucked behind sand.

1	Range (Grass)	Short Game	Putting Green	On-Site Rooms	Nearby Rooms	Altitude: 588'	Middle: N/A Front: 1,003 yds

Mariners Point Golf Center – San Mateo   ♦½

Bob Cupp & John Fought   www.marinerspoint.com
2401 E. 3rd Ave, San Mateo, CA 94404   (650) 573-7888
                1,233 yds   Par 27   Rating: 27.2 / 88   (1996)

Situated on a man-made headland just west of the San Mateo-Hayward Bridge, the Mariners Point Golf Center features an engaging nine-hole par-3 course built around an expansive practice facility by Bob Cupp and ex-PGA Tour player John Fought. Holes average 137 yards in length and include plentiful bunkering, as evidenced by the 142-yard centerline-bunkered 1st, the 123-yard 3rd and the 161-yard 6th. The course is flanked on three sides by San Francisco Bay and while those waters serve only as a scenic backdrop, a single pond does affect play, closely guarding the green of the 101-yard 9th.

1	Range (Both)	Short Game	Putting Green	On-Site Rooms	Nearby Rooms	Altitude: 22'	Middle: N/A Front: 774 yds

SANTA CRUZ COUNTY

DeLaveaga Golf Course – Santa Cruz   ◆◆½

Bert Stamps   www.delaveagagolf.com
401 Upper Park Rd, Santa Cruz, CA 95065   (831) 423-7214
                6,110 yds   Par 70   Rating: 70.1 / 134   (1970)

Living forever within the shadow of its high-profile near-neighbor, the vastly more famous Pasatiempo, the DeLaveaga Golf Course is a short but highly engaging facility laid out over similarly rolling, barranca-crossed terrain by Bert Stamps in 1970. Stamps' work isn't quite a match for Dr. Alister MacKenzie's, of course, and DeLaveaga's scale is surely less attractive to long-hitting modern golfers, but there is no shortage of interesting golf present. On a par-34 front nine measuring only 2,802 yards, trees are often a significant factor, notably off the tee at the 504-yard 1st, pinching aggressive drives at the 337-yard 2nd, invasively filling the corner at the 387-yard 6th (an early turning dogleg right) and impeding the left side at the 366-yard 7th. Also notable is the 164-yard 3rd (played across an overgrown barranca) as well as a similarly swale-fronted par 3 on the inward half, the 170-yard 15th, where a prominent right-side tree also affects play. Best known, however are a pair of full-sized back nine entries, the 590-yard 10th (a sweeping dogleg left around trees and a ravine – and one of the region's toughest par 5s) and the 454-yard 18th, a sharp dogleg left with water lurking beyond the corner. Pasatiempo this isn't, but unless one is fixated upon size, DeLaveaga represents a nice, downsized area alternative.

4	Range	Short	Putting	On-Site	Nearby	Altitude:	Middle: 5,704 yds
	(Mats)	Game	Green	Rooms	Rooms	315'	Front: 5,081 yds

Seascape Golf Club – Aptos   ◆◆

William Locke   www.seascapegc.com
610 Clubhouse Dr, Aptos, CA 95003   (831) 688-3213
                6,034 yds   Par 71   Rating: 71.8 / 131   (1926)

Built upon rolling terrain half a mile inland from the Pacific Ocean, the Seascape Golf Club began life in 1926 as a private William Locke-designed facility known as Rio Del Mar before closing for several years during World War II. It is widely listed as having been redesigned by David Gill before reopening at least a decade after the cessation of hostilities, but with all of its original corridors of play and greensites being retained, his work was surely far less than that of the original architect. Today's version is a tree- and housing-lined test which is short enough to include its 441-yard uphill 2nd, 452-yard 13th and 436-yard uphill 18th as par 5s – and which thus counts only the scenic 433-yard 3rd as a par 4 measuring in excess of 400 yards. Other brawnier entries include the 207-yard 6th, the 524-yard downhill (and narrow) 10th and the 192-yard 14th, which climbs from the bottom of an outlying canyon to a green angled behind front-left sand. Toss in the 349-yard 5th (played uphill to another bunker-fronted target) and the 349-yard 15th (whose fairway is marked by a centerline tree) and there are some interesting moments present – but for many, it is the attractiveness of the setting which will rate the highest.

4	Range	Short	Putting	On-Site	Nearby	Altitude:	Middle: 5,813 yds
	(Mats)	Game	Green	Rooms	Rooms	182'	Front: 5,525 yds

Pasatiempo Golf Club – Santa Cruz   ◆◆◆◆

Dr. Alister MacKenzie
20 Clubhouse Rd, Santa Cruz, CA 95060

www.pasatiempo.com
(831) 459-9155

6,495 yds   Par 70   Rating: 72.5 / 141   (1929)

One of the most intact American designs of Dr. Alister MacKenzie (and the site of the Good Doctor's final place of residence – a house just off the 6th fairway), the Pasatiempo Golf Club has long enjoyed a reputation as one of America's top public-access courses. The property was developed by 1921 U.S. Women's Amateur champion Marion Hollins as a real estate subdivision in the hills above Santa Cruz, a location which allows the stylish layout to boast views of the Pacific Ocean (and the distant Monterey Peninsula) as it winds its way over a verdant, barranca-dotted acreage. The peripatetic Dr. MacKenzie often allowed others to construct his designs after he'd traveled on, but given his choice to reside here, Pasatiempo is widely viewed as the project he devoted the most time and effort to, a point evidenced in some of the more significant contouring of layout's putting surfaces. Also highly relevant is the nature of the site, for beyond climbing nearly 250 feet from south to north, it possesses a slightly schizophrenic personality, with the front nine occupying a narrow, fairly open expanse which descends steadily towards the sea while the back climbs more precipitously and is marked by a barranca which manages to affect the majority of its holes. In part due to a new millennium Tom Doak restoration, Pasatiempo bears a far greater resemblance to its original layout than do most MacKenzie works, but it must also be noted that it played to a par of 73 at the time of its opening; the 1st, 2nd and 10th were all par 5s before higher volumes of traffic and expansion of the clubhouse area forced the removal of several longer tees. Of course, as downhill par 4s measuring 458 and 430 yards, the 1st and 2nd make for a strong getaway, and they are followed by the 222-yard uphill 3rd, a tough, heavily bunkered par 3. What comes next, however, is the layout's least appealing section, a run of five holes which, though neatly bunkered and attractively tree-lined, are wedged together tightly enough that expansion is simply not a possibility. Among this quartet, the 190-yard uphill 5th often draws some measure of acclaim, while the 567-yard 6th is an uphill par 5 wedged between right-side trees and left-side out-of-bounds – and, at 70 Hollins Drive, Dr. MacKenzie's residence. After crossing the club entrance road, the 492-yard uphill 9th is noticeably wider and, though obviously reachable, plays to a green angled behind three front-left bunkers. But it's the more elevated back nine which really soars here; indeed this is a loop which teems with memorable holes. Initially there is the 437-yard dogleg left 10th, the former par 5 which requires a barranca-crossing drive before sweeping leftward to a green tucked behind front-left sand. Then comes the 390-yard 11th (played sharply uphill and across the barranca) followed by the parallel downhill 12th, whose green sits just beyond the same hazard. The loop's mid-section is then filled by a trio of fine entries: the 426-yard 14th (barranca left), the tiny, neatly bunkered 142-yard 15th (routed across it) and the 392-yard 16th, MacKenzie's personal favorite and, with green perched beyond the barranca, one of the region's most frequently photographed tests. Finally, the 173-yard 18th (which crosses the barranca at its widest point) is a suitably distinctive finisher for a layout that is, by leaps and bounds, the top stop between the Monterey Peninsula and San Francisco. **(G: #59 USA GD: #98 USA, #16 Public, #14 State GW: #32 Classic)**

1	2	3	4	5	6	7	8	9	Out
458	430	222	378	190	567	347	176	492	3260
4	4	3	4	3	5	4	3	5	35
10	11	12	13	14	15	16	17	18	In
437	390	371	532	426	142	392	372	173	3235
4	4	4	5	4	3	4	4	3	35

5	Range (Both)	Short Game	Putting Green	On-Site Rooms	Nearby Rooms	Altitude: 396'	Middle: 6,093 yds Front: 4,366 yds

Spring Hills Golf Course – Watsonville

♦½

Ben Harmon   www.springhillsgolf.com
501 Spring Hills Dr, Watsonville, CA 95076   (831) 724-1404
                6,002 yds   Par 71   Rating: 69.9 / 123   (1965)

Though a single golf hole reportedly existed on a previous owner's land as early as 1927, the Spring Hills Golf Course began its present life in 1965 with nine holes (today's inward half) before a second loop was added four years later. The standard of design is mostly basic, with only a dozen bunkers present and very few tactical questions posed – and at only 6,002 yards (with par 4s averaging 359 yards), the degree of challenge is obviously fairly modest as well. Play does open on a high(er) level, however, with the 386-yard 1st bending sharply rightward around a large hillside, the 427-yard 2nd crossing a pair of creeks on approach, and the 356-yard 3rd being crossed by a ditch 20 yards shy of its green. The back nine offers a bit of back-and-forth routing up and down a hillside in the property's western half, with a pair of back-to-back par 5s (the 526-yard uphill 16th and the 508-yard downhill 17th) heading the run size-wise, and setting up the 271-yard 18th, a downhill, pond-fronted par 4 with a large man-made waterfall to the right of its green.

3	Range (Mats)	Short Game	Putting Green	On-Site Rooms	Nearby Rooms	Altitude: 119'	Middle: 5,851 yds Front: 5,359 yds

Boulder Creek Golf & Country Club – Boulder Creek   ♦½

Jack Fleming   www.bouldercreekgolf.com
16901 Big Basin Hwy, Boulder Creek, CA 95006   (831) 338-2111
                4,396 yds   Par 65   Rating: 60.7 / 101   (1961)

Recovering from 2020 wildfire damage at the time of this writing, the Boulder Creek Golf & Country Club is an above-the-median executive layout designed by Jack Fleming high in the Santa Cruz Mountains. Frequently flanked by housing, the course only achieves a par of 65 by counting three sub-450-yard holes as par 5s and the 225-yard opener as a par 4. However, there is a bit more interesting golf present than one might guess, particularly on a big nine which includes the 182-yard creek- and tree-bothered 10th, the 168-yard pond-crossing 11th and the 120-yard 18th, which plays through an extremely narrow gap among trees. This may not qualify as destination stuff but if one is in the neighborhood...

2	Range (Grass)	Short Game	**Putting Green**	On-Site Rooms	Nearby Rooms	Altitude: 809'	Middle: N/A Front: 4,027 yds

Casserly Golf Course – Watsonville   ♦

Robert Sanford   www.casserlygolf.com
626 Casserly Rd, Watsonville, CA 95076   (831) 724-1654
                1,264 yds   Par 27   Rating: - / -   (1966)

Bordering the regulation-sized Spring Hills Golf Course along its western flank, the nine-hole Casserly Golf Course offers a basic par-3 layout set upon an open, tree-less expanse. Holes average 140 yards in length, but this number is somewhat inflated by the presence of the 218-yard 6th; there are, in fact, four holes measuring less than 115 yards, with the 8th weighing in at only 88. With only two bunkers and two small ponds present, this is a facility well-suited to beginners and the less-skilled.

1	Range (Grass)	Short Game	**Putting Green**	On-Site Rooms	Nearby Rooms	Altitude: 184'	Middle: N/A Front: 1,158 yds

MONTEREY
PENINSULA

Corral de Tierra Country Club – Corral de Tierra   ♦♦

Bob Baldock   www.corraldeltierracc.com
81 Corral de Tierra Rd, Corral de Tierra, CA   93908   (831) 484-1112
            6,756 yds   Par 72   Rating: 73.2 / 134   (1959)

Often overlooked due to its proximity to so many famous golfing addresses, the Corral de Tierra Country Club is the easternmost of Monterey Peninsula area courses, lying nearly halfway to Salinas off the south side of the Monterey-Salinas Highway. The course was laid out by Bob Baldock and, per his norm, was a mostly functional test prior to a 2000 renovation by Todd Eckenrode and Mike Poellet, a project which retained all of Baldock's routing but injected considerably greater playing interest. Unchangeable, however, was Baldock's usage of the barranca-like Toro Creek, a sandy hazard whose biggest role is to artificially lengthen a trio of short par 5s whose fairways it crosses at distances that mandate laid-up tee shots: the 498-yard 9th, the 492-yard 13th and the 509-yard 16th. The rest of the layout offers a bit more room to operate, with the front nine being led by the 200-yard pondside 4th and the 378-yard 6th, whose fairway bunkering creates multiple tee shot options. The back then features the 175-yard 11th (which angles across Toro Creek) and the 432-yard tightly bunkered 18th. Though perimeter housing is plentiful, it is usually distant enough not to disfigure the surrounding mountain landscape too greatly.

6	Range (Both)	Short Game+	Putting Green	On-Site Rooms	Nearby Rooms	Altitude: 377'	Middle: 6,408 yds Front: 5,406 yds

Monterey Peninsula CC (Dunes) – Pebble Beach   ♦♦♦½

Seth Raynor & Robert Hunter   www.mpccpb.org
3000 Club Rd, Pebble Beach, CA   93953   (831) 373-1556
            7,089 yds   Par 72   Rating: 74.0 / 136   (1926)

As with nearby Cypress Point, the Monterey Peninsula Country Club's Dunes course was originally planned by Seth Raynor, but upon Raynor's 1926 passing, its construction was instead completed by Dr. Alister MacKenzie's partner Robert Hunter. Also like Cypress Point, the layout sits upon a wonderfully varied landscape, its first eight holes marching through beautiful, residence-dotted forest before play emerges into the sand dunes, then briefly touches the coastline. But while this was always a splendidly scenic track, it was surprisingly limited in terms of playing interest prior to a 1999 Rees Jones renovation, then a more comprehensive re-working by Tom Fazio in 2016 that has lifted the Dunes' stock considerably. After opening with three fairly modest par 4s, the front nine offers a run of fine golf led by the 234-yard 4th (played to a huge L-shaped green), the 467-yard dogleg right 6th, the attractive 416-yard creek- and tree-lined 8th and the 543-yard 9th, which breaks out of the forest to a another creek-guarded green, this one set amidst the dunes. There follows a run of eight wind-exposed holes closer to the Pacific, the most memorable of which may be the 171-yard 10th and the 169-yard 14th, the club's only actual seaside test. Among the closers, the 393-yard 16th bends leftward to an extremely shallow green, the 463-yard uphill 17th is a backbreaker, and the 536-yard 18th climbs steadily to a centerline-bunkered putting surface. Though Seth Raynor might not recognize the place, the Dunes can now hold its own with the best in this golf-rich neighborhood. **(G**: #85 USA **GD**: #80 USA, #10 State **GW**: #58 Classic**)**

7	Range (Grass)	Short Game	Putting Green	On-Site Rooms	Nearby Rooms	Altitude: 158'	Middle: 6,559 yds Front: 4,850 yds

Cypress Point Club – Pebble Beach   ◆◆◆◆◆

Dr. Alister MacKenzie & Robert Hunter
3150 17 Mile Dr, Pebble Beach, CA 93953   (831) 624-2223
6,524 yds   Par 72   Rating: 73.1 / 141   (1928)

It is difficult to imagine that anywhere on this planet there lies a golf course with a stronger mix of superbly conceived holes *and* scenic beauty than Alister MacKenzie's landmark Cypress Point. Of course, in this light, it is always interesting to recall that MacKenzie wasn't even the first architectural choice of club developer Marion Hollins; that honor went instead to Seth Raynor, who then passed away unexpectedly, leaving MacKenzie to fill the most desirable of pinch-hitter roles. But this unanticipated change of fortune certainly worked out nicely, for MacKenzie quickly produced one of the greatest routings in the history of the game, a sequence of play which runs a uniquely appealing path through silvery dunes, lush green forests and, ultimately, along the ocean for a spectacular clifftop run – all made possible by a site which Herbert Warren Wind once observed "possesses a diversity of terrain possibly unmatched." Against this uniquely special backdrop comes a seemingly endless procession of fine holes, with play opening with a tee shot across 17 Mile Drive, then an uphill drive angled across sand at the par-5 2nd. The 156-yard 3rd plays to a green framed attractively by a huge central sand dune, and then it's into the forest for a run of holes that features a pair of short-but-charming back-to-back par 5s at the 5th (a 491-yard dogleg left) and the 521-yard 6th, which plays to another dune-framed putting surface. The outward half then closes with two of golf's most distinctive short par 4s, the 369-yard 8th (a sharp dogleg right around a massive sandhill), and the 289-yard 9th, whose wild green is pitched high within the dunes. The back nine begins with one more detour into the woods at the 476-yard par-5 10th and the 440-yard 11th before emerging into the dunes for a trio of shorter par 4s highlighted by the 404-yard 12th (which curls rightward along another huge sandhill) and the 366-yard 13th, which descends towards the Pacific and a beautifully bunkered putting surface. The quirky 393-yard 14th skirts 17 Mile Drive, its fairway severely pinched by thick clumps of cypress trees, and then the player reaches the shoreline for perhaps the most famous threesome of oceanfront holes in all of golf. Initially there is the 135-yard 15th (which plays across a rocky inlet to a near-boomerang green), but this is immediately trumped by the 233-yard 16th, a uniquely spectacular par 3 requiring a long ocean carry to reach a green set far out on a rocky promontory; not surprisingly, this rates among the game's most photographed holes. And lastly there is the 386-yard 17th, a dogleg right requiring a windswept drive played diagonally across both the ocean and a gnarly wall of coastal rock. Of course, it must be noted that many a critic has referred to Cypress Point "the greatest seventeen-hole course in the world" due to the relative blandness of the 343-yard 18th, a quirky uphill dogleg right which was once adorned by several additional fairway bunkers. But this minor blemish is of little significance when weighed against the near-flawless opening 17 which, though obviously short by modern standards, still provide enough windblown danger to test even the skilled player – and a physical beauty *nonpareil*. Ultimately, it can safely be said that no serious golfer can call their career complete without having visited Cypress Point, and what higher recommendation is there than that?   (**G**: #2 USA, #2 World   **GD**: #3 USA, #1 State   **GW**: #2 Classic)

1	2	3	4	5	6	7	8	9	Out
420	549	156	383	491	521	170	369	289	3348
4	5	3	4	5	5	3	4	4	37
10	11	12	13	14	15	16	17	18	In
476	440	404	366	393	135	233	386	343	3176
5	4	4	4	4	3	3	4	4	35

6	Range (Grass)	Short Game	Putting Green	On-Site Rooms	Nearby Rooms	Altitude: 68'	Middle: 6,294 yds Front: 5,703 yds

Monterey Peninsula CC (Shore) – Pebble Beach   ◆◆◆◆

Mike Strantz   www.mpccpb.org
3000 Club Rd, Pebble Beach, CA 93953   (831) 373-1556
            6,942 yds   Par 72   Rating: 74.2 / 133   (2004)

The Monterey Peninsula Country Club's Shore course has, over more than half a century, experienced one of the more remarkable changes of fortune in the history of American golf architecture. Initially built by Bob Baldock in 1961 as the club's second layout, it occupies a site which includes a bit of forest near the clubhouse but also a vast expanse of open, windswept land narrowly separated from the Pacific Ocean by 17 Mile Drive. Unfortunately, the road's presence meant that there would be no genuine seaside holes, but so much sandy, open terrain still held considerable potential – which explains why Baldock's relatively pedestrian creation spent some four decades being widely viewed as one of the least-inspiring uses of prime seaside property in the history of golf course design. Early in the new millennium, the club elected to finally capitalize on this great potential by hiring former Tom Fazio associate Mike Strantz to perform a full makeover, a project which would largely retain Baldock's original routing (though with most of its mid-section reversed) but which otherwise would literally transform the entire golfing landscape around it. Sadly, Strantz had been diagnosed with cancer prior to commencing the project and, as he would pass away a year after its opening, put his heart and soul into this project knowing that it very well might be his last. Relying upon numerous sketches that he drew in the field, Strantz performed a comprehensive renovation that included the creation of copious artificial sand dunes, resulting in a vastly more engaging, hazard-laden layout whose aesthetic at times feels like a striking cross between rough-edged beauty and an over-the-top video game. Interesting holes abound, with the routing beginning to emerge from the woods at the downhill 155-yard 3rd, then really picking up steam as it moves northward at the 349-yard 5th (played across a right-side waste bunker to a narrow green set along a creekbed), the 548-yard double dogleg 6th and the 226-yard 7th, which features a steeply elevated target. The 454-yard 8th doglegs leftward around a prominent cypress tree before the action turns south at the stiff, into-the-wind 224-yard 9th, then enters a run of four holes moving (mostly) parallel to the ocean that includes the 181-yard Redan-like 11th, the 599-yard 12th (which bends gently rightward along 17 Mile Drive) and 434-yard 13th, whose narrow green is set between sand and a pair of statuesque cypress trees. The 415-yard 15th is a tactically engaging two-shotter that twists among some Strantz-made dunes before play turns inland for a closing trio led by the demanding 455-yard 17th (routed uphill to a green wedged tightly between sand and a right-side creek) and the 377-yard 18th, a dogleg right which requires more aggressive tee shots to thread a needle between two prominent bunkers and the mature trees that line the corner. Though Strantz's redrawing of the landscape may not look entirely natural, it did create an eye-catching strategic test with vastly more playing interest than that which existed before – a recipe strong enough to land the Shore course comfortably with both *Golf* and *Golf Digest*'s national top 100s. Further, the Shore is now teamed with Pebble Beach and Spyglass Hill as a tri-host of the AT&T Pebble Beach Pro-Am, guaranteeing major national exposure for years to come. Quite the change indeed. **(G**: #67 USA **GD**: #53 USA, #8 State **GW**: #29 Modern**)**

1	2	3	4	5	6	7	8	9	Out
505	391	155	401	349	577	226	455	225	3284
5	4	3	4	4	5	3	4	3	35
10	11	12	13	14	15	16	17	18	In
545	185	600	417	185	426	501	429	370	3658
5	3	5	4	3	4	5	4	4	37

7	Range (Grass)	Short Game	Putting Green	On-Site Rooms	Nearby Rooms	Altitude: 141'	Middle: 6,449 yds Front: 4,860 yds

Club at Pasadera – Monterey

Jack Nicklaus

100 Pasadera Dr, Monterey, CA 93940

www.theclubatpasadera.com

(831) 647-2400

6,713 yds   Par 71   Rating: 73.6 / 143   (2000)

Built adjacent to the public Laguna Seca Golf Ranch on the Monterey-Salinas Highway, the Club at Pasadera is a typically challenging Jack Nicklaus design routed through both open terrain and a trio of housing-dotted canyons. The layout's total yardage of 6,713 is misleadingly short, rendered such by its status as the rare modern track to be designed with six par 3s. The front nine is generally the less-inspiring half, though both the uphill 463-yard 4th and the 476-yard pond-guarded 9th are powerhouse par 4s, and the 380-yard 5th and 158-yard 6th are noteworthy for actually crossing fairways (an unavoidable concession to the confined canyon terrain). The inward half then stretches out over a pair of early ascending tests, the 208-yard 11th and the 452-yard 12th, the latter climbing significantly to a green wedged between two canyon walls. The 352-yard dogleg right 13th (where a centerline tree affects the drive) climbs even further up the canyon, setting the stage for the spectacular 206-yard 14th, which plays from one canyon rim to the other, requiring a carry across a 100-foot-deep abyss. The action then descends over three enjoyable holes, the 551-yard 15th, the 151-yard 16th (played over a gaping front bunker) and the 576-yard 17th, whose green angles behind a front-left pond. The uphill 469-yard creek-flanked 18th then makes for an imposingly big finish to a solid track largely overshadowed by so many high-profile Monterey area neighbors.

6	Range (Grass)	Short Game	Putting Green	On-Site Rooms	Nearby Rooms	Altitude: 418'	Middle: 6,245 yds Front: 4,927 yds

Preserve Golf Club – Carmel

Tom Fazio

19 Pronghorn Run, Carmel, CA 93923

www.santaluciapreserve.com

(831) 620-6700

7,138 yds   Par 72   Rating: 74.4 / 141   (2000)

Though located but a short drive from the Monterey Peninsula, the Preserve Golf Club might well be a million miles away, sitting, as it does, on a secluded expanse 1,500 feet up in the Santa Lucia Mountains. Generally known as an earthmover of epic proportion, Tom Fazio (with help from former USGA President Sandy Tatum and Mike Poellot) took rather a different approach here, essentially allowing his routing to follow the lay of the land, and building less than 50 bunkers (and nary an artificial water hazard) throughout. Perhaps because of this more natural tone, good holes abound, with the non-returning front nine opening with the 442-yard 1st (a downhill two-shotter routed among mature oak trees) and closing with the 458-yard 9th, a sharply downhill dogleg left. The back nine initially features a pair of longer entries, the 457-yard 11th (whose green is guarded by another prominent tree) and the 571-yard 13th, where the aggressive can skirt a left-side pond and bunker off the tee. The homeward run is equally brawny and includes the 477-yard 15th (a tough uphill/sidehill dogleg left), the 558-yard 17th (played over a ridge, then downhill to a bunkerless target) and the 450-yard dogleg left 18th, where the drive is played across an overgrown valley. Notably, The Preserve is one Tom Fazio design that has maintained most of its lofty initial rankings, as it remains a fixture among most top 20s in golf-rich California. Located close to Pebble Beach, perhaps, but as different a golfing experience as night and day. (**GD**: #103 USA, #12 State **GW**: 135 Modern)

7	Range (Grass)	Short Game	Putting Green	On-Site Rooms	Nearby Rooms	Altitude: 1,544'	Middle: 6,603 yds Front: 5,081 yds

Tehàma Golf Club – Carmel Valley   ♦♦♦

Jay Morrish   www.tehamagolfclub.com
25000 Via Malpaso, Carmel Valley, CA 93923   (831) 622-2250
               6,567 yds   Par 72   Rating: 72.8 / 138   (1999)

Built by a group headed by longtime local resident Clint Eastwood, the Tehàma Golf Club resides high upon a secluded mountaintop just a short drive southeast (and then a longer one up the mountain) from Monterey. In truth, this is by no means a top-shelf golf course; indeed, it would have been impossible to build something even approaching great on so tight and hilly a site. But Jay Morrish did succeed in wringing 6,567 yards worth of decent – and frequently exciting – golf out of it and this, combined with its impressive seclusion and scenic splendor, still add up to a fairly imposing package. The outward half is built primarily upon two large promontories and features numerous engaging entries led by the downhill 544-yard 1st, the 530-yard 4th (whose right edge plunges down a mountainside), the 280-yard 5th (driveable but heavily bunkered) and a pair of highly testing par 4s, the 407-yard 7th (which requires an uphill second) and the 417-yard dogleg right 8th. Following another plunging opener at the 444-yard 10th, the back nine is highlighted by the panoramic 457-yard 13th and the 222-yard 14th, the latter played across a steep fallaway to a small hillside green. The 145-yard ridgetop 17th is a pinpoint test played to a diminutive, ridge-divided target, while the 470-yard 18th is a stout two-shotter which descends steadily to a large putting surface. Surprisingly underrated given its exclusivity, but scenic and exhilarating most every step of the way.

5	Range (Grass)	Short Game	Putting Green	On-Site Rooms	Nearby Rooms	Altitude: 819'	Middle: 6,253 yds Front: 4,968 yds

Carmel Valley Ranch Golf Club – Carmel   ♦♦½

Pete Dye   www.carmelvalleyranchclub.com
1 Old Ranch Rd, Carmel, CA 93923   (831) 620-6406
                6,117 yds   Par 70   Rating: 71.2 / 130   (1981)

Occupying an attractive site six miles inland from the Pacific Ocean, the Carmel Valley Ranch features Pete Dye's lone Northern California design – a short and quirky layout which underwent significant alteration (largely in its bunkering) by Gene Bates in 2007. The compact and sometimes severe nature of the property greatly limited Dye's hand, so it is perhaps understandable that the result was, in the words of Tom Doak, "the most preposterous course Pete ever built." The somewhat forced routing includes 13 holes squeezed onto a valley floor and five more (numbers 10-14) climbing into much steeper country. The valley holes are often flanked (but never directly affected) by the Carmel River and are led by a pair of shorter holes, the 293-yard pond-guarded 2nd and the 151-yard over-water 5th. The alpine holes are exciting, yet also somewhat eccentric, with the 455-yard par-5 10th representing the former (it climbs more than 100 feet uphill, over a tree-pinched fairway), and the 394-yard 12th (with its extremely long putting surface) and the semi-blind 141-yard 13th the latter. If one doesn't judge this against the best of Dye's catalog, it might weigh in as quirky and fun – but it's obviously a second-tier choice relative to the more famous golfing options that lie just down the road.

4	Range (Grass)	Short Game	Putting Green	On-Site Rooms	Nearby Rooms	Altitude: 176'	Middle: 5,664 yds Front: 4,433 yds

Del Monte Golf Course – Monterey   ♦♦½

Charles Maud / Herbert Fowler   www.pebblebeach.com
1300 Sylvan Rd, Monterey, CA 93940   (831) 373-2700
                6,365 yds   Par 72   Rating: 71.6 / 131   (1897)

Easily the oldest of the Pebble Beach Company's four full-sized resort layouts, the Del Monte Golf Course cannot hold a candle to Pebble Beach, Spyglass Hill or the Links at Spanish Bay, but it remains a pleasant option as well as an historical one; indeed, this is the oldest continuously operated golf course west of the Mississippi. The layout began with nine holes designed by Charles Maud in 1897, was expanded to 18 in 1903, and was eventually redesigned by Herbert Fowler in 1921 during the same American visit which saw him famously convert Pebble Beach's 18th hole to a par 5. Today's course follows most of Fowler's routing (though plenty of bunkering has been added) and, with its confined, sloping property limiting expansion options, it remains a track short enough to have five par 4s measuring under 335 yards and only one (the 421-yard 16th) in excess of 400. Still, there are a some enjoyable holes here, led by the 328-yard 2nd (a tree-lined dogleg left), the 327-yard 5th (where bunkers tighten the driving zone), the 218-yard 14th and the 330-yard 15th, whose fairway is narrowed significantly by encroaching trees. Though serious players will likely find this best suited for a warm-up round, there remains a fair amount of timeless Monterey Peninsula ambience to be found here.

4	Range (Grass)	Short Game	Putting Green	On-Site Rooms	Nearby Rooms	Altitude: 92'	Middle: 6,085 yds Front: 5,435 yds

Pebble Beach Golf Links – Pebble Beach   ◆◆◆◆◆

Jack Neville & Douglas Grant   www.pebblebeach.com
1700 17 Mile Dr, Pebble Beach, CA 93953   (831) 622-8723
          6,828 yds   Par 72   Rating: 75.1 / 145   (1919)

America's best-known public-access facility, the Pebble Beach Golf Links boasts a layout strong enough to have hosted six U.S. Opens and five U.S. Amateurs, in addition to anchoring the PGA Tour's AT&T National Pro-Am (née the Bing Crosby) since 1947. As the flagship layout of the eponymous development company, the course was famously designed by a pair of local amateurs, five-time California champion Jack Neville and the comparably talented Douglas Grant. Their 1919 creation included enough rudimentary features to need considerable renovation, including the conversion of the 18th hole from a short par 4 into the world's most famous par 5 by Herbert Fowler in 1921, and a significant reworking of bunkers and greens by H. Chandler Egan prior to the 1929 U.S. Amateur. But Neville and Grant's greatest contribution, a figure-eight routing which allowed an unprecedented eight holes to border the Pacific, remains in play today, and might well be considered the layout's hallmark. This routing begins with a trio of inland holes led by the 511-yard 2nd, a smartly bunkered, swale-crossed par 5 that has been converted to two-shot status in recent U.S. Open play. The ocean is first encountered at the attractive drive-and-pitch 4th and the 192-yard 5th, the latter a 1999 Jack Nicklaus addition made after the Pebble Beach Company was finally able to repurchase clifftop land that had been sold off eight decades earlier. But the first truly famous oceanfront hole is the 506-yard uphill 6th, which is followed by the renowned 106-yard 7th, a downhill, sand-ringed one-shotter built upon a windy headland; it is among the most famously unpredictable tests in all of golf. Collectively, the first seven holes have long played much easier than the 11 to follow, with the challenge picking up markedly via as difficult a trio of successive par 4s as one might imagine: the 427-yard 8th (whose approach is played across a colossal ocean-filled chasm to a steeply pitched green), the 481-yard 9th (a clifftop monster stretched to 505 yards for the U.S. Open) and the 446-yard 10th, another dangerous beachside entry with alternate tees available ranging from 495 U.S. Open yards to a driveable 320-yard option adjacent to the 9th green. From here play returns inland for a solid, if unspectacular, stretch which includes the 373-yard 11th (played to one of the narrowest greens around), the testing 201-yard 12th and, most prominently, the 572-yard 14th, an out-of-bounds-flanked dogleg right whose elevated green had become so difficult as to mandate a complete rebuild in 2016. But Pebble Beach's crowning moments come at the close, first at the 177-yard 17th, a waterside test which can be stretched as long as 229 yards, and whose hourglass-shaped, bunker-ringed green has witnessed two of the U.S. Open's defining moments: Jack Nicklaus's near-hole-in-one to clinch the 1972 title and Tom Watson's legendary chip-in to put the 1982 edition on ice. And then there is the 543-yard 18th, a spectacular ocean-hugging par 5 which, very simply, is the most famous hole in all of golf. Stretchable to 7,040 yards via seldom-used U.S. Open tees, Pebble Beach's tiny greens and windswept landscape keep it highly testing in the modern era, helping it to stand as one of the game's genuinely iconic facilities. It is a playing experience that no serious golfer should retire without. **(G:** #11 World, #10 USA **GD:** #8 USA, #2 State, #1 Public **GW:** #9 Classic, #1 Resort**)**

1	2	3	4	5	6	7	8	9	Out
377	511	390	326	192	506	106	427	481	3316
4	5	4	4	3	5	3	4	4	36
10	11	12	13	14	15	16	17	18	In
446	373	201	403	572	396	401	177	543	3512
4	4	3	4	5	4	4	3	5	36

8	Range (Both) +	Short Game +	Putting Green	On-Site Rooms	Nearby Rooms	Altitude: 56'	Middle: 6,454 yds Front: 5,249 yds

Golf Club at Quail Lodge – Carmel   ♦♦½

Robert Muir Graves   www.quaillodge.com
8205 Valley Greens Dr, Carmel, CA 93923   (831) 620-8808
            6,464 yds   Par 72   Rating: 71.3 / 128   (1963)

Sitting five miles inland from the Pacific Ocean, the Golf Club at Quail Lodge is a flat, housing-permeated Robert Muir Graves design which, given the presence of eight lakes and the Carmel River, might well have turned out rather tougher than it did. Indeed, for its first half-century of existence, it was a shortish, housing-lined track whose period stylings seemed noticeably bland given the presence of several nationally elite facilities close by. But in 2015 Todd Eckenrode performed a renovation which, though unable to alter corridors of play, included a complete rebunkering, resulting in a more tactically rich, classic-feeling experience. Notably, its outward half is led by the 347-yard creek-crossed 6th, whose boomerang green dates back to Graves' day. But Eckenrode succeeded in improving all three of the loop's one-shotters, a group anchored by the pond-flanked 196-yard 5th and the 212-yard 8th. Coming home, the 388-yard well-bunkered 13th and 494-yard par-5 14th were also enhanced, as was the 408-yard 16th, a dogleg right enlivened considerably by the addition of a centerline bunker shy of the corner. Also worthy of mention is the 524-yard dogleg left 15th, where a greenside lake would make for a highly tempting second were several houses not blocking the route.

4	Range (Grass)	Short Game	Putting Green	On-Site Rooms	Nearby Rooms	Altitude: 72'	Middle: 6,043 yds Front: 5,009 yds

Links at Spanish Bay – Pebble Beach   ♦♦♦½

Robert Trent Jones II, Tom Watson & Sandy Tatum   www.pebblebeach.com
2700 17 Mile Dr, Pebble Beach, CA 93953   (831) 647-7495
            6,821 yds   Par 72   Rating: 74.0 / 140   (1987)

The newest of the Pebble Beach Company's four golf courses, the Links at Spanish Bay is built around a modern hostelry and occupies prime oceanfront land between the Monterey Peninsula Country Club and Asilomar State Beach. The work of Robert Trent Jones II, Sandy Tatum and Tom Watson, it is, in reality, a synthetic links, for many of the dunes through which the layout passes were created by the designers – though unlike many such American fabrications, the wind and rain that blow in off the Pacific are very real here. After opening with a 500-yard par 5 into the dunes, followed by a driveable 307-yard par 4 that runs back to the Lodge, the shorter front nine visits several solid par 4s, led by the 451-yard dogleg right 5th, whose fairway is dotted by three centerline bunkers. It then crosses 17 Mile Drive for three less links-like, wetlands-affected tests, the strongest perhaps being the 158-yard all-carry 8th. The back nine then slips behind the resort complex for four more not-so-links-like tests, but the 432-yard gully-fronted 12th and the tiny 126-yard 13th are both entertaining. The 576-yard 14th then rambles back to the shoreline, where the closers traverse back-and-forth among the dunes, with the 200-yard 16th and 413-yard 17th touching the beach, and the 571-yard 18th featuring a lay-up zone divided by a gorse-dotted gully. A bit compact in spots, Spanish Bay may not be a true links, but it provides much of the ambience of links golf and enough engaging holes to rate it among the region's best.   **(GD:** #30 State, #48 Public **GW:** #77 Resort**)**

6	Range (Grass)	Short Game	Putting Green	On-Site Rooms	Nearby Rooms	Altitude: 47'	Middle: 6,422 yds Front: 5,332 yds

Spyglass Hill Golf Course – Pebble Beach   ◆◆◆◆

Robert Trent Jones   www.pebblebeach.com
Spyglass Hill & Stevenson Dr, Pebble Beach, CA 93953   (831) 625-8563
6,960 yds   Par 72   Rating: 75.1 / 145   (1966)

In its early years, Spyglass Hill was legendary for its difficulty, with stories abounding regarding the torturous nature of its greens (Jack Nicklaus reportedly four-putted the 14th from inside of 20 feet), its unplayability in anything resembling a stiff wind, and the fact that it took several editions of the Bing Crosby Pro-Am before anybody broke 70. More than half a century later, however, modern equipment, rebuilt greens and several design alterations have combined to tone it down to a level that most seem comfortable with; the pros long ago stopped complaining and, at least if magazine rankings are to be believed, it is today widely viewed as the finest work of the ultra-prolific Robert Trent Jones. In truth, part of Spyglass's timeless appeal is its ambience, its combination of seaside dunes, lush pines and cypress forest creates a visually striking tableau that may only be matched in the entire golfing world by its immediate neighboring Cypress Point. But along with this splendid variety of settings comes one of modern golf designs most enduring questions: With acreage in the dunes being at premium relative to the plentiful land in the forest, why did Trent Jones elect to begin his layout close to ocean rather than end it there? Indeed, Spyglass opens with a scenic 595-yard dogleg left par 5 which descends more than 100 feet as it transitions from the forest to the dunes, its small green angled beyond three man-made bunkers. The 349-yard 2nd then enters the dunes directly and requires a tricky pitch to a green elevated among them, with the 172-yard 3rd then offering a drop shot as it descends nearly 60 feet, a tricky proposition in a heavy breeze. Trent Jones's personal favorite was the 370-yard 4th, where drives played down the right side open the ideal angle to a long and extremely narrow putting surface largely hidden behind a large front-left dune. The 197-yard 5th represents one final stop within this precious golfing terrain and then the action moves back into the forest, ascending sharply at the 446-yard 6th, then facing a reachable (but pond-guarded) par 5 at the 529-yard downhill 7th. The par-4 8th and 9th continue the climb back to the clubhouse before play begins on a back nine which, in truth, bears moments of repetitiveness in that three holes play to greens guarded by man-made ponds (a fourth, the par-5 11th, had another green-fronting hazard filled in shortly before the millennium). Nonetheless, two of these water-guarded tests are widely rated among the best holes on the Monterey Peninsula, the 178-yard 12th (which descends steadily to a narrow green benched into a slope above a front-left pond) and the 130-yard 15th, a mere pitch to a target set just beyond a similar hazard. Nicely mixed in among these water-oriented holes, however, are a pair of deluxe par 4s, the 460-yard uphill 13th and the 476-yard 16th, which doglegs right, past a prominent pine and annually ranks among the toughest two-shotters on the PGA Tour. Curiously, Trent Jones ratcheted down the challenge at the close, for the 325-yard 17th is little more than an iron-and-pitch while the 408-yard 18th is a shortish, straightaway test rated the sixth-toughest among the club's par 4s. No doubt this is a vastly more manageable layout today than it was in 1966, but its unique combination of challenge and Monterey Peninsula ambience still make Spyglass Hill a first-class stop for any visiting golfer. **(GD:** #51 USA, #7 State, #10 Public **GW:** #33 Modern, #11 Resort)

1	2	3	4	5	6	7	8	9	Out
595	349	172	370	197	446	529	399	431	3488
5	4	3	4	3	4	5	4	4	36
10	11	12	13	14	15	16	17	18	In
407	528	178	460	560	130	476	325	408	3472
4	5	3	4	5	3	4	4	4	36

8	Range (Both)	Short Game	Putting Green	On-Site Rooms	Nearby Rooms	Altitude: 206'	Middle: 6,538 yds Front: 5,381 yds

Bayonet & Black Horse (Bayonet) – Seaside   ◆◆½

Gen. Robert McClure   www.bayonetblackhorse.com
1 McClure Way, Seaside, CA 93955   (831) 899-7271
            7,104 yds   Par 72   Rating: 74.9 / 137   (1954)

Long a part of the Army's expansive Monterey area installation at Fort Ord, this imposing 36-hole facility was purchased by the City of Seaside following the base's 1994 closing. Both courses were originally laid out by the fort's commander, a golfing General named Robert McClure, but each was renovated in the aftermath of the purchase by Gene Bates. In the case of the older Bayonet course, beyond re-routing the 9th, 14th and 15th holes (and some minor re-sequencing), Bates mostly added/reconfigured bunkers and reshaped greens, for the Bayonet's cypress- and pine-lined routing was already a long and testing one. Play opens with the uphill 548-yard 1st, then the tight, downhill 436-yard 2nd, but the action doesn't really hit stride until the 613-yard 8th and the new 476-yard 9th, a demanding dogleg right. This run continues through "Combat Corner," an undulating three-hole stretch highlighted by the uphill 419-yard 12th (a very demanding dogleg left) and the 479-yard 13th, whose approach plays back down the hill, but into an ever-present ocean breeze. The terrain remains a factor hereafter, notably at the uphill 16th and the 225-yard 17th, a panoramic downhill par 3. Few have equated the renovated Bayonet with classic design, but it certainly rates among the toughest courses in the area.

7	Range (Grass) +	Short Game	Putting Green	On-Site Rooms	Nearby Rooms	Altitude: 252'	Middle: 6,641 yds Front: 5,229 yds

Bayonet & Black Horse (Black Horse) – Seaside   ◆◆½

Gen. Robert McClure   www.bayonetblackhorse.com
1 McClure Way, Seaside, CA 93955   (831) 899-7271
            7,025 yds   Par 72   Rating: 73.9 / 136   (1964)

From its inception in 1964 as the then-Fort Ord's second 18-hole course, the Black Horse operated as a more open, less-demanding facility, weighing in at under 6,400 yards and playing the standard role of a user-friendly "second" layout. Such is no longer the case, however, as Gene Bates' 2008 renovation added more than 600 yards of length, lots of modern, cape-and-bay-style bunkers and several new back nine holes to lift the layout's challenge to within site of the more celebrated Bayonet. Following the reconfigured 538-yard opener and the 246-yard 2nd, the front nine climbs to higher ground adjacent to the back nine of the Bayonet, where holes like the scenic 444-yard 4th and the uphill 265-yard par-4 6th (eminently driveable, but over sand and a prominent tree) lead the way. The inward half then shows its best stuff early at the 448-yard 11th (a demanding dogleg right), the 508-yard 12th (which twists among trees and left-side out-of-bounds to a narrow green) and the 459-yard 13th, the layout's longest par 4, but one nearly always played downwind. The finish is also notable, first at the uphill 192-yard 17th (a tree- and bunker-squeezed test), then at the 610-yard 18th, a long downhill three-shotter which bends gently rightward and boasts one final grand view of Monterey Bay.

6	Range (Grass) +	Short Game	Putting Green	On-Site Rooms	Nearby Rooms	Altitude: 268'	Middle: 6,542 yds Front: 5,040 yds

Laguna Seca Golf Ranch – Monterey   ♦♦½

Robert Trent Jones & Robert Trent Jones II   www.lagunasecagolf.com
10520 York Rd, Monterey, CA 93940   (831) 373-3701
            6,226 yds   Par 71   Rating: 70.2 / 129   (1970)

Located five miles inland along the Monterey Salinas Highway, the Laguna Seca Golf Ranch was built by Robert Trent Jones and son on a scale rather smaller than those of its more famous coastal neighbors. In part this was surely do to the site, which is somewhat small and slopes steadily from high ground in the north to the base of a large mountain ridge (and the highway) in the south. The resulting 6,226-yard layout is thus somewhat size-deprived, with seven par 4s measuring less than 390 yards (three weigh in under 350) and a collection of five par 3s averaging 155 – but with more than 60 of Jones' period cape-and-bay-style bunkers added to the undulating terrain, a fair degree of challenge is present. The course's one brawnier stretch comes through its mid-section and features the 404-yard sharply uphill 9th, the tumbling 415-yard 10th, the 560-yard downhill-then-uphill 13th (which sweeps leftward around a hillside) and the 547-yard 15th, where water must be crossed on both the second and third. Also noteworthy is the 506-yard 3rd, which descends to a very shallow, centerline-bunkered green. This is pleasant and scenic period stuff in a neighborhood loaded with expensive, high-end options.

4	Range (Grass)	Short Game	Putting Green	On-Site Rooms	Nearby Rooms	Altitude: 448'	Middle: 5,719 yds Front: 4,332 yds

Pacific Grove Golf Links – Pacific Grove   ♦♦½

H. Chandler Egan / Jack Neville   www.playpacificgrove.com
77 Asilomar Blvd, Pacific Grove, CA 93950   (831) 648-5775
            5,727 yds   Par 70   Rating: 67.9 / 113   (1932/1960)

Arguably the most overlooked layout in this golf-rich neighborhood, the Pacific Grove Golf Links lays at the northernmost tip of the Monterey Peninsula and enjoys a rather unique design pedigree. Its front nine, which does a narrow out-and-back through the village in vaguely St Andrews-like fashion, was built by two-time U.S. Amateur champion Chandler Egan in 1932 and is a short, fairly easy affair that thrives on its ambience – though it does include two full-sized par 5s as well as both the 312-yard tree-pinched 3rd and the 424-yard 8th, a sweeping dogleg right. The back nine, on the other hand, was added by original Pebble Beach co-designer Jack Neville in 1960 and is a completely different story, occupying a wide-open seaside expanse ripe with ice plant, sand dunes and often-stiff breezes. The action here centers on a run of four back-and-forth, dunes-lined holes of windblown distinction: the 513-yard dogleg right 12th, the 316-yard driveable 13th, the 356-yard 14th and the 397-yard 15th. This collectability rating hinges somewhat on both ambience and the cachet of the Monterey Peninsula, but the dunes holes do represent one of the more unique stretches of municipal golf in the country.

3	Range (Both) -	Short Game	Putting Green	On-Site Rooms	Nearby Rooms	Altitude: 47'	Middle: 5,571 yds Front: 5,305 yds

Poppy Hills Golf Course – Pebble Beach   ♦♦♦

Robert Trent Jones II   www.poppyhillsgolf.com
3200 Lopez Rd, Pebble Beach, CA 93953   (831) 622-8237
                    7,002 yds   Par 71   Rating: 74.4 / 144   (1986)

Owned and operated by the Northern California Golf Association, the Poppy Hills Golf Course enjoys one of golf's great addresses, being, at the time of its opening, the first course built within the Monterey Peninsula's sublime Del Monte Forest in two decades. Routed over significantly undulating ground just east of Spyglass Hill, the Robert Trent Jones II design is certainly a poster child for the forest's beauty, with endless stands of cypress and pines framing fairways, and the nearby Pacific Ocean often visible beyond their green curtain. Unfortunately, the golf course itself was not one of Jones' most engaging, prompting him to return for a 2014 renovation which completely rebuilt bunkering, carved out some faux "native" sandy areas along fairways and removed all of the layout's rough. The result has been fairly well-received, though in many eyes, the 11 holes on the south side of Lopez Road (numbers 1-9, 17 and 18) rate a bit higher than the seven to the north. Outbound favorites now include the 202-yard chasm-crossing 2nd, the 629-yard smartly bunkered 4th and the 535-yard 9th, which dares a long downhill second across a fronting swale. The back opens with the 527-yard reconfigured 10th (its green moved away from a left-side pond) and later features the 223-yard Redan-like 15th, the 444-yard dogleg right 16th and the 179-yard 17th, which sits aside a right-side ravine.

7	Range (Grass)	Short Game	Putting Green	On-Site Rooms	Nearby Rooms	Altitude: 438'	Middle: 6,501 yds Front: 5,415 yds

Monterey Pines Golf Club – Monterey   ♦½

Robert Muir Graves   www.monterey.navylifsw.com
1250 Garden Rd, Monterey, CA 93940   (831) 656-2167
                5,554 yds   Par 69   Rating: 66.3 / 111   (1963)

A part of the adjacent Naval Postgraduate School, the Monterey Pines Golf Club lies between its campus and the runways of Monterey Regional Airport, where its initial configuration was built by Robert Muir Graves in 1963. The layout has evolved a bit in the decades since but as it occupies limited acreage, it remains a short and fairly basic par-69 track whose routing circumnavigates a small collection of naval buildings and curls around the western edge of the airport. With both of its par 5s measuring less than 500 yards and the 402-yard lakeside 18th being the only par 4 in excess of 380, this is far from backbreaking stuff, and its overall standard of design leans more towards functional than short-course engaging. Perhaps not surprisingly, then, it is within the layout's handful of water holes that the most memorable golf lies, with featured entries including the 371-yard 10th (which bends rightward along a lake), the 348-yard 12th (a sharp dogleg left which requires the golfer to pick a water-crossing angle) and the aforementioned 18th.

2	Range (Mats)	Short Game	Putting Green	On-Site Rooms	Nearby Rooms	Altitude: 104'	Middle: 4,878 yds Front: 4,513 yds

The Hay – Pebble Beach

Tiger Woods
1700 17 Mile Dr, Pebble Beach, CA   93953

www.pebblebeach.com
(831) 622-8723

670 yds   Par 27   Rating: - / -   (2021)

Situated just up 17 Mile Drive from the Lodge at Pebble Beach, The Hay is a nine-hole pitch-and-putt layout originally built by longtime Pebble Beach professional Peter Hay in 1957. That loop was completely reconfigured by Tiger Woods' design company in 2021, however, resulting in a new course with holes averaging 74 yards in length and often named after Major championship winners at Pebble Beach. The featured entry is the 106-yard 2nd, whose green complex replicates that of Pebble's famed 7th hole, but without the Pacific Ocean as a backdrop. It is hard to imagine the serious golfer spending much time here given the resort's other golfing options, but it is a strong facility of its type.

1	Range (Both) +	Short Game +	Putting Green	On-Site Rooms	Nearby Rooms	Altitude: 144'	Middle: N/A Front: N/A

GONE BUT NOT FORGOTTEN

Every major American city has seen golf courses come and go, the departures often being rooted in simple economics – that is, the acreage used for early courses, frequently being close to city centers, simply became too valuable over time not to sell off for commercial or residential development. The San Francisco area has seen its share of such departures but, thankfully, relatively few of these courses were ranked among the region's best. Consequently, the following list of noteworthy losses is a relatively short one.

Ingleside Golf Club (1905)

San Francisco's Ingleside Golf Club was the rare golf course to be discarded by not one but two famous golfing organizations which, of course, is a story in itself. The course occupied acreage immediately north of today's San Francisco Golf Club and south of the San Francisco State University campus, on land which would become the huge Parkmerced apartment development immediately after World War II. The golf course's roots go back to 1905 when it was built by members of the San Francisco Golf Club who, growing tired of sharing their original nine-hole layout on the grounds of the Presidio with the exercises of their military landlords, opted to break away. They designed the new course themselves and if it was thus perhaps a shade rough around the edges, it was instantly popular and, inevitably, subject to a fair number of changes over time. The layout hit its peak of fame in 1915 when, at less than 6,000 yards, it hosted major amateur and professional events in association with the city's Pan-Pacific Expo, with reigning U.S. Open champion Walter Hagen claiming the professional title. When the San Francisco Golf Club moved to its present facility immediately to the south in 1920, the old course was taken over by the members of a new organization, the California Golf Club, who both renamed and continued improving the layout, expanding it to 6,132 yards by mid decade. But by any definition, even their improved track measured up well shy of its illustrious neighbors, which included the Olympic Club, Lake Merced and after 1925, the new municipal facility in Harding Park. Consequently, the California Golf Club membership purchased acreage five miles to the southeast and built a new facility – which following an eventual upgrading by Dr. Alister MacKenzie, became among the region's best. One last organization, the Ingleside Golf Club, gave the old course a shot before selling out to developers by the end of the World War II.

Lake Merced Golf Club (1922)

The Lake Merced Golf Club still exists, of course, and it continues to utilize both its original site and a number of original corridors of play – but today's layout is completely different from the club's more famous Golden Age version. The course was originally built by William Locke in 1922, but it didn't truly come into its own until a 1929 visit from Dr. Alister MacKenzie, who did little to its routing but made significant alterations to its bunkering and green approaches, resulting in a layout strong enough to host five playings of the PGA Tour's San Francisco Match Play event between 1931-1940. MacKenzie's bunkering was always an attention-getter, helping to make Lake Merced a widely photographed facility during those early years, with the center of attention generally being the 165-yard 17th, which played slightly downhill and across a valley to a green fronted by several very large and attractive bunkers carved into the hillside. The 17th was actually just a part of strong three-hole finishing run as the 444-yard 16th was an imposing par 4 which required a drive across a small ravine, then a long approach across a second depression to a tiny, hillside green, while the 425-yard 18th bent gently leftward en route to a narrow putting surface set between a pair of large bunkers. The course measured 6,450 yards following MacKenzie's work but it would be lengthened to over 6,800 by the mid-1950s, by which time the 13th had been reduced from a short par 5 to a stiff 440-yard two-shotter, while a pair of par 3s, the 225-yard 8th and the 230-yard 14th, retained all of the muscle that William Locke originally imbued them with. Unfortunately, while most of its acreage was to remain untouched, the northeastern flank of MacKenzie's layout was threatened by the early 1960s construction of Interstate 280, which marched directly across land housing the clubhouse and the 1st hole. Consequently the club hired Robert Muir Graves to perform a complete redesign, with Graves' work eventually being modified by a Rees Jones appearance in 1997.

Olympic Club (Ocean) (1924)

The Ocean course at The Olympic Club is another layout which, at least by name, still exists – but today's version of the Ocean course has absolutely no design connection with the famed club's long-lost original. That layout made its debut in 1924 after the club purchased the old Lakeside Golf Club and, desiring a genuinely first-class golfing facility, replaced it with 36 brand new holes designed by William Watson and Sam Whiting. One half of the new configuration, the Lake course, lay on the inland side of Skyline Boulevard and would eventually provide some foundation for the club's flagship Lake course of the modern era; it was not, however, Olympic's top layout in 1924. That honor instead went to the Ocean course which, as its name suggests, lay largely on the west side of Skyline Boulevard and included a trio of seaside holes as well as several more routed over hugely scenic terrain just above them. The crux of the action began at the 411-yard 8th and the 528-yard 9th, the latter teeing off from atop a cliff, then crossing heavily-undulating fairway en route to a deep, three-tiered putting surface. The centerpiece, however, was the 185-yard 10th, which descended towards the sea, its green framed by bunkers, the ocean and the distant Marin headlands, making it among the more beautiful par 3s in the history of American golf. The 10th also set the stage for the layout's three seaside holes: the demanding 421-yard 11th, the 380-yard 12th and the 504-yard 13th. Sadly, the Ocean course would survive for little more than a year as storms during the winter of 1925-1926 caused landslides, ruining key holes and rendering much of their acreage unsuitable for rebuilding. The club thus charged Sam Whiting (who'd stayed on as greenkeeper) with reconfiguring the entire property, resulting in the creation of a far lesser Ocean course, but also a Lake course that would soon become one of the nation's venerated tournament venues.

Alameda Municipal Golf Course (1927)

The first course to be built on the grounds of today's huge Corica Park golf complex, what was initially known as the Alameda Municipal Golf Course was laid out by Billy Bell near the end of his highly successful Southern California design partnership with George Thomas. The course was built just after the opening of the adjacent Oakland International Airport but was otherwise pleasantly isolated, with the San Leandro Channel forming its northern boundary and the area to its west (today's densely populated Harbor Bay Isle neighborhood) still an unspoiled wetlands. In its early days, Bell's creation weighed in at 6,135 yards (with a par of 71) and featured a pair of man-made water hazards, a wide, river-like creek which meaningfully impacted three holes and a narrow drainage canal which influenced two others. His original configuration survived relatively well through the Depression and World War II but in 1957, his son William F. Bell was hired to build a second layout on land to the south, requiring a resequencing to accommodate a new clubhouse. Numerous other minor changes took place prior to the layout being closed in 2018 for a full renovation, with reopening scheduled for late 2021.

Capuchino Golf Club (1927)

The Capuchino Golf Club is something of a mystery in Bay Area golfing history, due in large part to its surviving little more than 15 years with its existence being poorly documented. What is known is that the 18-hole layout bordered today's Green Hills Country Club on that facility's northern boundary, and that it opened its doors in (or very close to) 1927. It has been reported that Dr. Alister MacKenzie and his partner Robert Hunter submitted initial plans for Capuchino's layout (hardly a stretch as they also built Green Hills) but those plans apparently went unused, as the club ultimately selected Max Behr as its designer, with the layout's construction being supervised by Olympic Club greenkeeper Sam Whiting. The 1928 edition of the *American Annual Golf Guide* listed the course at 6,371 yards with a par of 72 and it occupied a typically rolling site which, like Green Hills, climbed significantly towards its western reaches. One thing that made Capuchino different from its fellow San Francisco Peninsula clubs of the period, however, is that it was created with a real estate component as a central aspect, with a residential neighborhood planned for the course's center. Few houses were ever actually constructed there prior to the club's mid-1940s subdivision, but the present Juanita Avenue and Park Boulevard define the original neighborhood's perimeter, while today's Capuchino High School was constructed in 1950 in the golf course's easternmost corner.

Sharp Park Golf Club (1932)

Like several other courses in this section, Sharp Park very much still exists – but in a form rather different from its original 1932 incarnation. Situated along the ocean in the southern suburb of Pacifica, the course was designed in 1932 by Dr. Alister MacKenzie and featured numerous memorable holes highlighted by a pair of seaside par 4s, the 323-yard 3rd and the 383-yard 7th. There were also several entries routed along the shoreline of a large interior lake, two of which (the 338-yard 5th and the 392-yard 10th) included dual fairways. Not surprisingly, despite being a compact facility which measured less than 6,200 yards, MacKenzie's Sharp Park clearly ranked among the nation's top municipal layouts - for about a decade. World War II-era storms did significant damage to the seaside holes (only the 7th remains, as today's 16th) which in turn led to the construction of four entirely new (and poorly matched) replacements on the inland side of Pacific Coast Highway, fundamentally changing the layout's timber. Further, while roughly 13 of MacKenzie's original corridors of play remain, nearly all are missing most of their original bunkering, green shapes, etc. There is optimism that at least some of these things can be restored, potentially to a level that allows the layout to no longer be considered "lost" – but it appears that for a variety of environmental and logistical reasons, rebuilding the course to anything resembling original overall specs is out of the question.

San Geronimo Golf Club (1965)

One of the very last design projects completed by Irish-turned-Canadian architect A. Vernon Macan (the course actually opened after his 1964 death), the San Geronimo Golf Club was a popular public facility situated on either side of Sir Francis Drake Boulevard in the hills northwest of San Rafael. At 6,801 yards, and carrying a 73.3 rating, it was a fairly challenging test whose front nine occupied mostly lower ground south and east of the clubhouse before the back was routed through a narrow valley to the northwest. While the Pacific Northwest-centric Macan certainly offered a fine design pedigree, a good deal of the layout's new millennium challenge owed to Robert Muir Graves, who performed a 1989 renovation which included the addition of bunkering, the building of a new (and wildly shaped) 9th green and the reconfiguring of the 406-yard 18th hole around a new left-side lake. Also of note were a pair of strong, downhill par 4s that fell early in the back nine, the 421-yard 11th (whose approach angled through trees and across a creekbed) and the 415-yard tactically strong 12th, where drives carrying left-side sand opened the ideal line of approach. Following a bit of legal wrangling, and a failed local election to save it, the course eventually fell victim to a battle with environmentalists, being purchased by Marin County in an eminent domain-like move and then being allowed to return to the wild.

The Ranch Golf Club (2004)

Located just west of the Silver Creek Valley Country Club, the Ranch Golf Club was a 2004 addition to the San Jose area's golfing landscape and was built by Casey O'Callaghan over some very hilly terrain on the southeast side of town. The layout followed a wildly expansive routing which flanked several residential neighborhoods, included over 400 feet of terrain variance, and required so many long, steep, switchback-laden cart rides that the prospect of one's vehicle having mechanical problems might well have presented a life-threatening situation. The course measured only 6,656 yards from the tips but it was fairly demanding due largely to the terrain, particularly on a front nine which included a number of holes benched into a steep hillside, and thus carrying the prospect of shots missed to the wrong side tumbling into oblivion. It was also something of a puzzle design-wise in that despite the huge amount of acreage covered by such a routing, its two back nine par 3s measured all of 99 and 115 yards. Thus while some wildly shaped greens, several barrancas and multiple spectacularly situated holes combined to provide a level of playing interest, this was the sort of track reviled by traditionalists and critics of "cart ball," and thus had a fairly quiet send-off upon closing in 2019.

SAN FRANCISCO GOLF TIMELINE

1890s

1893
• The Burlingame Country Club puts golf's first Bay Area footprints on the ground, reportedly constructing a three-hole course which is one of several to lay claim to being the first American layout built west of the Mississippi River. It will be expanded to nine holes by decade's end, and a new 18-hole facility will be built in the early 1920s by British architect Herbert Fowler, with apparent input from William Watson as well.

1896
• The San Francisco Golf Club opens its initial nine-hole course, a 2,143-yard loop which is built among sand dunes on acreage that lies within the Presidio army base. A nearby clubhouse is built on leased land immediately adjacent to the base.

1897
• The nine-hole Del Monte Golf Course (part of today's Pebble Beach resort) opens in Monterey, likely designed by English émigré Charles Maud, and it will later become California's first recorded 18-hole facility upon its expansion in 1903. Also opening this year is the Oakland Golf Club, a relatively short-lived nine-hole facility laid out – depending upon varied published reports – by either one P.E. Bowles or a "Mr. Robertson."

1900s

1901
• The Northern California Golf Association is formed, though it will not conduct its first Amateur Championship until 1903. In the decades to follow, winners of that title will include Jack Neville and Douglas Grant (the original designers of Pebble Beach), architect Norman MacBeth, George Von Elm, Lawson Little, Bob Rosburg and Roger Maltbie, among many others.

1905
• With their original nine-hole course built within the Presidio frequently being used as a military training ground, the San Francisco Golf Club moves southward to the Ingleside area, opening a new, member-designed 18-hole course on acreage not far from their present site. Those who remain behind at the Presidio form a new private club, eventually expanding the layout into a new 18-hole facility in 1910.

1910s

1915
• The first major professional golf tournament to be played in the region is hosted by the San Francisco Golf Club as a part of the Pan-Pacific Exhibition, and it boasts a field which includes a number of national-level stars. The 72-hole event is won by reigning U.S. Open champion Walter Hagen, whose 286 total is eight better than runner-up John Black.

1916
• The prestigious Western Amateur is played at the Del Monte Golf Course, in Monterey. The winner is Heinrich Schmidt, who vanquishes Douglas Grant 7 & 6 in the final, with the event helping to establish golf as a centerpiece of the area's soon-to-be full speed development.

1917
• The San Francisco City Championship makes its debut at the Lincoln Park Golf Course, which will be permanently joined in hosting the event by Harding Park upon its 1925 opening. It will become one of the oldest continuously played tournaments in the United States, with its list of champions including Pebble Beach co-designer Jack Neville (1922 and '24), Hall-of-Famer Ken Venturi (1950, '53 and '56), U.S. and British Amateur champion E. Harvie Ward (1955) and 1969

Masters champion George Archer (1963), as well as future LPGA Tour players Juli Inkster (twice), Shelly Hamlin (thrice) and Jan Ferraris (four times consecutively, from 1962-1965).

1918

• Having lost the lease on the site of their second golf course, the San Francisco Golf Club moves to its present site, opening a new member-designed 18-hole layout. Within two years, the club will adopt plans drawn up by famed architect A.W. Tillinghast, leading to the construction of the world-famous layout still in play today.

1919

• The Pebble Beach Golf Links makes its debut in late February, designed by first-time course architects (but prominent amateur players) Jack Neville and Douglas Grant. Though its signature figure-eight seaside routing is impressive, the layout's hazarding and conditioning are met with lukewarm acclaim, leading to a series of alterations, including work done by Herbert Fowler in 1921 that converts the 18th hole from a short par 4 into the world's most famous par 5.

1920s

1923

• Making a rare Northern California appearance, the sometimes-PGA-Tour-recognized California Open is contested at the San Francisco Golf Club, with trick shot artist Joe Kirkwood defeating Macdonald Smith by two shots (77-79) in a playoff after the pair deadlock on 299.

1924

• The downtown-based Olympic Club opens a new 36-hole golf facility on the coastal site of the old Lakeside Golf Club, which the Olympians had taken over six years earlier. Both new layouts are designed by William Watson and constructed by Sam Whiting, but after suffering severe storm damage, they are heavily redesigned by Whiting in 1927, resulting in the creation of the major championship-worthy Lake course as we know it today.

1925

• Marking a brief window where the California Open alternates between northern and southern sites, the event is played at the Olympic Club, with Macdonald Smith beating Monterey native Abe Espinosa by two.

1926

• Pebble Beach's first major professional event, the one-time Monterey Peninsula Championship, is won by "Lighthorse" Harry Cooper, who beats Larry Nabholtz by two.

• Another one-time event, the Santa Clara Valley Open, is won by "Wild" Bill Mehlhorn, who walks away from Tommy Armour by four at the San Jose Country Club.

1927

• The California Open makes its final Bay Area appearance as a PGA Tour-recognized event, being played at the Burlingame Country Club, where Willie Hunter defeats Burlingame's pro, Harold Sampson, by six shots in a playoff after the pair tied on 302.

1928

• Designed by Dr. Alister MacKenzie and Robert Hunter, the Monterey Peninsula's Cypress Point Club opens to unanimous acclaim, it mix of woods, sand dunes and clifftop holes securing the layout an immediate place among the world elite.

• Former two-time U.S. Amateur champion H. Chandler Egan performs a significant renovation of Pebble Beach, retaining all of the layout's original routing but adding length and lots of bunkering, and reshaping most green complexes. It is Egan's work which will come to most define the Pebble Beach layout as it is known today.

1929

• The USGA visits California for the first time when it brings the U.S. Amateur to the newly renovated Pebble Beach. Harrison "Jimmy" Johnston defeats Dr. O.F. Willing 4 & 3 in the final to claim a surprise victory – a "surprise" because two-time defending champion Bobby Jones enters the week as a heavy favorite, only to be upset by Johnny Goodman in the first round.

• The world's hottest professional golfer, Horton Smith, wins a one-time PGA Tour-recognized event known as the Bay District Open, beating Billy Burke by three at the Berkeley Country Club.

1930s

1930
• Its inaugural edition played at the Olympic Club, the San Francisco Match Play makes its debut in December, with Leo Diegel beating Al Espinosa 6 & 4 to claim the title. Save for 1933, the Match Play will be contested every year through 1941, at various Bay Area venues, with all 11 playings today being recognized as official by the PGA Tour.

1934
• Famed architect Dr. Alister MacKenzie, creator of several of Northern California's timelessly elite courses, dies in Santa Cruz, where he has lived in a home beside the Pasatiempo Golf Club's 6th fairway since 1931.

1935
• Having already won both the U.S. and British Amateur titles in 1934, Monterey resident Lawson Little becomes the only man ever to claim both titles in back-to-back years, claiming the U.S. Amateur at The Country Club (in Pepper Pike, Ohio) and the British crown at Royal Lytham & St. Anne's. After turning professional, he will record another Major triumph in the state of Ohio by winning the 1940 U.S. Open at Canterbury.

1937
• The PGA Tour's Oakland Open makes its debut at the Claremont Country Club, with this first edition being historically significant as the maiden victory recorded outside of West Virginia by Sam Snead, who edges the world's hottest golfer, Ralph Guldahl, by two.
• The USGA's second visit to the region sees the U.S. Amateur Public Links come to Harding Park, where Bruce McCormick edges Don Erickson 1 up to take the title.

1938
• The Oakland Open moves to the Sequoyah Country Club, where it will remain through 1944 before expiring during wartime. Harry Cooper wins this second playing (by one over Jimmy Hines and Charles Sheppard) and he will be followed by Dick Metz, Jimmy Demaret and Leonard Dodson in the three editions immediately to follow.
• Future Hall-of-Famer Jimmy Demaret records his first official PGA Tour victory at the San Francisco Match Play, defeating Sam Snead 4 & 3 at the old Ingleside Golf Club. Demaret will win the title again in 1940, when he dispatches Willie Goggin 2 & 1 at Lake Merced.

1940s

1940
• Pebble Beach hosts its first major women's event, the U.S. Women's Amateur, with future Hall-of-Famer Betty Jameson rolling past Jane Cothran 6 & 5 to take the title.

1941
• Johnny Revolta runs away from Harry Cooper by a 7 & 6 margin to win the final edition of the San Francisco Match Play, which is contested at the Presidio Golf Club.

1942
• Byron Nelson wins the Oakland Open at the Sequoyah Country Club, his six-under-par 274 total proving good enough to pull away from famed California amateur Johnny Dawson by five.
• Played the week after the Oakland Open, the San Francisco Open makes its debut at the old California Country Club, where Ben Hogan rolls past Sam Snead by three to claim the title.

1944
• Following a one-year wartime absence, the Oakland Open is revived for one final playing at the Sequoyah Country Club, with Australian Jim Ferrier edging Ky Laffoon by one to take the title.

• Also returning from a year of wartime darkness is the San Francisco Open, which is won by Byron Nelson (who runs away from Jug McSpaden by six) at Harding Park. A second playing of the event is staged in December (in lieu of a 1945 edition) and Nelson successfully defends his title, edging Jim Ferrier by one.

• Joining the fray this year is another PGA Tour-recognized event, the Richmond Open, which is played at the Richmond Country Club and won by Sam Snead, who edges Charles Congdon by a single shot. Following a dark year in 1945, the event will return for three more playings, with Toney Penna, George Schoux and Dutch Harrison emerging as champions.

1946

• The fourth and final playing of the San Francisco Open is staged at the Olympic Club with Byron Nelson claiming the title for the third year in succession, this time in a nine-shot runaway over Herman Barron.

1947

• The U.S. Amateur returns for a second visit to Pebble Beach, with Robert "Skee" Riegel beating famed developer-to-be John Dawson 2 & 1 to raise the trophy.

• After six playings in the San Diego suburb of Rancho Santa Fe (and four years off due to World War II), Bing Crosby brings his celebrity pro-am to the Monterey Peninsula, where it will find a permanent home at Pebble Beach and several nearby courses, with the first 19 editions being tri-hosted by Cypress Point and the Monterey Peninsula Country Club. Spyglass Hill and the Dunes course at the Monterey Peninsula Country Club will later join the rotation, and the event will officially be known as the AT&T Pebble Beach Pro-Am beginning in 1986. This maiden 1947 playing results in a tie between George Fazio and Ed Furgol, who card 213 totals over 54 holes.

1948

• Lloyd Mangrum wins the second Pebble Beach playing of the Bing Crosby Pro-Am, beating Stan Leonard by five shots. Mangrum will win the title again in 1953, this time by a four-shot margin over fellow Hall-of-Famer Julius Boros.

• One year after entertaining the U.S. Amateur, Pebble Beach hosts its second U.S. Women's Amateur, with Connecticut's Grace Lenczyk beating Helen Sigel 4 & 3 to win the title.

• The final playing of the Richmond Open is won by Dutch Harrison (who edges Jimmy Demaret by two) but this edition will hold an important footnote in history: Having been denied duly earned spots in the field because of their race, black stars Bill Spiller, Ted Rhodes and Madison Gunter file a lawsuit against the PGA of America, the first step in a protracted struggle that will eventually see the demise of the PGA's infamous "caucasians only" clause some 13 years later.

1949

• Ben Hogan wins the Bing Crosby Pro-Am by two shots over Jim Ferrier. Hogan will win again the following week in Long Beach, then lose a playoff (to Jimmy Demaret) in Phoenix before embarking on the drive back to Texas during which he is nearly killed in a head-on collision with a Greyhound bus – a near-catastrophe which, following a long and arduous recovery, leads to the greatest competitive comeback in golfing history.

1950s

1950

• In its first year of operation, the LPGA Tour visits the Monterey Peninsula for a 36-hole event known as the Pebble Beach Weathervane, which is won by the legendary Babe Zaharias, who beats fellow Hall-of-Famer-to-be Patty Berg by two. The tournament will be contested once more in 1951 (with Berg reversing fortune by defeating Zaharias by four) before disappearing from the landscape thereafter.

1951

• Now a mostly retired part-time golfer, Byron Nelson claims the last of his 52 PGA Tour victories at the Bing Crosby Pro-Am, where he shoots 71-67-71 to beat Dr. Cary Middlecoff by three.

• Three years after saying goodbye to the PGA Tour, the Richmond Country Club hosts the LPGA's Richmond Open, with Babe Zaharias capturing the inaugural version, narrowly beating

Louise Suggs by one. Patty Berg will raise the trophy (in a four-shot walkaway) in 1952 before the event vanishes for two years, returning for a final bow in 1955, when Betty Jameson beats Mary Lena Faulk by one to retire it.

1952

• The Dunes course at the Monterey Peninsula Country Club hosts the fourth playing of the U.S. Girls' Junior with a 17-year-old Mickey Wright making her debut in the national spotlight but taking the title, edging Barbara McIntire 1 up in the final.

1953

• The fledgling LPGA Tour makes a one-time visit to the Presidio Golf Club for the San Francisco Weathervane, a 36-hole event which sees Louise Suggs beat Betsy Rawls by two.

1955

• The U.S. Open makes its Northern California debut at the Olympic Club, where Ben Hogan gamely seeks a record fifth Open title. Hogan appears on track to win until little-known Jack Fleck birdies the 72nd hole to tie him, then famously upsets Hogan in an 18-hole playoff, winning by three when Hogan double-bogeys the 18th hole.

• Having finished second to Byron Nelson in 1951, Dr. Cary Middlecoff wins the Bing Crosby Pro-Am, cruising past Julius Boros and Paul McGuire by four shots. Middlecoff will successfully defend his title in 1956, when he rolls past Mike Souchak by five.

1956

• The Western Open makes its lone Bay Area appearance, being played within the U.S. Army base at The Presidio. Mike Fetchick claims the second of his three PGA Tour wins but not without a fight, as he beats Doug Ford, Jay Hebert and Don January in a sudden death playoff.

• The U.S. Amateur Public Links makes its second visit to Harding Park, where James Buxbaum win the title, beating W.C. Scarbrough 3 & 2.

1957

• Four years after its previous visit, the LPGA returns to the Presidio Golf Club for another one-time event, the United Voluntary Services Open, a 54-hole tiurnament in which Wiffi Smith runs away to a seven-shot victory.

1958

• Three years after hosting the U.S. Open, the Olympic Club entertains the U.S. Amateur, with Charlie Coe beating future PGA Tour star Tommy Aaron 5 & 4 to emerge victorious.

• Billy Casper earns the fourth victory of his PGA Tour career at the Bing Crosby Pro-Am, riding a second round 66 to an eventual four-shot triumph over Dave Marr. Casper will win the Crosby again in 1963, when he edges a group of five players (which includes Jack Nicklaus and Gary Player) by one.

• Thomas Robbins defeats John Dawson (by this time a well-known Southern California desert developer) 2 & 1 to win the U.S. Senior Amateur at the Monterey Peninsula Country Club.

1959

• Known in its first playing as the Golden Gate Open, the Lucky International, a high-profile PGA Tour event, makes its debut at Harding Park. This maiden edition is claimed by Mason Rudolph, who beats Dow Finsterwald and Bob Goalby by two. The tournament will be contested (with one dark year) through the entirety of the 1960s, always at Harding Park.

• The Stanford University Golf Club hosts the U.S. Junior Amateur, with Larry Lee defeating Michael McMahon 2 up to claim the title.

1960s

1960

• San Jose's Almaden Country Club hosts the first of six Almaden Opens, an event which will have four of its playings retroactively recognized as official by the PGA Tour. This maiden edition (won by San Francisco native Ken Venturi) is not one of them, but subsequent victories by Jim Ferrier (1961), Al Geiberger (1963), Billy Casper (1964) and Gary Player's brother-in-law Bobby

Verwey (1965) will all go down as official in the Tour's record book.

1961

• Having already won his first U.S. Amateur title two years earlier at The Broadmoor, Jack Nicklaus records his first of several major successes at Pebble Beach by claiming the Amateur title for a second time, routing Dudley Wysong 8 & 6 in a one-sided final.

• Behind a dazzling closing 65, Gary Player records his third PGA Tour victory at the Lucky International, beating George Bayer and Don Whitt by two.

1963

• Hall-of-Famer Jack Burke Jr. records the 16th (and final) victory of his PGA Tour career at the Lucky International, closing with a 67 to beat Don January by three at Harding Park.

1964

• In a summer to make all San Francisco golfers proud, native son Ken Venturi comes back from a series of debilitating wrist injuries to win the U.S. Open at the Congressional Country Club in June. Three weeks later, fellow local Tony Lema captures the British Open at St Andrews, giving San Francisco a rare double of Major champions. For his part, Lema has already raised local spirits by claiming his fifth career PGA Tour victory at the Bing Crosby Pro-Am in January, beating Gay Brewer and Bo Wininger by three shots.

• Closing 65-66, Chi Chi Rodriguez records his second PGA Tour victory at the Lucky International, beating Don January in a playoff.

1965

• San Francisco native George Archer records his first PGA Tour victory at the Lucky International, closing with a 68 to tie Hall-of-Famer Bob Charles on 278, then winning in a playoff.

1966

• The U.S. Open returns to the Olympic Club and sees Billy Casper claim one of the more memorable Open victories on record. Casper trails Arnold Palmer by seven shots through 63 holes before his final-nine 32 (combined with an epic Palmer collapse) allows him to draw even and force an 18-hole playoff. Though trailing early, Casper eventually storms back to win the playoff by four, capping the greatest comeback victory in Major championship history.

• Hometown hero Ken Venturi records the last of his 14 career PGA Tour victories at the Lucky International, closing with a 66 to edge Frank Beard by one over the Harding Park layout upon which Venturi learned the game as a child.

1967

• Jack Nicklaus wins the Bing Crosby Pro-Am, closing with a 68 at Pebble Beach to walk away from Billy Casper by five shots. Nicklaus will win the Crosby twice more, beating Johnny Miller in a playoff in 1972, then defending that title a year later when sudden death will again be necessary, this time to dispatch Raymond Floyd and Orville Moody.

1968

• A new PGA Tour event, the Kaiser International Open, makes its debut at Napa's Silverado resort, with Kermit Zarley winning the inaugural edition by one over Dave Marr. The tournament will remain on the Tour schedule through 1980, remaining at Silverado for its entire run.

• Playing over the Monterey Peninsula Country Club's Dunes course, Carolyn Cudone wins the first of her unmatched five consecutive U.S. Senior Women's Amateur titles, her 236 total running away by 10 shots in an event then contested at medal play.

1969

• After its scheduled January playing is limited to 36 holes by rain, Jack Nicklaus wins a second edition of the Kaiser International in November, beating George Archer, Billy Casper and Don January in a playoff.

• Steve Spray claims his lone PGA Tour victory in the final playing of the Lucky International, riding a second round 63 to an eventual one-shot triumph over 1964 champion Chi Chi Rodriguez at Harding Park.

• The LPGA debuts its Lincoln-Mercury Open at Contra Costa County's Round Hill Country Club, where Donna Caponi beats Kathy Whitworth in a playoff to claim the title. The event will survive for five years, with Sandra Haynie winning the final two editions (in 1972 and '73) and the legendary Whitworth finishing runner-up in 1970 and '71 as well.

1970s

1970
• Gene Andrews wins the U.S. Senior Amateur at the California Golf Club of San Francisco, defeating James Ferrie 1 up in the final.

1972
• The U.S. Open is played at Pebble Beach for the first time and the occasion proves memorable, as Jack Nicklaus wins his third Open title, beating Bruce Crampton by three. Nicklaus clinches the victory with one of the era's iconic shots: a 1 iron which hits the pin and sets up a tap-in birdie at the famous par-3 17th.

1973
• Recording what many consider the greatest round of golf ever played, San Francisco native Johnny Miller closes with an eight-under-par 63 to win the U.S. Open at Pennsylvania's famously difficult Oakmont. Beginning the final round six shots off the lead, Miller's electric performance ultimately sees him home one better than John Schlee to claim his first Major championship.

1974
• Johnny Miller records the first of the eight victories that will define his career-best 1974 season at a 54-hole rain-shortened edition of the Bing Crosby Pro-Am, beating Grier Jones by four. Miller will then win the Phoenix and Tucson Opens over the next two weeks, jumpstarting his epic campaign.
• In September, Miller records the eighth victory of his season at the Kaiser International, running away from Billy Casper and Lee Trevino by a resounding eight shots. Though Miller's 1975 campaign will prove far less fruitful, he will return to successfully defend his Kaiser title, beating Rod Curl by three.

1975
• William Colm wins the U.S. Senior Open at what is today know as the Quail Lodge Golf Club (née Carmel Valley Golf & Country Club), beating Stephen Stimac 4 & 3 in the final.

1976
• The U.S. Senior Women's Amateur returns to the Dunes course at the Monterey Peninsula Country Club with Cecile Maclaurin emerging victorious, beating Carol Bowman by seven shots with a 230 aggregate.

1977
• The PGA Championship makes its Northern California debut (and only its second Golden State appearance overall) at the Pebble Beach Golf Links, where future Hall-of-Famer Lanny Wadkins captures the title. Wadkins begins the final round six behind a 47-year-old Gene Littler, who stumbles home with a 76, allowing Wadkins to tie him (on 282) with a 70, then take the title with a par on the third playoff hole.
• Tom Watson kicks off a breakout season that will include two Major championship victories by winning the Bing Crosby Pro-Am, his 15-under-par 273 total proving just enough to slip past future Hall-of-Famer Tony Jacklin by one. Watson will successfully defend this title a year later, closing with 69 to tie Ben Crenshaw on 280 before winning in sudden death.
• Three years after the demise of its Lincoln-Mercury Open, the LPGA returns to the Round Hill Country Club with a new event, the Sarah Coventry. Jane Blalock wins this inaugural edition (beating Debbie Austin and Pat Meyers by three) but the tournament will witness only one more playing, with Donna Caponi taking the 1978 title, breezing past Blalock by five.

1978
• Tom Watson wins the recently renamed Anheuser-Busch Classic (née the Kaiser International) at the Silverado Resort, beating Ed Sneed by three shots.

1980s

1980

• Ben Crenshaw wins the final paying of the Anheuser-Busch Classic, a closing 71 seeing him home four shots clear of Jack Renner at the Silverado Resort.

• The LPGA debuts its new Inamori Classic at the Almaden Country Club, with Amy Alcott claiming a four-shot victory over Beth Daniel and Patty Hayes in the inaugural. The event will remain at Almaden for two more years (with Hollis Stacy and Patty Sheehan recording wins) before moving to the San Diego area in 1983.

1981

• Nathanial Crosby, son of legendary crooner (and fine golfer) Bing, scores a surprise victory in the U.S. Amateur at the Olympic Club, eliminating Brian Lindley at the 37th hole. Seldom even rated the best player on his University of Miami golf team, Crosby enjoys his career week close to Burlingame, the community in which he grew up.

• In its second season of operation, the PGA Tour Champions brings an event to Harding Park, the Eureka Federal Savings Classic. It will survive for only one year with this lone edition being won by the tour's reigning Player of the Year Don January, who edges Bob Goalby by one.

1982

• Ten years after its first visit, the U.S. Open returns to Pebble Beach for another epic edition. Once again Jack Nicklaus is in the mix, closing with 69 to post a four-under-par 284 total – a number which looks good enough to at least guarantee playoff with Tom Watson, who is also four under but mired in the shortside rough beside the 17th green. However, in one of the game's iconic moments, Watson chips in for birdie, then birdies the par-5 18th to win by two, denying Nicklaus his fifth Open title.

1983

• With the Inamori Classic moving to San Diego, the LPGA brings a new event to the Almaden Country Club, the Konica San Jose Classic, which will remain there for the entirety of its seven-year run. Kathy Postlewait wins this debut edition (edging Charlotte Montgomery by one), and she will be followed by four Hall-of-Fame champions over the next six playings: Amy Alcott (1984), Patty Sheehan (1986), Jan Stephenson (1987) and Beth Daniel (1989).

1985

• Mark O'Meara wins the Bing Crosby Pro-Am, edging Curtis Strange, Larry Rinker and Kikuo Arai by one shot. O'Meara clearly finds the event to his liking as he will go on to win it a remarkable five times, adding victories in 1989 (by one over Tom Kite), 1990 (by two over Kenny Perry), 1992 (in a playoff with Jeff Sluman) and 1997.

1986

• San Jose native and UCLA All-American Kay Cockerill wins the U.S. Women's Amateur at the Pasatiempo Golf Club in Santa Cruz, routing Kathleen McCarthy 9 & 7 in the final. Cockerill will successfully defend her title the following year at the Rhode Island Country Club, where she beats Tracy Kerdyk 3 & 2

1987

• The U.S. Open returns to the Olympic Club for the third time, with Scott Simpson closing with 68 to edge Tom Watson by one and claim the title. This victory will frequently be cited as a third time that Olympic has produced the "wrong" champion (following Fleck upsetting Hogan in 1955 and Casper vanquishing Arnold Palmer in 1966) despite the fact that Scott Simpson actually sits above Watson in the Official World Golf Ranking entering Open week.

• A 39-year-old Johnny Miller ends a four-year victory drought by winning the Bing Crosby Pro-Am, closing 68-66 to slip past Payne Stewart by one shot.

1988

• After debuting in Texas a year earlier, the PGA Tour's season-ending Tour Championship is played at Pebble Beach, with Player of the Year Curtis Strange beating Tom Kite in sudden death to claim the title.

1989

• The PGA Tour Champions debuts what will become a long-running event in Napa, known for most of its existence as the Napa Valley Championship. It will ultimately include 14 playings (all at the Silverado Resort) and its list of champions will include Hall-of-Famers like Billy Casper (1989), Lee Trevino (1990 and '95), Bob Charles (1992) and, eventually, Tom Kite, who wins the event's final playing in 2002.

1990s

1990

• The U.S. Junior Amateur makes its second Bay Area appearance, with Matthew Todd edging Dennis Hillman 1 up to take the title at the Lake Merced Golf Club.

1992

• The U.S. Open returns to Pebble Beach for the third time, with Tom Kite emerging victorious to record his only Major championship victory. On a Sunday which sees the Pacific Ocean breezes greatly affect play, Kite battles his way to a closing 72, which proves good enough to edge Jeff Sluman by two.

1993

• The PGA Tour brings its Tour Championship to the Olympic Club for the first of two playings, with Jim Gallagher Jr. winning the title by one shot over Greg Norman, Scott Simpson, David Frost and John Huston. A year later, the second playing is taken by Mark McCumber, who beats Fuzzy Zoeller in a playoff.

1994

• Recording the 25th (and final) victory of his PGA Tour career, 46-year-old Johnny Miller scores a stunning triumph at the Bing Crosby Pro-Am, carding a third round 67 before staggering across the finish line with a closing 74 – just good enough to edge a quartet of players (including a 44-year-old Tom Watson) by one.

1997

• Forty-year-old Mark O'Meara wins his fifth Bing Crosby Pro-Am, stringing together four straight rounds of 67 to finish one better than the imposing duo of David Duval and Tiger Woods.

1998

• Six years after its most recent Pebble Beach playing, the U.S. Open returns to San Francisco's Olympic Club, where Lee Janzen claims his second Open title. Janzen trails leader Payne Stewart by five shots after 54 holes before closing with a 68, which proves good enough to triumph by one when Stewart stumbles home with a 74.

• Closing with a 67, Phil Mickelson edges Tom Pernice Jr. by one to win a 54-hole, rain-shortened Bing Crosby Pro-Am. Though it will take 21 years, Mickelson will eventually match Mark O'Meara as a five-time winner of the event, with subsequent titles coming in 2005 (by four over Mike Weir), 2007 (by five over Kevin Sutherland), 2012 (by two over Charlie Wi) and in 2019, when he beats England's Paul Casey by three shots at age 48.

1999

• The U.S. Amateur returns to Pebble Beach and is won by two-time University of Texas All-American David Gossett, who runs away from South Korea's Sung-yoon Kim 9 & 8 in the final.

2000s

2000

• In one of golf's greatest-ever performances, Tiger Woods wins the U.S. Open's centennial edition by a record-setting 15 shots upon the Open's return to Pebble Beach. Woods opens with rounds of 65-69 to take a six-shot halfway lead, then expands that lead to 10 with a Saturday 71. His closing 67 then sees him home on 272, matching the then-tournament record and setting a margin-of-victory standard that is likely to stand for decades, if not centuries.

• Four months prior to his U.S. Open victory, Tiger Woods wins at Pebble Beach in altogether different fashion, needing a closing 64 to beat Matt Gogel and Vijay Singh by two at the Bing Crosby Pro-Am.

• Having debuted its Samsung World Championship in 1980, the LPGA Tour brings this traveling event to Vallejo's Hiddenbrooke Golf Club for a three-year run, with winners including Juli Inkster, Dorothy Delasin and Annika Sorenstam. After leaving the area in 2003, it will return five years later for one final Bay Area playing, with Mountain View native Paula Creamer taking the title in 2008 at the Half Moon Bay Resort.

2001

• Davis Love III closes with a 63 to edge Vijay Singh by one and claim his 14th career PGA Tour victory at the Bing Crosby Pro-Am. Love will win again at Pebble Beach in 2003, when a Sunday 68 sees him home one better than Tom Lehman.

• The PGA Tour Champions debuts a new event, the Siebel Classic in Silicon Valley, which played at the Coyote Creek Golf Club in Morgan Hill. The tournament will survive for only two playings and produce period Champions stalwarts Hale Irwin and Dana Quigley as champions.

2004

• The Olympic Club hosts the U.S. Junior Amateur, with South Korean Sihwan Kim edging American David Chung 1 up to win the title.

• The PGA Tour Champions begins a new event at the Pebble Beach Golf Links, a tournament initially known as the First Tee Open which will operate under numerous sponsors and names throughout its existence. Craig Stadler wins this inaugural edition, but the tournament will eventually be dominated by a pair of three-time winners, Jeff Sluman (who prevails in 2008, '09 and '11) and Kirk Triplett (2012, '13 and '19).

• Carolyn Creekmore wins the U.S. Senior Women's Amateur at the Pasatiempo Golf Club, beating Liz Haines 1 up in the final.

2006

• Having been played around Sacramento since its 1996 inception, the LPGA Tour's Longs Drugs Challenge moves to Danville's Blackhawk Country Club for its final five playings, with this 2006 edition featuring a battle of Hall-of-Famers, as Australia's Karrie Webb edges Annika Sorenstam by one. Subsequent champions will include Suzann Pettersen (who beats Lorena Ochoa in a playoff in 2007), In-Kyung Kim (2008), Sophie Gustafson (2009, in a four-shot walkaway) and Beatriz Recari (2010).

2007

• Southern Methodist University star Colt Knost win the U.S. Amateur at the Olympic Club, beating fellow future PGA Tour player Michael Thompson 2 & 1 in the final.

2009

• With a 15-under-par 201 total, Dustin Johnson claims his second PGA Tour victory at the Bing Crosby Pro-Am, beating Mike Weir by four. A year later, Johnson will successfully defend his title, sharing the 54-hole lead with Paul Goydo before stumbling home with 74 – but still hanging on to beat David Duval and J.B. Holmes by one.

2010s

2010

• The U.S. Open's fifth playing at Pebble Beach sees Northern Ireland's Graeme McDowell score a breakthrough triumph in another memorable Open. McDowell trails leader Dustin Johnson (a two-time defending champion of the Bing Crosby Pro-Am) by three after 54 holes, but Johnson staggers home with an 82, allowing McDowell's closing 74 to prove just good enough to edge upstart Gregory Havret by one and Ernie Els by two.

• Having been played since 2007 at Arizona's Grayhawk Golf Club, the PGA Tour's Frys.com Open moves to CordeValle, where it is won by popular Rocco Mediate in truly spectacular fashion. He edges Bo Van Pelt and Alex Prugh by one – but only after holing four shots of over 100 yards during the 72 holes of play, one during each round.

2012

• The U.S. Open visits the Olympic Club for a fourth time, with Webb Simpson breaking through to claim his first Major title. Simpson begins the final round four behind co-leaders Jim Furyk and Graeme McDowell, then closes with a 68 to edge McDowell and Michael Thompson by one.

• Exactly 60 years after its last visit, the U.S. Girls' Junior returns to the Bay Area, with Australian Minjee Lee beating Alison Lee 1 up to take the title at the Lake Merced Golf Club.

2013

• Brandt Snedeker records his fifth PGA Tour victory at the Bing Crosby Pro-Am, closing with a 65 at Pebble Beach to beat Chris Kirk by two. Snedeker will claim the title again in 2015, when a tournament record 265 total beats Nick Watney by three.

• Having won the 2012 title at Pennsylvania's Hershey Country Club, Ellen Port defends her U.S. Senior Women's Amateur crown at CordeValle, beating Susan Cohn 3 & 2 in the final.

2014

• After four editions at CordeValle, the PGA Tour's Frys.com Open moves to Napa's Silverado Resort, where Sang-moon Bae wins the first playing, beating Australia's Steven Bowditch by two.

• After a three-year absence, the LPGA Tour returns to Bay Area, debuting the Swinging Skirts LPGA Classic at the Lake Merced Golf Club. Seventeen-year-old Lydia Ko claims her third LPGA Tour victory (but her first as a professional) in this 2014 edition, then returns to successfully defend her title in 2015, when she beats Morgan Pressel in a playoff. Japan's Haru Nomura will claim the third and final edition (beating South African Lee-Anne Pace by four) before the event goes on a one-year hiatus and, eventually, a sponsorship change.

2015

• The Olympic Club's Lake course hosts the inaugural edition of the U.S. Amateur Four-Ball, with 2013 Walker Cup teammates Nathan Smith and Todd White defeating Sherrill Britt and Greg Earnhardt 7 & 5 in the final.

2016

• With the former Frys.com Open changing its name/sponsorship to the Safeway Open, Brendan Steele closes 67-65 to win the title, edging Patton Kizzire by one at the Silverado Resort. Steele will successfully defend his title in 2017, when he holds off Tony Finau by two.

• The U.S. Women's Open makes its first-ever visit to the Bay Area, with Brittany Lang capturing the title at CordeValle, but not without controversy. Lang and Sweden's Anna Nordqvist tie on six-under-par 282 and engage in a three-hole aggregate playoff, a contest heavily swayed by a two-shot penalty assessed to Nordqvist on the second hole for moving sand in a bunker – but about which the players aren't informed until they approach the green of the third extra hole.

2018

• The LPGA brings new event to the Lake Merced Golf Club, the Mediheal Championship, and this debut edition is won by Lydia Ko, who beats Minjee Lee with an eagle on the first hole of sudden death.

• San Francisco-born Yealimi Noh wins the U.S. Girls' Junior at the Poppy Gills Golf Course, beating 13-year-old Floridian Alexa Pano 4 & 3 in the final.

2019

• The U.S. Open is played for the sixth time at Pebble Beach, where long-hitting Gary Woodland emerges victorious. Opening with rounds of 68-65, Woodland takes a two-shot halfway lead over Justin Rose, then remains one ahead of Rose through 54 holes before a closing 69 sees him home three better than two-time defending champion Brooks Koepka, who gamely attempts to join Willie Anderson as the only man ever to win the Open three straight times.

2020s

2020

• The PGA Championship makes its San Francisco debut at the layout now known as the TPC Harding Park. With no crowds in attendance due to the COVID-19 pandemic, 23-year-old former

University of California star Collin Morikawa claims his first Major title, closing 65-64 to beat Dustin Johnson and Paul Casey by two.

• Forty-six-year-old Stewart Cink closes 65-65 to break an 11-year victory drought and win the Safeway Open at Silverado, beating Harry Higgs by two.

SAN FRANCISCO'S MOST COLLECTABLE COURSES
(Includes the Monterey Peninsula)

Cypress Point Club
Pebble Beach Golf Links

Olympic Club (Lake)
San Francisco Golf Club

California Golf Club
Monterey Peninsula Country Club (Shore)
Pasatiempo Golf Club
Spyglass Hill Golf Course
TPC Harding Park

Claremont Country Club
CordeValle
The Institute
Mayacama Golf Club
Meadow Club
Monterey Peninsula Country Club (Dunes)
Links at Spanish Bay
Stanford University Golf Course

Bayland Golf Links
Golf Club at Boulder Ridge
Cinnabar Hills Golf Club
Coyote Creek Golf Club (Tournament)
Diablo Country Club
Half Moon Bay Golf Links
Hiddenbrooke Golf Club
Lake Merced Golf Club
Menlo Country Club
Olympic Club (Ocean)
Orinda Country Club
Club at Pasadera
Poppy Hills Golf Course
Preserve Golf Club
Ruby Hill Golf Club
Silverado Country Club & Resort (North)
Sonoma Golf Club
Tehàma Golf Club
TPC Stonebrae
Course at Wente Vineyards

SAN FRANCISCO'S TOUGHEST COURSES
(Includes the Monterey Peninsula)

10
The Institute

9
CordeValle
Olympic Club (Lake)

8
Eagle Vines Golf Club
Pebble Beach Golf Links
Ruby Hill Golf Club
Spyglass Hill Golf Course

7
Bayonet & Black Horse (Bayonet)
Bridges Golf Club
California Golf Club
Coyote Creek Golf Club (Tournament)
Coyote Creek Golf Club (Valley)
Eagle Ridge Golf Club
Half Moon Bay Golf Links (Old)
Monterey Peninsula Country Club (Dunes)
Monterey Peninsula Country Club (Shore)
Poppy Hills Golf Course
Poppy Ridge Golf Course
Preserve Golf Club
Shoreline Golf Links
Silverado Country Club & Resort (North)
Sonoma Golf Club
TPC Harding Park
TPC Stonebrae
Course at Wente Vineyards

INDEX OF COURSES

Pacific Grove GL	130	Saratoga CC	87
Palo Alto Hills G&CC	86	Sea Ranch GL	41
Paradise Valley GC	54	Seascape GC	114
Pasadera, C at	123	Sebastapol GC	43
Pasatiempo GC	115	Sequoyah CC	74
Peacock Gap GC	29	Sharon Heights G&CC	107
Pebble Beach GL	126	Sharp Park GC	110
Peninsula G&CC	107	Shoreline GL	96
Petaluma G&CC	35	Silverado CC & Resort (North)	47
Pleasanton G Cen	82	Silverado CC & Resort (South)	47
Poplar Creek GC	109	Silver Creek Valley CC	88
Poppy Hills GC	131	Sonoma GC	36
Poppy Ridge GC	78	Spanish Bay, L at	127
Preserve GC	123	Spring Hills GC	116
Presidio GC	24	Spring Valley GC	96
Pruneridge GC	100	Spyglass Hill GC	128
Quail Lodge, GC at	127	Stanford University GC	88
Rancho del Pueblo GC	100	Stone Tree GC	30
Rancho Solano GC	55	Sugarloaf GC	43
Redwood Canyon GC	79	Sunken Gardens GC	101
Richmond CC	63	Sunnyvale Muni GC	97
Rio Vista, GC at	55	Tehama GC	124
Rooster Run GC	40	Tilden Park GC	69
Rossmoor	63	TPC Harding Park	25
Round Hill CC	64	TPC Harding Park (Fleming)	26
Ruby Hill GC	73	TPC Stonebrae	74
San Francisco GC	22	Valley of Moon C	41
San Jose CC	87	Villages G&CC	89
San Jose Muni GC	95	VillagesG&CC (Short)	101
San Ramon GC	69	Vintners GC	49
Santa Rosa G&CC	35	Wente Vineyards, C at	79
Santa Teresa GC	95	Windsor GC	42
Santa Teresa GC (Par 3)	100		